CH

D0394371

*f*P

ACROSS THE GREAT DIVIDE

ROBERT STUART AND
THE DISCOVERY OF THE
OREGON TRAIL

LATON McCARTNEY

FREE PRESS

NEW YORK LONDON TORONTO SYDNEY SINGAPORE

FREE PRESS
A Division of Simon & Schuster Inc.
1230 Avenue of the Americas
New York, NY 10020

FREE PRESS and colophon are
trademarks of Simon & Schuster, Inc.

For information about special discounts for bulk purchases,
please contact Simon & Schuster Special Sales:
1-800-456-6798 or business@simonandschuster.com

Manufactured in the United States of America

1   3   5   7   9   10   8   6   4   2

Library of Congress Cataloging-in-Publication Data

McCartney, Laton.
    Across the Great Divide : Robert Stuart and the discovery of
the Oregon Trail / Laton McCartney.
        p. cm.
    Includes bibliographical references and index.
    1. Oregon National Historic Trail—History. 2. West (U.S.)—
Discovery and exploration. 3. Oregon—Discovery and
exploration. 4. Stuart, Robert, 1785–1848—Journeys—West
(U.S.) 5. Tonquin (Ship) 6. Pioneers—West (U.S.)—Biography.
7. Pioneers—Oregon—Biography. 8. Overland journeys to the
Pacific. I. Title.
F880.M455 2003
979.5'03—dc21   2003044874

ISBN 0-7432-4924-0

TO THE THREE WHO MATTER MOST:

NANCY, PAT, AND MIKE

CONTENTS

ACROSS THE
GREAT DIVIDE

FOREWORD

IN JUNE 1812, NOT QUITE SIX YEARS AFTER THE RETURN of Meriwether Lewis and William Clark from the far reaches of the American frontier, another expedition set out to cross the western half of the continent.

Led by a young, Scottish-born fur trader and explorer, Robert Stuart, this seven-man party discovered a gateway through the Rocky Mountains as well as much of the overland route across the western half of the continent that would become the emigrant trail to Oregon and California. This is an account of Stuart's remarkable journey and the events that led up to it.

Today, Stuart's expedition has largely been forgotten, but it ranks as one of the great adventure odysseys of nineteenth-century North America. For me, it is an intensely personal narrative. Stuart was my ancestor, a paternal grandfather four generations removed. I grew up in the late 1940s and early 1950s on a remote ranch in southeastern Wyoming, the son of a hard-drinking, Yale-educated cattleman from Colorado and his New Haven–born wife. Set against the eastern slope of the Medicine Bow Range, our ranch was traversed by an offshoot of the century-old emigrant road Stuart had been the first to travel.

In the spring, when the wagon tracks were clearly visible in the new grass, my sister and I used to follow the trail northwest toward Elk Mountain in search of arrowheads as well as artifacts discarded by the pioneers as their wagon trains struggled to ascend the foothills. Each year we'd discover new treasures—pieces of crockery, cartridge casings, broken furniture, a cast-iron stove half submerged in the mud at the edge of Dutton Creek, even the badly weathered torso of a wooden doll.

The trail and its history loomed large in my imagination. Lying awake with the relentless Wyoming wind whistling outside our ranch house, I read about the Grattan Massacre, a dispute over an emigrant's stray cow that triggered twenty-five years of warfare with the Sioux; the ill-fated Donner expedition; and Marcus and Narcissa Whitman's pilgrimage to Oregon to salvage the souls of the Cayuses and Flatheads.

Owen Wister's *The Virginian* was set outside the town of Medicine Bow, just northeast of my family's ranch, and old Fort Laramie lay to the east on the far side of Laramie Peak. There, the young Francis Parkman made copious field notes for *The Oregon Trail,* and tens of thousands of emigrants rested and reconnoitered after coming up the Platte River Road, the first leg of their long westward journey.

Robert Stuart was the first nonnative American to travel the length of this road. A junior partner in one of John Jacob Astor's fur-trading ventures, he sailed to the mouth of the Columbia River in 1810. There, he and his shipmates established Astoria, the first American settlement on the Pacific Coast and the headquarters for what Astor hoped would develop into a frontier empire in the Northwest.

In June 1812, Stuart, then twenty-seven, was chosen to lead a small overland expedition back to St. Louis and New York. Two American-led expeditions had crossed the continent before him, that of Lewis and Clark in 1803–1806 and Wilson Price Hunt's, another of Astor's traders, in 1810–11. But Lewis and Clark's Corps of Discovery and Hunt had both journeyed up the Missouri and over the rugged, nearly impassable northern Rockies. Traveling from west to east for more than three thousand miles by canoe, on horseback, and ultimately by foot, Stuart and his six companions followed the mountains south until they came upon South Pass, the one gap in the three-thousand-mile-long Rocky Mountain chain that was passable by wagon. From there they continued east along the Sweetwater and Platte Rivers across present-day Wyoming and Nebraska. The path that this obscure young Scot and his eastbound companions blazed became the central route of America's expansion, the emigrant road that opened up the Far West to settlement.

A daguerreotype of Stuart and his wife, Betsy, hung in my grandmother's house in Denver—venerated icons that embodied what my grandmother described as "the pioneer spirit." Stuart, the long-dead family patriarch, seemed a stern and foreboding figure whose dark, probing eyes seemed to scrutinize disapprovingly my tomboy sister, Dillon, and me whenever we came down from the ranch to visit.

As a boy I listened attentively to my grandmother's stories about Stuart's exploits, but I was far more partial to Indians, gunfighters, and cowboys than fur trader–explorers. Then, too, I associated Stuart with the Scottish side of the family and specifically my father, a difficult, domineering, sometimes violent man from whom I was estranged for much of my adult life. After being sent east to boarding school, I distanced myself from him—and my western roots—eventually settling in New York, a city my father loathed and feared in equal measure. It was only after my father finally gave up drinking in the mid-1970s that we reconciled and I began joining him on fishing trips out West.

It was on the last of those excursions, a weeklong trip to Wyoming in late July, that I first considered writing about Stuart and my western heritage. At the time, my father was suffering from throat cancer. Both of us knew he hadn't much time left.

We'd started our trip in Jackson Hole, fishing on a privately owned ranch just outside Teton Park, and then driven down to Pinedale, where we fished the Green and the New Fork rivers. Neither of us had much luck that last morning. We caught several middling rainbow trout and a few whitefish that my father would haul in impatiently and then discard, throwing them to the riverbank in disgust. Once whitefish got in a stream, he claimed, they proliferated and drove away the trout. He killed as many of them as he could.

Normally, we would have fished until the fading light made it impossible to see our flies on the river, but my father's dwindling energy reserves were spent, and a dark, malignant-looking thunderstorm was working its way down the Wind River Range in our direction. With thunder sounding in the distance, we decided to head on back to town rather than wait for the rancher who was coming to pick us up at dusk and risk getting soaked.

Walking back to Pinedale, we suddenly came upon a Sublette County historical marker that was partially obscured by a stand of lodgepole pines. Although we'd been fishing in the area for several days, neither of us had noticed it before. "I'll be damned," my father said. "Look at this." He read the inscription aloud:

A Pause on the Journey

On Oct. 16, 1812, the Astorians Robert Stuart, Ramsay Crooks, Robert McClellan, Joseph Miller, Benjamin Jones, Francis LeClair and Andy Valle, traveling from Astoria to St. Louis, all their horses having been stolen by Indians, passed this way by foot and forded Pine Creek near here, the first whites known to have seen it. From Stuart's journal: "We forded another stream whose banks were adorned with many pines—near which we found an Indian encampment deserted about a month ago, with immense numbers of buffalo bones strewed everywhere; in center of camp a great lodge of pines and willows at west and three persons lay interred with feet to east; at head of each a large buffalo skull painted black; from lodge were suspended numerous ornaments and moccasins." Six days later on Oct. 22nd, they made the memorable discovery of the South Pass.

I had enough of the Irish mystic in me from my mother's side of the family to view our discovery as an epiphany, a sign from beyond the great veil. Here I was fishing with my dying father on a remote Wyoming outback, and we found that we'd been treading exactly the same path our ancestor had traversed nearly two centuries earlier. The dead greet the dying, appropriately at the site of what once had been an Indian burial lodge.

For an instant, I could envision Stuart and his men, gaunt and spectral, reconnoitering the deserted Indian lodge. My father, I'm sure, had a similar revelation. Certainly, he looked as if he had seen a ghost. "Imagine being the first white man to see this country," he said in a quiet voice.

We lingered at the marker for a few minutes, lost in our own thoughts, and then continued on into town, beating the rain by a matter of minutes.

Soon after, my father took his own life rather than endure further the cancer and the chemotherapy that left him racked with pain and nausea. In accordance with his wishes, my mother, sister, and I had him cremated in Denver, his hometown, and then drove up to an old friend's ranch in Wyoming to scatter his ashes over a favorite fishing hole on the North Platte.

MONTHS LATER, IN GOING through some of my father's possessions that had been in storage, I discovered the framed daguerreotype of the Stuarts that had hung in my by-then-deceased grandmother's living room in Denver.

There was also a privately published two-volume edition of Stuart family letters and a rare 1935 edition of *The Discovery of the Oregon Trail: Robert Stuart's Narratives of His Overland Trip Eastward from Astoria*, edited by the late Western historian Philip A. Rollins. The latter includes the remarkable journal Stuart had kept during his ten-month-long trek across the continent. He'd written it using sap, berry juice, and even his own blood after he'd run out of ink. The original journal and traveling memoranda (the latter written after the expedition) had been used by Washington Irving without attribution as the basis for much of *Astoria*, his account of Astor's ill-fated trading venture. Years after Irving's death the journal was discovered tucked away in a cupboard in the author's Hudson River valley house, Sunnyside.

Of Stuart's narrative, which eventually found its way into the William Robertson Coe Collection at the Beinecke Library at Yale University, Rollins wrote, "Compared with all the other overland diaries of the United States . . . Stuart's product seems to be outranked only by the journals emanating from the Lewis and Clark expedition."

Stuart arrived in Oregon in 1811, returning in 1813. A few years later he went into business with Astor running the field operations of Astor's American Fur Company (AFC) from remote Mackinac Island in northern Michigan. I discovered copies of the AFC letters, including hundreds to and from Stuart, in various historical archives, including the New-York Historical Society, only a few blocks from my home on Manhattan's Upper West Side.

Months later, in a conversation with a distant cousin, I learned that my grandmother's late sister in St. Paul had owned a collection of previously unpublished family letters including hundreds written by Robert and Betsy Stuart and their oldest daughter and her husband, Mary and Dr. George Franklin Turner, my forebears. Before she died, my great-aunt, an intensely private woman, indicated she wanted the letters destroyed because of their personal revelations. Happily, one of her daughters ignored her dictate and donated this vivid chronicle of frontier life to the Minnesota Historical Society.

Stuart's journals, the AFC records and correspondence, and the family letters lent Robert Stuart humanity and animation, revealing him as vulnerable and more appealing than I'd imagined. His journals make clear that Stuart, the seemingly intrepid, resolute voyager, had his moments of self-doubt, trepidation, and wrongheadedness. He was, after all, an entrepreneur, not an explorer. He'd come to the Pacific Northwest simply to make his fortune in the fur trade, yet during his stay in the wilderness, he emerged as a pioneer western naturalist of the first rank, a perceptive student of Native American cultures, and one of America's most important, if least known, explorers.

The earlier Lewis and Clark expedition had turned the nation's eyes to the vast wilderness west of the Mississippi, but it was really Robert Stuart who opened the door to westward expansion.

CHAPTER 1

MR. ASTOR'S PROPOSAL

IN FEBRUARY 1808, THOMAS JEFFERSON, SIXTY-FIVE years old and in the waning months of his second term as president, received a letter from the New York merchant John Jacob Astor asking him to support a far-flung trading venture beyond the Mississippi.

Astor had already begun to amass an enormous fortune in trading furs and exporting and importing goods, yet he was not widely known outside New York and Montreal, where he did much of his trading. The president had never met Astor—in fact, he had likely never heard of him, though Astor cited his fellow New Yorker, George Clinton, Jefferson's vice president, as someone who could attest to his good character and accomplishments. Based on the ambitious proposal Astor outlined in his letter to Jefferson, however, the nation's chief executive may well have concluded its author was either a man of great ambition and vision or perhaps someone suffering from delusions of grandeur.

Astor wanted to create a great fur-trading company that would operate through a network of posts he intended to build along the route followed by Lewis and Clark from St. Louis all the way to the Pacific. To be called the American Fur Company (AFC), this enterprise would put the entire fur trade in the northern half of Louisiana Territory—all the area included in the Louisiana Purchase of April 30, 1803—under U.S. control within four or five years, Astor asserted. To succeed, the company needed the president's blessing as well as the full support of the American government.

The proposal captured Jefferson's attention. Assuming Astor had the resources and business and organizational acumen to mount such an ambitious and costly endeavor—and the president was well aware that few men in the United States possessed such qualifications—this fur-trading enterprise of his might well serve Jefferson's own agenda for bringing Louisiana into the bosom of the Republic.

In 1803, Jefferson received congressional approval and an appropriation of twenty-five hundred dollars to send a military expedition to explore the upper Missouri River to its headwaters in the Rocky Mountains. From there, what would become known as the "Corps of Discovery" was to follow the first westward-flowing river the explorers came upon to the Pacific Ocean. Jefferson had chosen his private secretary, Captain Meriwether Lewis, to lead the expedition. In turn, Lewis asked his friend William Clark to serve as coleader. Their chief objectives were twofold: advance the geographic and scientific knowledge of the continent and pave the way for advancement of the American fur trade to the various Indian tribes they encountered on their journey. In the three years that elapsed between the time Lewis and Clark began to organize their expedition in the summer of 1803 and their return to St. Louis in the fall of 1806, the Corps of Discovery had traveled eight thousand miles and had accomplished its mission, setting the stage for expansion into the trans-Mississippi West.

The commercial gains that Jefferson had assured Congress would come as the result of the expedition, however, had been slow to materialize. By the time Jefferson received Astor's letter, almost five years since the United States had acquired Louisiana from France and eighteen months since the return of Meriwether Lewis and William Clark, the president's enemies were still characterizing the Louisiana Purchase as a costly folly. Worse, the government's efforts to extend America's commercial reach beyond the Mississippi had faltered badly, especially in upper Louisiana Territory, then known as the Old Northwest. There, two major Canadian trading companies—North West Company (NWC) and the more recently formed Michilimackinac, a NWC subsidiary—were securing huge quantities of furs from the Indians of the region while turning these tribes against the United States.

At the time, the fur trade ranked as perhaps the largest business in North America. Some six million pelts—mostly beaver for felt hats worn by European and American gentry; sable, ermine, and marten for coats, fur muffs, and trimming; as well as less valuable muskrat, fox, buffalo, and raccoon hides—were sold annually at prices ranging from fifteen cents to five thousand dollars per pelt.

With the North West traders encroaching on the upper Missouri and Old Northwest and Michilimackinac rapidly gaining control of the upper Great Lakes and Mississippi, American traders were being excluded from their own territory by what had emerged as a quasi-monopoly. Moreover, the pelts secured by the Canadians and British traders in U.S. territory were sold at a significant premium within the United States, which imported three-fourths of its furs from Canada and England. In other words, Americans were paying more for furs that had been trapped within their own borders than were the British.

Jefferson had done what he could to counter the Canadian influence. In 1807, he sent William Clark back to St. Louis to serve as superintendent of Indian affairs. Meriwether Lewis was scheduled to join Clark there in March, when he would take office as governor of Missouri Territory. Jefferson was counting on the two former Corps of Discovery commanders to be his eyes and ears on the frontier and do what was needed to aid in the further development of Louisiana.

The government had also dispatched an expedition lead by Zebulon Pike up the Mississippi to warn off British traders while convincing a reluctant Congress to fund the building of trading posts west of the Mississippi on the Arkansas, Natchitoches, and Bellefontaine rivers. Subsidized by the government, these outposts would, Jefferson hoped, serve as supply bases for American traders and a means of attracting the Indians with prices that were far more competitive than those being paid by the British.

But, by itself, the American government didn't have the resources to match the Canadians. Together the NWC and Michilimackinac had a capitalization of close to two million dollars, almost as much as the entire federal budget at the time. Then, too, three years into his second term and getting ready to retire, Jefferson had shifted his own focus, out of necessity, to foreign affairs.

WITH GREAT BRITAIN and Napoleonic France at war, both countries routinely blockaded U.S. shipping and seized American vessels with impunity. On one such instance, on June 22, 1807, the HMS *Leopard*, acting under the orders of British Vice Admiral George C. Berkeley, fired repeated broadsides at the defenseless American frigate *Chesapeake* after Commodore James Barron, in command, refused to allow the British to search for English deserters. Three Americans were killed and eighteen wounded.

Enraged, Jefferson responded by enacting the Embargo Act of 1807, which prevented all exports and most imports, and put himself in charge of enforcing it, a role that normally would have fallen to Secretary of the Treasury Albert Gallatin. Intended to force the British and French to recognize American sovereignty without provoking outright war, the embargo proved largely counterproductive and hugely unpopular, especially in the Federalist Northeast, which suffered most from the lack of foreign commerce.

In the meantime, the president was receiving reports of British agents operating on the western frontier and raids on American trading parties by the Aricaras and other tribes along the upper Missouri. Jefferson suspected that the British traders had incited these attacks.

Astor's proposal had come at a propitious time. Perhaps his chain of commercial trading posts would serve to keep the British and Canadians in check, acting as a commercial barricade extending to the western sea. But who exactly was this man? What were his bona fides? Jefferson asked Secretary of War General Henry Dearborn to find out all he could about Astor from New York Governor De Witt Clinton. "Governor speaks well of Astor, as a man of large property & fair character, and well acquainted with the fur & peltry business," Dearborn reported on April 8, 1808. That was enough to satisfy Jefferson. A few days later, he gave the New Yorker his blessing for the plan to undertake trans-Mississippi trade with the western Indians.

"ALL BEYOND THE Mississippi is ours exclusively, and it will be in our power to give our own traders great advantages over their foreign competitors," Jefferson wrote Astor. "You may be assured that in order to get the whole of this business passed into the hands of our own citizens, and to oust foreign traders, who so much abuse the privilege by endeavoring to excite the Indians against us, every reasonable patronage and facility in the power of the Executive will be afforded."

In July, the president wrote excitedly to Meriwether Lewis in St. Louis, now governor of Missouri Territory, informing his friend and former secretary that a powerful company was being formed to carry on the Indian trade on a large scale with the intention of securing for the United States "exclusive possession of that commerce." This new enterprise would be under the command, Jefferson explained, of "a most excellent man, a Mr. Astor, of New York, long engaged in the business and perfectly master of it."

CHAPTER 2

A HIGHLANDER'S PROGRESS

SIX MONTHS BEFORE JOHN JACOB ASTOR MADE HIS
initial overtures to Thomas Jefferson, a twenty-two-year-old Scot
named Robert Stuart boarded one of the immigrant ships that
departed regularly for Canada from Glasgow. Among the hundreds of
passengers aboard—crofters and tradesmen with their families, min-
ers, mill workers, and fishermen—Stuart stood out. He was tall and
lean with what some described as an imperious bearing, an impressive head of wavy, dark brown hair worn swept back from his broad
forehead and handsome, finely delineated features. He might have
been taken as the scion of a laird family, a bit down on his luck by the
look of his somewhat shopworn clothes, or a righteous young minister ready to take on his first assignment. In fact, he was nearly penni-
less with the promise of a job as his only asset. During the
three-week voyage across the Atlantic, he paced the decks restlessly,
eager to meet whatever destiny awaited him in Canada.

Like many Scottish immigrants at the time, Stuart was a Highlander, one of fifteen thousand who relocated to Canada between
1770 and 1815. The third of nine children, he was born February 19,
1785, in the Parish of Callander on the southern fringes of the High-
lands and baptized the following day in the neighboring parish of
Balquhidder in an ivy-covered chapel on the banks of Loch Voil.

The Balquhidder district is a wild, harshly beautiful region that
figures prominently in Scottish history and literature. Here in the valley of the Balvaig, Clan Alpine's fiery cross "glanced like lightning"
when summoning men to battle, Philip Rollins notes. In Robert Louis

Stevenson's *Kidnapped*, Robin Oig bested Alan Stewart in duel here, with bagpipes being the weapon of choice. This is also Rob Roy country, the home of the MacGregor clan. Robert "Roy" MacGregor is buried in the old parish churchyard along with generations of Stuarts.

Robert Stuart's mother, Mary, whom he remembered fondly as "an affectionate, gentle, innocent Highland mother," was a Buchanan from the nearby hamlet of Ruskachan. His father, John Stuart, a quiet, scholarly man who was known in Gaelic as Ian Mohr na Coille ("Big John of the Woods"), served as the parish schoolmaster and operated the small family farm, or croft.

The Stuarts, or Stewarts as the name was alternatively spelled, of Balquhidder took great pride in their bloodline. Robert Stuart's bachelor uncle, David, liked to boast that his kinsmen weren't descended from the Royal Stuarts but that the Royal Stuarts were descended from them. The family traced its lineage back to Walter Steward, the sixth high steward of Scotland, who in 1314 won the hand of Majory, daughter of Robert the Bruce, king of Scotland. Their son, the feckless Robert II, ruled Scotland from 1371 to 1390 as the first in a long line of Stuart monarchs.

Robert Stuart's more immediate ancestral role models were the chieftains of Clan Stuart of Balquhidder, who, like their counterparts in other Highland clans, controlled the ancestral lands, parceling out some acreage for their favored kin to manage and leasing the rest at nominal fees to tenants, who acknowledged the chief's authority, accepted his protection, and soldiered in the clan regiment wherever a dispute arose. "The clans were miniature courts in each of which a petty prince attended by guards . . . kept a rude state, dispensed a rude justice [and] waged wars," noted the British historian Thomas Macaulay.

The Stuart coat of arms, which Robert and his uncle David later brought with them to the New World, bore the crest of a rampant demi-lion with the motto above it *Nobilis ira est leonis* ("Noble is the anger of the lion"), contracted by usage to *Nobilis ira*. These weren't a people to trifle with. In his introduction to *Rob Roy*, Sir Walter Scott described an encounter in the early 1700s between Roy and the Stuarts. At dispute was a small hill farm in Balquhidder. The Stuarts owned the farm at the time, but the MacGregors, who lived mainly

Robert Stuart

by stealing cattle and selling "protection" to wealthy English land-holders, claimed it by right of ancient occupancy.

As MacGregor and his followers were planning to take possession, several hundred heavily armed Stuarts marched down from the hills, angry, rough-hewn men clearly primed for battle. Seeing his clansmen outnumbered, MacGregor prudently decided not to dispute Stuart ownership. Fearing, though, that his followers might think he had conceded too readily, MacGregor invited any of the Stuarts "to exchange a few blows with him for the honor of their respective clans."

Alaster Stuart, Robert's Jacobite great-grandfather and then second chieftain of the Stuart tribe, accepted the challenge, inflicting a slight gash on one of MacGregor's arms during the course of their exchange. Reputedly the finest swordsman in Scotland, MacGregor immediately dropped his broadsword to show he was conceding and gamely congratulated Stuart on being the first man to ever draw his blood in a duel. The two later became close friends, and before he died, MacGregor presented Stuart with an armchair and candlestick

Alexander Mackenzie Esq.
COURTESY OF NATIONAL LIBRARY OF CANADA.

holder that he'd fashioned himself, gifts that remained in the Stuart family for generations.

HAD ROBERT STUART been born in an earlier time, he likely would have assumed his role as a leader of the Stuart clan, but by the late 1700s, the British, in an effort to bring the wild, rebellious Highlanders to heel, had largely dismantled the clan system. Clan chieftains were stripped of their hereditary powers by the English, their lands given over to approved factors, often Lowlanders. Non-Gaels and often Whigs who opposed the Highland Jacobites and their support for the house of Stuart, the Lowlanders had more in common with the British than their Highland countrymen. They promptly replaced the black cattle the clans had raised for generations with sheep, mutton being far more economical than beef to produce.

The Stuart family fortunes suffered markedly as a result of these measures. In the years when Robert Stuart was growing up, the small family farm, "Tigh-na-cuilt" ("House in the Woods"), was all that remained of the clan's once considerable landholdings in Balquhidder. It was only marginally self-sufficient, and with his modest stipend from teaching, John Stuart was barely able to support his large family. "We were poor and had to get through life in the hardest manner," one of Robert Stuart's brothers later recalled.

As a boy, Stuart was known as "Little Robert of the Hills." He inherited his mother's wry, felicitous humor, a side of his personality that was, in later years, often masked by his seemingly reserved and often-dour composure. From his father he received a thorough, secular schooling, and was, as one of his biographers noted, "educated according to the usages of the Presbyterian Church in its doctrinal belief and in the religious regard for the Sabbath, a reverence for the Sacred Scriptures as the word of God, and a respect for the ministry."

Like his siblings, Stuart grew up speaking both English and Gaelic. His later letters and journals indicate that, as a youth, he read voraciously: Shakespeare, Cervantes, the English philosopher John Locke, and his countryman Robert Burns, who shared Stuart's impoverished, agricultural background and would become his favorite poet. He also developed into an enthusiastic amateur naturalist.

With his uncle David, who migrated to the New World when Stuart was still a boy, and his two older brothers James and John, Stuart would roam the rugged, harshly beautiful countryside hunting red deer, alpine hare, ptarmigan, and grouse, or fishing for salmon and gray trout in the lochs and rivers. This interest in nature would serve him well when Stuart eventually set out to record his observations of the uncharted American West and its animal and plant life.

Impressed with young Stuart's energy and quick intelligence, a wealthy relative after whom he was named, General Robert Stuart of the East India Company's private army, asked the then-teenager to accompany him to the East Indies. All the arrangements were made, but at the last minute, Mary Stuart couldn't bear to lose her son, and the trip was canceled. Instead of sailing off to the Orient, Stuart was left behind to help out his father on the farm until he found a way to make a living.

The options were few. As part of its efforts to rid the glens of troublesome clansmen, the government in London shrewdly offered military commissions in the Black Watch, the Forty-Second Royal Highland Regiment, to clan chieftains, thus ensuring that their followers would enlist as well. Before retiring to the family farm in Balquhidder, Stuart's grandfather, James Stuart, a loyalist, had served as a captain in the Black Watch with such distinction that the National War Museum in Edinburgh Castle added his Andrea Ferara broadsword to its collection. Yet Robert Stuart had no apparent interest in a military career. Nor was there a future for him in agriculture. By custom his oldest brother James was to inherit the family farm.

Probably at the urging of his father, Stuart ventured into teaching. For a time he assisted his father with his teaching duties locally. In 1807, he was serving as tutor to the children of Lord Macdonald of Skye when John Stuart died unexpectedly sitting in his chair before the fire at "Tigh-na-cuilt." He was fifty-one.

Not long after receiving the news of his father's death and returning home, Stuart received a letter from his Uncle David in Canada. An agent with the powerful NWC, then the most successful fur trading company in North America, David offered to find his nephew a job as a clerk with the firm if he came to Montreal, where the NWC was headquartered. To a young Scot with few prospects, the offer was irresistible. This time Mary Stuart would not be able to keep her son from leaving his homeland. Like so many Highlanders, Robert Stuart's future lay on the far side of the Atlantic.

AS PROMISED, David Stuart had secured his nephew a job with the NWC as an apprentice clerk. For the first year, the position paid a modest salary, roughly one hundred pounds plus room and board in the dormitorylike clerks' quarters at the company house on St. Gabriel Street.

Stuart was now engaged in a business the British had originally dominated, thanks to the Royal Charter signed by Charles II in 1670 that had invested the English-owned Hudson's Bay Company with exclusive rights over the vast watershed of Hudson Bay. By the early 1780s, however, the NWC, a consortium of mostly Scottish traders led by Simon McTavish, an energetic Highlander with a genius for business organization, had leapfrogged its Hudson Bay rival and begun to carve out a vast trading empire in the West.

By the time the younger Stuart joined the company, the Nor'Westers—the "Lords of the Lakes and Forest," as Washington Irving dubbed them—had gained control over nearly 80 percent of Canadian fur sales. Led by trader-explorers such as Alexander Mackenzie, who had traveled overland all the way to the Pacific Ocean in 1793, a full ten years before the departure of Lewis and Clark, and the Englishman David Thompson, the NWC was already trading beyond the Great Divide and had opened up most of the Northwest, from Lake Superior to the Pacific Ocean and from the headwaters of the Mississippi to the Arctic Sea.

In their brightly painted "canots du maitre," the great birch-bark Montreal canoes that were up to forty feet long and six feet wide, and the smaller, more maneuverable "canots du nord," the Nor'Westers transported the merchandise they traded to the Indians through a far-reaching network of posts that extended from the company's inland trading hub, Fort William, near the head of Lake Superior.

A fur-trading scene.

At the NWC headquarters in Montreal, where all the pelts were eventually collected, Stuart and his fellow clerks supervised the opening of the bales of furs, bound in buffalo hides and bearskins, that the traders brought back with them each fall. The intake was enormous: in one year totaling more than 100,000 beaver skins, 32,000 marten, 11,000 mink, 17,000 muskrat pelts, and tens of thousands of additional furs. Working in the semidark expanses of the vast NWC warehouses, clerks counted and inspected the pelts, making sure each was free of dust and moths. When that chore was completed, the clerks sorted, graded, and valued each skin. Finally, the entire collection of pelts would be stored for the winter to harden before being shipped off to England.

It was tedious, repetitious work that consumed twelve to fourteen hours a day, six days a week. Holidays were few, the longest being Christmas week when the St. Lawrence River often froze over and the clerks celebrated Christmas at a rousing banquet in the feast room of the company house.

As the novelty of his new post wore off, Stuart found life in Montreal increasingly monotonous and often bleak, especially during the long winters. With its iron-shuttered wooden houses, the city was as gray and gloomy as a prison, its dirt streets clouded with dust in the summer and ankle-deep in mud during the winter and spring. Far from home and his family, Stuart had few diversions beyond carousing occasionally with his fellow clerks and perhaps brief interludes with prostitutes and shop girls.

Intensely ambitious, Stuart hadn't come to Canada to pass his days processing pelts in the damp chill of the NWC's waterfront warehouses. From the outset, he had hoped to be sent to the interior. Not only did a wilderness posting appeal to his adventuresome nature, but Stuart also knew that such assignments were often the most direct route to advancement.

A year after Stuart started with the NWC, a distant cousin named John Stuart, an agent with the company, had accompanied the irascible Simon Fraser, one of the company's partners, on Fraser's expedition west through Canada's interior to find a water route to the mouth of the Columbia. Though Fraser reached the Pacific, as had Mackenzie before him, he failed to find a so-called Northwest Passage to the Columbia. Even so, the company honored Fraser while putting his lieutenant John Stuart in charge of one of its most important western districts.

Robert Stuart did what he could to prepare for a similar assignment, should one be offered him. He was a frequent visitor to the Montreal Library with its two thousand French and six thousand English volumes. There, or in the NWC's own far more modest library, he read Alexander Mackenzie's account of his 1793 journey to the Pacific as well as the journal Patrick Gass had kept while with the Lewis and Clark's Corps of Discovery expedition, published in 1807. With a Catholic priest at the Saint-Sulpice Seminary, Stuart also began studying French, the language of the French Canadian voyageurs and engages, common laborers who were treated as indentured servants, and many of the Indians with whom they traded.

Still, he remained in Montreal, growing increasingly restless.

TRADING IN NOVA SCOTIA and the coast of Labrador, David Stuart came to Montreal perhaps twice a year. On those occasions he'd spend as much time with his nephew as possible. Twenty years older than Robert, David Stuart was a wiry gamecock of a man with a great shock of prematurely white hair and craggy features that looked as though they had been forged on the frontier. He bore a prominent facial scar from a wound received fighting Indians and usually had a pipe clenched between his teeth.

A later daguerreotype shows him to be a formidable-looking character, and, indeed, a colleague described him as "one of those intrepid souls who are born without fear." But the elder Stuart was also a gentle, avuncular man with a great sense of dignity. An experienced frontiersman, he had a talent for dealing with the Indians, with whom he had lived and traded on cordial terms for much of his adult life.

During his visits to Montreal, David Stuart counseled his nephew to be patient regarding a promotion and promised to put in a good word for the younger man whenever the opportunity arose. By one unsubstantiated account, Robert Stuart considered leaving the fur trade altogether for a position in the office of the attorney general of Lower Canada. At the urging of his uncle, however, he remained with the NWC.

David Stuart's own prospects within the company weren't especially promising. He had served as a clerk and agent with the NWC for well over a decade and still hadn't been made a partner. Moreover, since many of the existing partners were still relatively young men far from retirement, admission into the company's inner circle was hard to come by.

Still, David Stuart urged his nephew not to do anything rash. Sooner or later, an opportunity would come along—perhaps for both of them.

CHAPTER 3

HIDDEN AGENDA

LATE IN THE SUMMER OF 1809, JOHN JACOB ASTOR SET off from New York to Montreal on his fall buying trip, a journey he had been making annually for more than a decade. In those early years in the fur trade, he would take a sloop up the Hudson to Albany, where he'd secure a horse, wagon, and trading goods to exchange with the Indians for pelts. Then he would make his way north through the still-wild backcountry en route to Canada.

For an enterprising frontier entrepreneur who didn't mind sleeping on the kitchen floor in front of the open fire at Peter Sailly's house in Plattsburgh or getting lost on a miserable night in the forest after straying from the Indian trail, the fur trade held an undeniable appeal. Few businesses required so little capital and generated such fabulous returns. "Many times I have seen John Jacob Astor with his coat off, unpacking . . . a lot of furs he had bought dog-cheap off the Indians and beating them out, cleaning and repacking them in more elegant and salable form to be transported to England and Germany, where they would yield him 1,000 per cent on the original cost," one of his early associates wrote.

In 1809, Astor was forty-six, a short, stout man with a formidable jaw, hook nose, and what one biographer described as "deep-set, intent eyes." His traffic in furs plus a growing real-estate portfolio and a highly prosperous import-export business had already made him one of the wealthiest and most influential merchants in North America. His marriage to Sarah Todd, whose family had strong maritime ties, helped secure his success, providing Astor with access to many of the city's sea captains and shipowners.

For all his wealth, however, Astor was never accepted as a member of Knickerbocker society. Many in New York and Europe dismissed him as boorish, an arriviste bereft of culture or taste. The son of the village butcher in Waldorf, Germany, Astor spoke English with a thick, guttural accent, exhibited an uncertain mastery of English syntax in both the written and spoken word, and showed little aptitude for social niceties. "Mr. Astor is horrid," wrote James Gallatin, son of Jefferson's secretary of the treasury Albert Gallatin, seeing Astor wipe his hands on the sleeve of his dinner partner's gown. On another such occasion, Astor scandalized the guests by devouring his peas with a knife.

Montreal, the capital of the North American fur trade, was perhaps where Astor felt most comfortable. In recent years, he had traveled there as much to fraternize with the powers of the Canadian fur trade as to traffic in pelts, often staying a month or two at summer's end. Inevitably, as the NWC's biggest and perhaps oldest customer, Astor was accorded the full measure of Canadian hospitality. His hosts were men with whom he had much in common—immigrants like himself, most of them Scots, who had made their own way in the world, mastering a hard wilderness trade. They dominated the commercial and social life of young Canada much in the same manner that the tobacco lords held sway in Virginia.

On these trips, Astor was frequently a guest at banquets held by the famous Beaver Club, a social organization made up of what the club rules defined as, "a set of men highly respectable in society who had passed their best days in a savage country and had encountered the difficulties and dangers incident to a pursuit of the fur trade in Canada."

At the club banquets, scenes of Hogarthian excess, the members seemed determined to make up for whatever deprivations they'd experienced in the wilderness. Astor, for instance, attended a club dinner on September 17, 1808, at Mr. Dillon's Montreal Hotel on Place d'Annes. Astor and several dozen other guests and members among them consumed 32 dinners, 29 bottles of Madeira, 19 bottles of port, 14 bottles of porter, 8 quarts of ale, 7 suppers, and unspecified quantities of gin and brandy. The bill, which included cigars and tobacco as well as three broken wineglasses, came to just over twenty-eight pounds.

On these visits, William McGillivray, the NWC's chief executive officer, always asked Astor to dine at his lavish home, Chateau St. Antoine, at the base of Mont Royal, as did another NWC principal, Joseph Frobisher. A sixty-nine-year-old Englishman, Frobisher had been the first white man to penetrate the wilderness of northwestern Canada as far as the Churchill River. During an 1806 visit, when Astor had come to Montreal with his oldest daughter, Magdalen, Frobisher hosted a ball at his home, Beaver Hall, in honor of the rather plain young woman whom the New Yorker hoped to marry off with a dowry of twenty-five thousand dollars. In Canada, at least, she found no suitors.

For Astor, Montreal was a second home, a place where new money and accomplishment counted more than social pedigree. Still, although he owned property there including a fur warehouse, Astor remained an outsider and was increasingly seen as a competitor. He had come to Canada the previous summer several months after getting the go-ahead for his western trading enterprise from Jefferson. On that visit, he met with the Nor'Westers, who controlled both the NWC and Michilimackinac, to discuss possibly partnering with them or buying Michilimackinac outright. These talks had gone nowhere, largely because, with Jefferson's embargo in effect, neither Astor nor those associated with him could export or import furs.

But the U.S. government had finally lifted the increasingly unpopular trade ban a few months prior to Astor's most recent trip to Montreal. The Canadians, of course, were well aware of this and were looking forward to renewed talks with Astor. On this 1809 visit to Montreal, however, Astor's plans for the AFC had changed significantly. His primary concern wasn't buying furs or partnering with the Canadians. He had an altogether different agenda, one he intended to conceal from his hosts for as long as possible.

BY ANY MEASURE, Astor was an exceptionally able businessman, a brilliant strategist and organizer who rarely misstepped. He combined a robust energy and drive with enormous patience, and the self-assuredness to ride out a long-term investment until it paid off. Usually, he got what he wanted when he wanted it—if necessary, through intimidation or deception. As an example, Astor had been less than forthright with President Jefferson in securing backing for the AFC, implying that the trans-Mississippi trade was to be carried out by a syndicate of American investors, all of whom would share in the profits. From the outset, however, Astor intended to retain absolute control of the new enterprise. "It was his purpose to concentrate the western fur trade in the hands of only such American citizens as had been born in Waldorf, Germany, in 1763, and had arrived in the United States from London in the spring of 1784," his biographer Kenneth Porter noted.

Astor's real genius lay in his ability to think and operate effectively on a global scale, juggling disparate initiatives in different parts of the world until he was able to make them converge in ways that almost invariably earned him unseemly large sums of money. It was this desire to extend his reach well beyond U.S. borders that caused Astor to rethink his approach in proceeding with the AFC.

Since 1786, Astor had been trading on an international basis, importing musical instruments, armaments, dry goods, and the like from England and Europe, and from the Orient, souchong teas and India silks. In turn, Astor would send furs to London or Canton, where they were highly valued and drew top prices. At first, these trading efforts had been relatively modest. Astor would charter space for shipments of furs on a ship bound for Hamburg or the Orient. He would use some of the merchandise, such as blankets and cutlery that came back in exchange for the Indian trade, and sell the rest to the public. "Jacob Astor," notices in the *New York Packet* and the *Daily Advertiser* proclaimed, had "just imported an elegant assortment of Piano Fortes which he will sell on reasonable terms." They went on to note that Astor also bought and sold all kinds of furs for cash on the barrelhead.

Several of Astor's in-laws were sea captains in the China trade. Acting with their guidance, he began buying interests in various trading ships. The first was the 280-ton *Severn*. Under the command of Stuart Dean, the husband of one of Sarah Astor's nieces, the ship sailed for Canton in late April 1800 with a cargo consisting of close to fifty thousand pelts, including 30,573 sealskins. Upon the ship's return a year later, Astor and his partners quickly sold out the goods acquired in the Orient—nutmegs and cloves, silks, Nankin fans, chinaware, and silver. Astor was so encouraged that he promptly acquired complete ownership of the *Severn* in 1804, and soon was ordering other vessels to be built specifically for trade with Canton.

Jefferson's embargo put an end to trading with both Europe and China, although Astor did manage to get one ship, the *Beaver*, through to Canton after receiving special clearance from the president. Jefferson granted approval based on an appeal from Latham Mitchell, senator from New York, whom Astor, operating from behind the scenes, used as an intermediary. Mitchell claimed that a prominent Hong Kong merchant wanted desperately to return to his homeland to attend his grandfather's funeral and be reunited with his family.

The appeal was entirely bogus. The supposed merchant proved to be a Chinese laborer whom Astor had dressed in expensive silks and given the unlikely name of the Punqua Wingchong. The Federalist newspapers had a field day with the story, once poor Punqua had been exposed; Jefferson was deeply embarrassed. Astor banked another significant profit after the *Beaver* returned from the Orient carrying merchandise worth two hundred thousand dollars more than the cargo she took with her upon leaving New York.

Even so, the two-year-long embargo cost Astor dearly. Once restrictions were lifted on March 1, 1809, he pressed vigorously to make up for lost opportunities. Within a few months, he acquired a new ship, the brig *Sylph*, obtained partial interest in another, and dispatched the *Beaver* to Canton and the brig *Fox* to Calcutta. In June, he also met the Russian consul general to America, Andrew Dashkoff. Dashkoff had come to the United States to seek assistance from newly elected President James Madison—Jefferson had retired to his beloved Monticello in January—in dealing with a problem concerning the Russian-American Company, which controlled the fur trade along the Northwest coast from the Bering Strait to Vancouver Island.

With Czar Alexander's government busy annexing Finland and engaged in a prolonged war with Persia, supply ships from St. Petersburg to the Russian settlements were infrequent. As a result, the Russians had to rely on irregular visits from American traders, who supplied the Indians in the area with guns and ammunition in exchange for valuable sea-otter pelts, which were in great demand in China. In so doing, the Americans were not only poaching on Russian turf but also were endangering the lives of Russian settlers by arming local natives. Dashkoff wanted the American government to step in and rectify the situation. Madison begged off. He hadn't the resources to police the Northwest coast, but suggested that perhaps Mr. Astor of New York could be of assistance.

SOON AFTER, the Russian consul general sent his representatives to feel out Astor and later met with the merchant himself. In the course of their discussions, Dashkoff suggested that Astor establish a great trading enterprise at the mouth of the Columbia River. It was not the first time Astor had heard such a plan proposed. One of his mentors in the trade, old Alexander Henry, had come up with the idea of establishing forts on the rivers of the Northwest coast in 1786. At the time, such a proposal seemed unfeasible, but that had been before Lewis and Clark had ventured up the Columbia, wintering not far from the river's mouth—and before Astor established the AFC with the intention of eventually building posts on the Columbia himself.

Dashkoff's suggestion triggered an epiphany of sorts. Astor abruptly decided that instead of building posts west from St. Louis—his initial approach with the AFC—he would start in reverse order, establishing his base at the Columbia's mouth. His friends, the Canadians, had a similar strategy in mind, he suspected.

Astor was well aware of the Nor'Wester Simon Fraser's failed attempt to reach the Columbia during the previous year. Ever since Mackenzie's 1793 crossing, the Canadians had been searching in vain for a water route from the north to the Columbia. "Whatever road one follows on leaving the shore of the Atlantic Ocean, one must join the Columbia in order to reach the great Pacific Ocean," Mackenzie believed. Before the Canadians tried again, Astor would leapfrog them and lock up the Northwest coast and the Columbia trade for himself.

To Dashkoff, Astor proposed that the AFC supply everything the Russian settlements needed from Europe and North America but refrain from dealing with Indians in Russian territory or providing them with armaments of any sort. In exchange, the Russians would not deal with other American or Canadian traders or traffic with the Indians in the Columbia area. Dashkoff not only agreed but also suggested that an Astor agent seal the agreement with Governor Baranov at New Archangel, on Sitka in southeast Alaska, where the Russian Fur Company was headquartered.

For Astor this new approach held enormous promise. From a hub at the mouth of the Columbia, Astor would establish satellite bases on the river's tributaries and tap into the rich bounty of furs in the Pacific Northwest. Equally important, he would be able to dispatch furs directly from the Columbia River to China at far less cost and time than sailing all the way from New York.

The potential was enormous, but Astor knew that mounting this initiative would be far more costly then building bases incrementally from east to west. He needed more capital, and most of all, he needed experienced men who could head up such a venture. But the only place to find such people was in Canada among the ranks of seasoned traders who knew the far frontier. In August, Astor left for Montreal intent on discreetly recruiting some of the NWC's key men. He would adhere to his usual routines, all the while extending feelers to the right people. He knew that ultimately, of course, the Nor'Westers would get wind of what he was up to. Certainly it wouldn't do to underrate the Canadians. His best hope was that they would underestimate him.

CHAPTER 4

IN PURSUIT OF
CASTOR CANADENSIS

THE PRIZE JOHN JACOB ASTOR WAS PURSUING IN FORMING the AFC was a large aquatic rodent distinguished by its outsize molars, its aptitude for building and engineering, and its pelt. Beaver, or *Castor canadensis,* are blessed—or cursed—with a handsome, richly luxuriant coat, which is also warm and largely waterproof, thanks to an underfur made up of tiny barbs. The barbs trap a layer of insulating air that keeps the beaver comfortable even in the coldest waters—and the wearers of beaver-felt hats dry in the most inclement weather, no small consideration prior to widespread use of the umbrella.

Traditionally, Europeans obtained their furs—the shaggy bearskin for the tall hats worn by the guardsmen at Buckingham Palace, the regal ermine used to trim royal robes—from Russia and Scandinavia, but these supplies had been largely exhausted by the sixteenth century. At about the same time, England, France, Holland, and Spain began acquiring North American furs, especially beaver. Soon these gentle creatures became the most widely hunted animal on the continent. They were killed—hunted and later trapped by Indians at the urging of white traders—primarily for their pelts.

The Pilgrims, as well as other colonists, used beaver skins they obtained from the natives to repay the English merchants who had funded their journey to the colonies. By 1632, pelts were already scarce in the Boston area and rapidly disappearing from other regions

John Jacob Astor by John Wesley Jarvis.
COURTESY OF NATIONAL PORTRAIT GALLERY, SMITHSONIAN
INSTITUTION; GIFT OF MRS. SUSAN MARY ALSOP.

including the Delaware River valley, where the Dutch and Swedes had been acquiring as many furs as the Indians there could produce. After 1638, when the English parliament passed an act prohibiting the making of hats from any material other than "beaver stuff and beaver wool," demand was so great that as many as two hundred thousand pelts were sent to Europe annually. Their local supplies dwindling, pioneer entrepreneurs from eastern Massachusetts such as William Pynchon of Roxbury moved to what at the time was the frontier, resettling near present Springfield, Massachusetts. From his trading post on the banks of the Connecticut River, Pynchon shipped nine thousand beaver skins to England between 1652 and 1658.

To the north and west, the French aggressively pursued the fur trade as well, dealing largely with their allies the Hurons, at least until the jealous Iroquois violently interceded. In their canoes, or plodding across the frozen north country in snowshoes, French traders and explorers, "coureurs des bois," often in tandem with Jesuit missionaries, traversed the wilderness in search of pelts. They were the first to navigate the Mississippi and settle the Mississippi River valley, founding New Orleans and St. Louis, the latter of which would later become the fur-trading center of the West; they were also the first to enter the basins of the Red and Saskatchewan rivers. The earliest whites in what is now Minnesota were two French fur traders who arrived from Quebec in 1655. Returning to Montreal, they told of the riches in fur to be found in the Minnesota country.

Not to be outdone, the British cavalierly laid claim to vast areas of present-day Canada, some of which was already under the French flag. A trading charter granted in May 1670 by Charles II to a syndicate headed by his cousin Prince Rupert created the Hudson's Bay Company (HBC). The charter gave the newly formed company an area of one and a half million square miles, known later as Rupert's Land. It encompassed most of present northern Ontario and northern Quebec, all of Manitoba, much of Saskatchewan, the southern half of Alberta, a large part of the Northwest Territories, and considerable chunks of Minnesota and North Dakota. Rupert and his fellow shareholders—a group of British nobles and merchant princes who had never visited the New World and never would—left the Indian trade to HBC recruits and agents, collected the dividends, and occasionally issued ill-informed edicts to their agents abroad, which went largely ignored.

The motto of the HBC was *Pro pelle cutem* ("skin for skin") and its logo was two rearing bull moose flanking a shield depicting four beaver. With a trading monopoly over much of the prime beaver country in North America, the company was generating a yearly profit of 200 percent on invested capital and yielding substantial dividends. To its credit, the company had developed a well-organized and reasonably equitable approach in dealing with Indian hunters. Under the HBC system, which quickly became pervasive throughout Rupert's Land, beaver pelts became the coin of the realm. Tally-stick in hand, a hunter matched the value of the pelts he brought to an HBC outpost with trade goods. A single beaver pelt brought the hunter a gallon of brandy or one and a half pounds of gunpowder; in exchange for six pelts, natives received a much-coveted Hudson Bay blanket, while the hunter with twelve prime winter beaver pelts could earn a musket.

For the short term at least—before the rum and whiskey that became the mother's milk of the fur trade took its toll on the native people and beaver populations were decimated throughout much of the continent—both whites and Indians benefited from the HBC system. "The relation of the trader to the Indian was the most natural and congenial of any which the two races have ever sustained toward each other," fur trade historian Hiram Chittenden noted. "Properly conducted, it fitted perfectly with the Indian's previous mode of life . . . and enabled him to pursue his natural occupation of hunting."

THE HBC RETAINED the fur trade in its increasingly complacent grip until 1783–84, when a confederation of freewheeling independent traders decided to launch the rival NWC based in Montreal.

Most of the NWC's founders were Jacobite Highlanders. They had no love for the British and were perfectly willing to poach on HBC territory. Their approach to the fur trade differed markedly from that of the HBC in several important respects. While the HBC's governors never ventured to the New World and their employees were indentured servants—mostly Orkney Islanders who returned to their homes as soon as their stint of duty was up—the Nor'Westers were largely Canadians. Based mostly in Montreal, they knew the Indian trade intimately and had canoed and portaged for years throughout the North American outback. Moreover, HBC's traders were largely stationary, manning the posts the company had built around the Hudson Bay. Native traders had to come to them, often traveling great distances in canoes laden with pelts. In contrast, the NWC's explorer-traders were constantly on the move. They brought the fur trade to the Indians, probing deep into previously uncharted territories. They established a wilderness headquarters, Fort William, near the head of Lake Superior. From there, they set up satellite outposts that were manned by so-called wintering partners, who remained with the natives throughout most of the year, often taking an Indian mistress—an occupational perk referred to as "bits of brown."

This aggressive, freewheeling approach gave the NWC traders first crack at the prime pelts and yielded such significant dividends that by the time John Jacob Astor was petitioning Thomas Jefferson for support, the NWC controlled almost 80 percent of Canadian fur sales. One of the few areas that still remained beyond the company's reach was the Pacific Northwest. With his AFC, Astor fully intended to emulate the approach that had proven so successful for his Canadian rivals.

CHAPTER 5

STARTING OVER

BY LATE WINTER 1810, ASTOR'S COLUMBIA RIVER CAMPAIGN was gathering momentum but not without encountering several unexpected hitches along the way. On his return to New York from Montreal, Astor recognized what should have been obvious from the outset: In order to attract the caliber of men he was seeking, he needed to offer equity in his new trading venture. No matter how dissatisfied they may have been working for the NWC, veteran Canadian traders were not likely to join an unproven start-up—even one backed by an American millionaire—without a partnership agreement and stock.

This presented an immediate problem. In his attempt to retain absolute control of the AFC, Astor had structured the company to exclude ownership by anyone other than himself. Consequently, he had to create an entirely new organization, the Pacific Fur Company (PFC), to deal with the Columbia River trade.

Back in New York, Astor also decided to send two expeditions to the mouth of the Columbia: one by land, along the route Lewis and Clark had followed, and the other by sea. Mounting a single expedition to the far side of the continent was an enormously costly and taxing endeavor. Costs for the Lewis and Clark expedition exceeded forty thousand dollars, a substantial sum at the time. Dual expeditions would require Astor to draw upon every resource at his command, a commitment he was willing to make in order to better his odds at beating the Canadians to the Columbia.

THE THREE MEN who opened an office in Montreal in early 1810 were there expressly to recruit additional traders for John Jacob Astor's newly formed PFC. Two of Astor's three emissaries were prominent figures in the fur trade. The flamboyant Alexander McKay, a former NWC partner who was known for his boisterous sense of humor and enormous physical courage, had been Alexander Mackenzie's lieutenant in the 1793 expedition down the Bella Coola River to the Pacific. Astor had met the well-liked Nor'Wester at Beaver Club banquets during his visits to Montreal.

Born in Scotland on June 12, 1783, Donald Mackenzie was a cousin of Alexander. He had studied for the ministry but soon switched to the fur trade, serving with the NWC for ten years in the interior as a clerk and agent. A superb marksman, Mackenzie had enormous energy, an outsize ego, and a girth to match, weighing in at close to three hundred pounds. Among his peers he was known simply as "Fat."

The third member of the delegation, Wilson Price Hunt, was new to the fur trade. Born in New Jersey, he moved as a young man to St. Louis, where he had emerged as one of the city's leading merchants. He likely came to Astor's attention through Charles Gratiot or another of the New Yorker's former business associates in St. Louis. Largely for political reasons, Astor wanted an American to head up the PFC operations and quickly became convinced that Hunt was his man. In his correspondence to Jefferson, Astor described Hunt as a "very respectful gentleman from Trenton, N.J." and a "Real American."

Hunt left St. Louis in November 1809, stopping in New York to meet with his new boss and sign a partnership agreement. From there, he went on to Montreal to join McKay and Mackenzie, both of whom had already committed to the new venture. Operating openly in the Nor'Westers' own backyard, the threesome set about recruiting clerks and additional partners from a short list of candidates McKay and Mackenzie had drawn up. Among the prospects were the well-respected David Stuart and his nephew, Robert—who by now had established himself as among the more able of the NWC clerks, a man who was clearly ready for advancement.

Both Stuarts knew of Astor. David likely met the New Yorker on one of his visits to Canada. They were impressed by the scope of Astor's plan as detailed in the gilded prospectus McKay and the others showed them. What really sold David and his nephew, though, was the quality of men who had already committed to the new company, McKay in particular. McKay's participation in the venture gave the PFC instant credibility. Few men in all of North America were as qualified to help Astor get established in Indian country as Alexander McKay.

For all his bluster, Donald Mackenzie was also a seasoned frontiersman, a valuable man to have on a venture that was clearly fraught with danger and uncertainty. And while Wilson Price Hunt knew nothing about the wilderness and little about the fur trade, he was a levelheaded, quietly assertive businessman. Hunt was only two years older than Robert Stuart, yet Astor had put him in charge of the overland expedition as well as the entire Columbia River venture. Clearly, as Robert Stuart noted, Astor hadn't any qualms about giving responsibility to able young men. Inspired by their fellow Scots' confidence in Astor's venture and attracted by the offer of partnerships in the fledgling firm, the Stuarts were among the first Nor'Westers to sign on, agreeing to terms on June 10.

Drawn up by hand on twenty pages of legal paper, the agreement between Astor and his new partners spelled out what was expected from both the New Yorker and his new, largely Scottish-born associates. The agreement specified that Astor would furnish "all the means requisite to establish a fur trading post at, or in the vicinity of the Columbia River, including vessels, goods, wares, merchandises, provisions, arms, ammunition and men." In total, he would put up as much as four hundred thousand dollars, an enormous fortune in 1810, to finance this venture. In exchange, he was to receive legal interest on every penny his partners spent, and he retained fifty percent equity, fifty of the one hundred shares in the newly formed PFC.

The Stuarts and Astor's other partners, each of whom received from two to five shares in the venture, were to send Astor all the furs they acquired, with the understanding that he would sell them without taking his usual commission and would pump the profits back into the company.

In addition, under the agreement, the senior partners such as

David Stuart, McKay, Mackenzie, and Duncan McDougall—another Scot and former Nor'Wester recruited in Montreal—could not retire from the company for five years. Robert Stuart and the other junior officers were obligated to remain on the payroll even longer, "until they shall have been seven years in the Indian country as partners."

CHAPTER 6

FINAL PREPARATIONS

ONCE THE NECESSARY PAPERWORK HAD BEEN DRAWN up, Astor's new partners split into two groups. Upset that he hadn't been chosen the sole leader of the overland expedition, "Fat" Mackenzie quarreled with Hunt, arguing they should restrict their recruiting to Canadian lads. Hunt, on Astor's instructions, pushed to include as many Americans as possible in the party. Still bickering, this mismatched pair left Montreal in a canot du maitre on July 2, bound eventually for St. Louis, where they were to join forces with the other members of the overland party and recruit additional partners.

By mid-July, the sea-bound Astorians were also ready to leave Montreal for New York. In addition to the Stuarts, the group included Duncan McDougall and Alexander Ross, a one-time schoolmaster who had signed on as a clerk.

The Stuart party set off to New York on a commercial sailing ship, leaving on July 20, 1810. Meanwhile, with his characteristic flair, McKay decided to make the nearly four-hundred-mile journey in a traditional Nor'Wester birch-bark canoe by way of Lake Champlain and the Hudson River. With him went Gabriel Franchere, the gregarious son of a Montreal merchant, who'd been recruited as a clerk; McKay's teenage son Tom, who also had signed on as a clerk; a half dozen voyageurs; and Adam Fisher, a sailor.

The Stuarts, Ross, and McDougall arrived at the end of July, McKay a week later on August 3. McKay knew how to make a proper entrance. Reaching the city on a Saturday night, he and his crew drew crowds along the shoreline, among them Astor, with their wildly enthusiastic renditions of the French canoe-men songs. "We sang, and the sight of a birch-bark canoe attracted crowds of people to the quays," Franchere recalled. Astor was so delighted when the group came ashore—McKay's powerful voyageurs easily lifting the enormously heavy canoe out of the water—that he stood them to drinks.

AT THE TIME, New York was a robust metropolis with a surging economy and a population of more than ninety thousand, ten times that of Montreal. It was home to thirty-two churches, eight markets, numerous newspapers, two theaters and hundreds of taverns and saloons, and what was probably the first building in the United States to be erected specifically as a hotel, the City Hotel on lower Broadway.

The city's popular, progressive mayor, De Witt Clinton, had founded the Orphan Asylum and the New-York Historical Society and was overseeing completion of a new city hall on Chambers Street, an impressive half-million-dollar edifice built from white marble brought down by wagon from the quarries of Stockbridge, Massachusetts.

On the streets, merchants in horse-drawn wagons sold watermelons, strawberries, and produce of all sorts. A London import, Sheridan's *She Stoops to Conquer,* was the hit of the theatrical season. Opium was sold openly and legally, and the front pages of *The New York Post* and the city's other newspapers advertised sizable rewards for the return of runaway slaves.

The Canadians, accustomed as they were to somber, slow-paced Montreal, were dazzled by the city's diversity and energy. "I found New York most agreeable," Gabriel Franchere observed. "The elegance of the public and private buildings, the cleanness of the streets, the shade of the poplars that lined them, the markets overflowing with every foodstuff required by man, the then-flourishing commercial activity, the many ships of all nations that lined the docks—all helped to emphasize the difference between the busy seaport and my native town which I had practically never left before."

Upon their arrival, the Stuarts and McDougall promptly reported to Astor's offices at 71 Liberty Street, where their new employer enthusiastically briefed them regarding the upcoming expedition. In

David Stuart, "Old Uncle."
COLLECTION OF THE AUTHOR.

recent months, Astor had been busy preparing for the sea expedition. In May, he'd hired an experienced captain to pilot his men to the Columbia, a thirty-year-old American naval officer named Jonathan Thorn. Thorn had been granted a two-year furlough to work for Astor even though war between the United States and England was a growing likelihood. Their new employer assured the Stuarts and McDougall that Thorn was well qualified to transport his traders to the Pacific Northwest.

A skilled and practical navigator who prided himself on his robust physique and undisputed courage, Thorn had fought with distinction in the 1801–1804 war against the Barbary States. That conflict had come about after Tripoli had demanded the United States pay tribute to its pasha so that American ships could pass unmolested through Mediterranean waters. Thorn had commanded a gunboat in the February 16, 1804, bombardment of Tripoli, earning commendations from his superiors. In 1806, he was appointed first commandant of the New York Navy Yard, and the following year was made a full lieutenant, the highest rank he would attain in the Navy.

With Thorn on his payroll, Astor still needed a ship to transport his men and supplies. Earlier in the summer, he had acquired the *Tonquin* for $37,860. A 269-ton, three-masted bark designed to carry twenty-two guns, the vessel had been built in 1807 at the New York shipyard of Adam and Noah Brown under the supervision of its first owner, Captain Edmund Fanning, an early hand in the China and Pacific trade and the discoverer of the Fanning Islands in the South Pacific. The *Tonquin* had earned the reputation of being a fast-sailing ship and had already made two tours of the Pacific circuit, one of them in an impressively expeditious ten months, a month less than the trip usually took. Despite its ninety-six-foot length, twenty-five-foot width, and twelve-foot depth, the *Tonquin* would prove too small to transport in comfort an extensive cargo, a full crew, and some thirty-three passengers on a prolonged and dangerous ocean voyage. When Astor finally took possession of the ship in early August, she had been idle for more than six months. Astor pressed Thorn to have her overhauled in record time and to finish assembling a crew.

For months, Astor continued to lead the Nor'Westers in believing he was going to let them participate in this venture. Now that he was proceeding without them, he feared that the British were planning to try to thwart his efforts. From his contacts in Washington, Astor had heard that an armed brig from Halifax, probably at the instigation of the NWC, was hovering off the coast with the purpose of intercepting the *Tonquin* and impressing the Canadians and British on board. Astor detailed these concerns to his new partners, assuring them, however, that they had little to worry about. To ensure that the *Tonquin* got off to a good start, he'd pulled strings in Washington to have the ship escorted out of New York harbor by none other than the USS *Constitution*, "Old Ironsides." Ready or not, the *Tonquin* would leave on September 6.

DURING THE COURSE of the meeting with Astor, Robert Stuart received some news that would cause him to reconsider his commitment to the venture. In their rush to recruit new men, Astor's representatives had given out fifty-two shares in the new enterprise when only fifty were available. As a result, Stuart, who in terms of experience was junior to the other partners, wasn't going to be allocated two shares after all. Without equity, he remained a clerk, no matter how his agreement with the AFC read.

This meant, for starters, that while his uncle, McDougall, and McKay, who arrived with the other expedition members in August, were provided with comfortable accommodations at Mrs. Saidler's boarding house in Manhattan, Stuart had to stay with the clerks across the East River. There, on behalf of Astor, he was put in charge of the group, paying their expenses for their month-long stay, a sum that totaled sixty-eight dollars according to the company books. He was also charged with ensuring that his boisterous fellow clerks obtained U.S. citizenship, a requisite for all Astor's men, and that they stay clear of trouble, especially in the rough waterfront taverns and bawdy houses across the East River. A number of Stuart's charges were in their late teens or early twenties and viewed the weeks before the long, dangerous voyage as a holiday, perhaps their last. Stuart had given up his post at the NWC and had come to New York, it seemed, to play nursemaid.

At least Stuart knew people in Brooklyn: a big, gregarious family like his own named Sullivan. Stuart met Mary Sullivan and her twin sons Robert and John in Montreal. In 1807, several months after she was widowed, Mary Sullivan had traveled to Montreal with the twins, who were then twelve, to enroll them in the College of Montreal on Rue St. Paul. They studied for the next three years there under the Sulpican fathers, with whom Stuart was then studying French.

Stuart was made welcome at the Sullivan home, a handsome, four-story brick house on the southwest corner of Fulton and Nassau Streets in the village on Long Island that would later become Brooklyn. The house had been built several years earlier by Mary Sullivan's late husband, John, a well-born Irish patriot from Cork who, according to family legend, fled to America to escape the British hangman. A supporter of Irish nationalist Robert Emmet, Sullivan had become a prosperous wholesale grocer and a prominent figure in New York City politics and the Catholic Church.

In addition to the twins, Mary and John Sullivan had five other children, four daughters and a son, ranging in age from six to twenty-four. A frequent guest at family dinners in Brooklyn, Stuart patiently responded to the twins' questions about the fur trade and his upcoming trip to Indian country, while the younger children—

Quintin, Nelly and Jane Theresa—were intrigued by this stranger with his Scottish accent and gentle, teasing manner. But it was Elizabeth Emma "Betsy" Sullivan who quickly became the focus of Stuart's attention.

While John and Mary Sullivan had agreed to rear their sons as Roman Catholics, Mary, the socially ambitious daughter of a well-to-do ship captain and his second wife, insisted that their daughters be brought up as Protestants. Betsy Sullivan, their second surviving daughter, had attended the Moravian Seminary in Bethlehem, Pennsylvania, graduating in 1804. At eighteen, she was a refined, gregarious, intelligent young woman with raven black hair and the poise and confidence of someone who was thoroughly at home in New York society.

Theirs was an unlikely pairing—the outgoing, somewhat spoiled Betsy Sullivan and her seemingly somber, resolute Celt who was seven years her senior. Yet Stuart clearly was taken with her and she with him. Betsy Sullivan later described him as a handsome, manly, genteel, and somewhat shy suitor. "He had the diffidence which young Scotchmen possess," she would say.

During the month before Stuart's departure, he and Betsy spent as much time as possible together, talking in the Sullivan parlor in hushed tones and taking walks along the waterfront past the enclosed basin not far from the Sullivans' house. There, gunboats were drawn almost out of the water and a heavily guarded military barrack had recently been built, an unhappy reminder of the impending threat of war. They saw each other almost every day and exchanged frequent notes on those occasions when they couldn't be together.

My Dear Betsy,
Being somewhat indisposed it is possible that I shall not have the happiness of seeing you this evening; therefore, I will be glad to hear how you are and what you mentioned from your window on my departure last night. Do not be alarmed as I am not seriously ill & and may likely be well in a few hours.
    Yours affectionately,

                                                            Robert Stuart
                                                            Sat.—2pm

With his departure date nearing, Stuart became increasingly reluctant to leave Betsy behind. The idea of being apart from her for the seven years he was required to serve in Indian country was becoming unthinkable. They talked of marriage—in later years Betsy would tell friends that she and Stuart were secretly married that summer, but there is no record of their union—and she suggested that instead of sailing for the Columbia, he take a job at the family emporium as had one of her brothers-in-law, a former sea captain.

Clearly the idea of staying behind had some appeal to Stuart, especially since he hadn't been given PFC stock. A few days before the *Tonquin* was to leave, he conferred with his uncle about resigning only to discover that David Stuart had some qualms as well about making the journey. Unbeknownst to Astor, David Stuart and McKay, both of whom were anxious about their fate, as well as that of their men, if war broke out, had visited the British minister in New York, Francis James Jackson. Having ignored Astor's request that they become naturalized citizens, they informed Jackson that they were all British subjects about to trade under the American flag and wanted to know how they and their fellow Canadians would be dealt with if the *Tonquin* was captured. Jackson weighed the question carefully and assured his visitors that since their mission was purely commercial in nature, "they should be respected as British subjects and traders."

Reassured, David Stuart had decided to honor his commitment to Astor, and he urged Robert to do the same, generously giving his nephew two of his five PFC shares. Stuart was deeply touched. "To him I owe everything," he would later say of his uncle.

As much as he cared for Betsy, remaining in New York was now out of the question. Stuart was less a romantic than several of his younger colleagues, but still the prospect of this great adventure was enormously compelling. Moreover, with equity in the PFC, he was now a partner, albeit a very junior partner, with the wealthiest man in North America. He now had the opportunity to accumulate a modest fortune of his own.

CHAPTER 7

ABOARD THE *TONQUIN*

New York to the Falkland Islands

ON SEPTEMBER 5, 1810, THE DAY BEFORE THE *TONQUIN* was scheduled to depart, Stuart said good-bye to Betsy, assuring her with all the conviction he could muster that he would return safely. Theirs was a bittersweet parting. A few days earlier, Mary Sullivan had given Stuart permission to marry Betsy. They planned to wed upon his return.

In Manhattan later the same day, Stuart met with his fellow partners and Astor. With the *Tonquin*'s departure imminent, Astor seemed both enthusiastic and anxious. After all, he was entrusting his new company—and a sizable fortune—to men who had been strangers to him only a few months earlier. Would these Scots remain loyal in case of war? Would they betray Astor to his rivals, the Nor'Westers? If McKay, the Stuarts, and McDougall switched allegiances once, they might do so again for the right price. Astor was counting on Captain Thorn to keep close watch on them for the duration of the voyage.

Eager that the trip be as trouble free as possible, Astor presented his partners with a letter urging them to cultivate harmony and unanimity. Naively, he recommended that all differences of opinion connected with the voyage be discussed by the whole and decided by a majority of votes. To Captain Thorn, who was assuming his first command, he issued similar instructions. Astor urged him to promote good humor and harmony onboard ship, adding, "To prevent any misunderstanding will require your good management."

Captain Jonathan Thorn.

Prophetically, Astor cautioned Thorn to be wary in dealing with the Indians. "I must recommend you to be particularly careful on the coast and not to rely too much on the friendly disposition of the native. All accidents which have as yet happened there arose from too much confidence in the Indians."

THE *TONQUIN* was moored off Water Street along with dozens of other ships, a number of them part of Astor's growing commercial fleet. What awaited Stuart and the others when they arrived at the dock shortly after sunup was anything but encouraging. To build a permanent commercial outpost on the far side of the continent, the traders needed tools, materials, and weapons as well as enough clothing and food to survive until the next of Astor's supply ships arrived. With war on the horizon, no one knew when that would be.

They were also transporting a vast inventory of goods for trade with the Indians: rolls of brightly colored cloth, madras handkerchiefs, and dozens of tomahawks. There were cases of utensils,

knives, pewter spoons, hundreds of fishhooks, kettles, cod line, pad-
locks, gunflints by the score, saws, beaver traps and trap chains, lead
pencils, ice chisels, hundreds of pounds of leaf tobacco, axes, frying
pans, coffee, souchong tea, chocolate, kegs of rice, salt, molasses, rum
and gin, hammers, balls, duck and goose shot, and enough gunpowder to conduct a small war. The PFC men were even bringing the
frame and timber needed to build a small schooner for the coast trade.

With a crew of twenty-one and all this cargo the *Tonquin* was
already cramped, and now Thorn was confronted with the prospect
of taking on some thirty-three passengers, each with his personal
belongings in tow. A ship twice the *Tonquin*'s ninety-foot length
would be hard-pressed to accommodate a group of this size even if it
weren't overloaded with trading goods.

The *Tonquin*'s crew tried frantically to find a place for everything
and secure the cargo, as Captain Thorn supervised the loading from
the quarterdeck, barking orders and scarcely acknowledging the passengers as they boarded one by one. "All was bustle and confusion on
the deck, and every place on the ship was in such topsy-turvy state
with what sailors call live and dead lumber, that scarcely anyone
knew how or where he was to be stowed," Alexander Ross noted.

Stuart and his uncle had just found the small cabin under the forward mast they were to share when a dispute erupted on deck. Several
of the ten clerks in the party had discovered they had been assigned to
the same quarters as the common sailors, a cramped airless space
before the mast. They complained loudly to Thorn, arguing that under
the terms of their employment they were to be accorded the same
treatment as the other clerks who were in steerage.

When the disgruntled group produced copies of the terms of
their engagement and brandished them in front of his face, Thorn
became enraged. They not only would have to remain in the same
quarters, he informed them, but also be required to perform the
duties of common sailors during the course of the trip.

The clerks immediately appealed to the Stuarts and the other
partners. When the Canadians protested, Thorn threatened to put
them in irons. At this point, a hungover and irritable McDougall,
Astor's proxy on the voyage, produced a pistol and swore he would
shoot the captain where he stood. So much for Astor's homilies
about maintaining harmony aboard ship. The *Tonquin* might never

have left the dock had David Stuart not intervened and brought the dispute to an end, temporarily at least, with his conciliatory manner.

When they finally set off, the wind promptly vanished, and the ship spent the afternoon tacking and drifting until Thorn finally decided to anchor off Staten Island. There, Thorn again asserted his authority, ordering his passengers, partners included, to retire to their bunks and douse their lights at precisely 8:00 P.M.

Still within sight of New York harbor, the *Tonquin*'s passengers had already had their fill of their choleric captain. "He was very self-conceited and extremely irritable," Stuart would later say. A disillusioned Franchere was ready to turn back. It was on these disquieting notes the *Tonquin* began its long voyage.

THORN EXPECTED the journey would take anywhere from six and a half to seven months. He planned to take the ship southeast all the way to the northwestern coast of North Africa, then vector sharply southwest to the Falkland Islands. From there, the *Tonquin* would round Cape Horn before detouring northwest to the Sandwich (Hawaiian) Islands where Astor had trading interests. The last leg of the voyage would take the ship northeast across the Pacific to the Oregon coast.

On departing New York, Thorn's immediate concern was the British. After clearing the bar within sight of the Sandy Hook lighthouse, the *Tonquin* was escorted out to sea by the *Constitution*. The feared British frigate from Halifax never materialized, and at dusk, Astor's ship and its escort parted company. Fortuitously, the wind picked up, moving the *Tonquin* at a lively clip through choppy waters. Many of the clerks and the voyageurs had never been to sea before and became violently ill. Pallid and unshaven, they emerged periodically from their cramped, poorly ventilated quarters to line the ship's side-rails and heave up whatever remained in their bellies as Thorn looked on in disgust.

It was several weeks before the passengers gained their sea legs. Gradually settling into the routine of a long ocean voyage, they amused themselves as best they could. When a school of dolphins began following the ship, some of the Canadians put out fishing lines and caught two of the mammals. The cook, a free Black named Thomas Work, prepared them for supper that night, a meal the passengers judged delicious. Soon after, the fishermen landed a shark, one of several that had ominously circled the *Tonquin* during a flat calm. It tasted like sturgeon, Franchere reported. The same day, a canary appeared aboard ship. Stuart and the others pampered this tiny mascot until it finally flew off.

Often on mild evenings, the Astorians gathered on deck to smoke their pipes and exchange war stories. The younger Stuart pressed McKay to recount the story of his passage to the Pacific with Alexander Mackenzie. Departing from Fort Chipewyan on Lake Athabasca, Mackenzie, McKay, seven voyageurs, and two Indians traveled by foot and canoe across the Rocky Mountains and reached the Pacific on July 22, 1793. On a rocky outcrop near the present-day town of Bella Coola, British Columbia, Mackenzie had written in vermilion paint, "Alexander Mackenzie, from Canada, by land, the twenty-second of July, one thousand seven hundred and ninety-three." As the voyage progressed, these evening soirees grew larger with clerks, voyageurs, and even members of the crew joining in, many of whom were beginning to chafe under Thorn's military command. McKay, a Falstaffian figure, led the group in choruses of ribald boat songs.

In the lingering light of a late September evening, the partners decided to take target practice. Stuart had taken a brace of pistols with him on the trip, but he hadn't done much shooting in years. McKay had taken a liking to the younger man. An excellent shot, he offered to give Stuart some pointers.

Firing at a target suspended from the ship's stern, Stuart suddenly noticed smoke issuing from the lifeboat secured beneath the target. Shouts of "Fire!" set off a mad scramble. Everyone on deck ran to and fro in search of water as passengers and crew began dousing the fire with water from mugs and decanters. Someone called frantically for help in breaking open the precious water casks; one of the passengers even descended to the galley to snatch away the cook's broth and his dishwater. In their panic, no one had the presence of mind to dip buckets over the side for water.

To the immense relief of everyone aboard, the fire was quickly extinguished. Gun wadding had ignited some old junk in the lifeboat. Naturally, Thorn was angered—only this time he directed his rage at Ben Fox, the amiable first mate. A Bostonian whose uncle had drowned off the Oregon coast on an earlier voyage (probably that of Captain Robert Gray in 1792), Fox had become friendly with Robert Stuart and the partners, which irked the captain no end. Thorn summarily suspended him from duty and ordered him below where he was confined to quarters for three days.

DURING THE EARLY weeks of the voyage, the tensions between Thorn, his crew, and the *Tonquin's* passengers continued to flare up. In the ten years he had been a naval officer, Thorn had dealt with sailors who snapped to at the sound of his voice. In the captain's eyes, he was now stuck with an undisciplined, ragtag crew and a lubberly collection of passengers who seemed singularly unsuited for a sea voyage. Worse, in Thorn's view these were foreigners, many of them British citizens, possibly the soon-to-be enemy in another war with Great Britain. Among the artisans and laborers there was a Russian carpenter; a cooper from New York; Job Aitken, a rigger and chalker from Scotland; Augustus Roussel, who had signed on as a blacksmith from Canada; and an apprentice boy, William Perrault, who had also been hired in Montreal. Somehow, Thorn had become convinced, erroneously, that the Canadians in the group were petty criminals who had fled Montreal to escape the law.

Of the voyageurs, the captain had an even lower opinion. In their surcoats made of blankets, leather leggings, moccasins fashioned from deerskin, and brightly colored belts of variegated worsted, the French Canadians resembled the Barbary pirates Thorn had fought in the Mediterranean a few years earlier. They came aboard, eleven of them including the young Lapensé brothers and Joseph Nadeau, laughing and joking in French. Thorn's spine stiffened at the prospect of transporting this unruly lot all the way to the Columbia.

Ross, Franchere, and the eight other clerks, only two of whom, James Lewis and Russell Farnham, were Americans, fared no better in Thorn's estimation. Most were from respectable families and had spent their brief professional lives teaching school or tallying ledger sheets in some back office or dusty warehouse. They had never been among the Indians, never before ventured into the wilderness. Thorn promptly dismissed them as pampered dilettantes who did nothing but complain: "When thwarted of their cravings for delicacies," Thorn would later write Astor, "they would exclaim that it was d——d hard they could not live as they pleased upon their own property, being on board of their own ship, freighted with their own merchandise.'

The captain vowed never to take them to sea again "without having a Fly-market on the forecastle, Convent-garden on the poop, and a cool spring from Canada in the maintop."

When he discovered that two of their number—Ross, the former schoolmaster, and Franchere—were taking notes and keeping journals detailing the events of the voyage, Thorn delighted in disparaging their literary pretensions. Ross, in particular, was the object of his scorn. Thorn dismissed him "as foolish a pedant as ever lived."

As for the partners, Thorn was especially hostile to the younger Stuart. He likely viewed Stuart as a glorified clerk who had been elevated to a partnership purely as a result of nepotism. With his rigid sense of rank and discipline, Thorn was also irritated that the partners fraternized on deck with common seamen and mechanics. It annoyed him no end when, in his presence or in the company of his younger brother, another of the ship's officers, the partners spoke Gaelic and the voyageurs French. He understood neither language and was certain the passengers were mocking him or plotting to take over the ship.

Thorn was determined to bring these fur traders to heel. He insisted that all passengers below the rank of partner carry out his orders. Those who dallied or made lubberly mistakes were so severely reprimanded that Franchere decried "the brutal way the ship's officers treated our young Canadian boys." Thorn put a stop to the after supper gatherings on deck. He banned the clerks altogether from the quarterdeck and restricted the partners to the quarterdeck's starboard side. The *Tonquin* was Thorn's ship, and he would run it as he saw fit.

DURING THE FIRST week in October, the *Tonquin* passed in sight of the rugged terrain of the Cape Verde Islands off Africa. The passengers pressed Thorn to stop to take on fresh water, but he refused, asserting that he didn't want to expose the ship to the English warships that frequented the area. "They [the passengers] were determined to have it said they had been in Africa and therefore insisted on my stopping at the Cape Verdes," he complained later to Astor.

Thorn's concerns were apparently justified when an armed brig appeared to leeward just as the *Tonquin* caught the trade winds southwest, bound now for the South American coast. The brig carried twenty guns (the *Tonquin* was also pierced for twenty guns but the ten cannons in the forward ports were dummies) and bore no flag. Although the *Tonquin* ran under full sail with a good wind, the mystery ship continued to draw closer. Fearing an attack, Thorn ordered all the crew and passengers on deck to prepare for action, but after an hour or so, the brig changed course, allowing the *Tonquin* to continue on without incident.

In a rare display of good spirits, Thorn declared October 25 a holiday to mark their crossing of the equator. By tradition, the crew dunked sailors who were entering the Southern Hemisphere for the first time. Robert Stuart and several of the clerks went for a swim, as well, to cool off. At midday, the temperature reached ninety-two degrees in the shade. "The customary ceremony of ducking and shaving was performed in high style," McDougall reported in his log.

In the night sky, Stuart marveled at the Clouds of Magellan, brilliant clusters of stars and nebulae that were now visible to the south-southwest. Immense flocks of aquatic birds passed overhead. In heavy swells, the captain lowered a boat to catch a giant tortoise. The fresh food had long since run out, and the ship's water supply was dangerously low. Thorn imposed rationing—three half pints a day for each man.

On November 4, the *Tonquin* crossed the tropic of Capricorn at a lively clip, but she soon began to lose the trade winds. The weather, which had been oppressively hot, abruptly turned cold and rainy. A week later, a violent gale howled from the northeast. "The sea looked as if it was on fire, and we had to batten down the hatches," Franchere wrote. Tremendous waves that Ross described as resembling "rolling mountains" and a tempestuous gale reduced the sails to shreds. Six of the cannons were torn from their lashings and rolled thunderously across the decks until the crew secured them again. The sailor who'd been at the tiller was thrown from one side of the vessel to the other like a rag doll. Sailors and passengers clung desperately to the rigging. Remarkably, no one was washed overboard or killed.

ON THE EVENING of December 3, one of the officers at the masthead shouted "Land! Land!" The Falklands lay directly to the west, but foul weather prevented the *Tonquin* from casting anchor in Port Egmont for three days.

Thorn stopped to replenish the *Tonquin's* supply of fresh water. The islands loomed barren and foreboding. They were uninhabited and unfrequented except for occasional visits by South Sea whalers. Stuart and the other passengers couldn't wait to go ashore. It had been three months since they had set foot on land.

Accompanied by several of the clerks, both of the Stuarts, McKay, and McDougall went off to hunt and explore the islands while the remainder of the passengers and the crew set about refilling the water casks and repairing the damage the *Tonquin* had suffered during the storm. The hunters marveled at the profusion of geese, ducks, albatross, eagles, hawks, and vultures that lined the ledges and rocks. "Wild fowl of all kinds stunned our ears with their noises and darkened the air with their numbers," Ross noted.

"Had excellent diversion shooting sea-lions, seals, foxes, geese, ducks and penguins, all of which are very numerous in these parts," McDougall added.

Foxes barked like dogs at the intruders who followed well-worn paths back into the hills, hoping to find goats or other fresh meat. Instead, they discovered a deserted fisherman's cabin crudely fashioned from whalebone, and the graves of two sailors: one had been killed by a fall from the rocks, according to what was written on the weathered board marking his grave, and the other by smallpox.

Among them, the hunters shot scores of geese and ducks and even several seals to restock the ship's larders. On shore, some four hundred yards from where the *Tonquin* was anchored, they pitched a tent to serve as a sporting rendezvous.

There, early on the morning of November 11, the Stuarts,

McDougall, Franchere, Ross, and half a dozen others gathered to prepare for a final few hours of sport. Its riggings repaired and its water supply now fully replenished, the *Tonquin* was scheduled to depart that afternoon. The hunters were about to set off when Thorn, who fancied himself a marksman, came ashore to join in the hunt. Earlier, one of the clerks, the high-spirited Russell Farnham, caught a gray goose, which he had tied to a stone midway between the shore and the tent. Seeing the goose and eager to display his prowess with a musket, Thorn shot the bird without realizing it was tethered. When it fluttered, seemingly wounded, the Captain ran to catch it before the goose could fly off.

Looking on, Stuart and the others contained themselves until the instant that Thorn discovered his mistake, and then erupted into gales of laughter. Livid, the captain turned on his heels and stalked back to the ship, the raucous taunts of the Canadians following him all the way.

EARLIER, THORN HAD given notice that the *Tonquin* would set sail at 2:30 P.M. Robert Stuart returned to the ship about 11:00 that morning, but his uncle and McDougall had gone off to the south end of the island in search of more game. Ross, McKay, Franchere, and four others also remained on shore. They'd gone up to repair the two sailors' graves they'd discovered earlier and gather to grass to feed several pigs the *Tonquin* had onboard. "At 1PM . . . the captain fired his gun and set sail notwithstanding it yet lacked an hour and a half of the time he had set for sailing," Stuart recalled years later.

At the sound of a cannon shot signaling the ship's departure, the men onshore panicked. "The ship's off!" one of the party shouted. "We knew too well the callous and headstrong passions of the wayward Captain to hesitate a moment in determining what to do," Ross explained. "With hearts, therefore beating between anxious hope and despair, some made for the boat, whilst others kept running and firing over hill and dale to warn Messrs. McDougall and Stuart."

Once David Stuart and McDougall had been found, the nine men left onshore—three of them Astor partners—squeezed into a tiny canoe they found and frantically made after the *Tonquin*, which was already three miles at sea. Meanwhile, Robert Stuart was growing anxious. At first, he thought Thorn was merely bluffing—a cruel payback for the derision the captain had suffered that morning—but when he confronted the captain on the quarterdeck, Thorn said he had no intention of stopping for Stuart's uncle and the others. Expert hunters that they were, Thorn noted sarcastically, the Canadians could surely live off the game they killed until another vessel came along and took them off.

From the deck, Stuart could see his uncle and the others floundering in increasingly rough seas as the *Tonquin* pulled away. Like Thorn, Stuart had a quick, dangerous temper. In later years, he would beat a voyageur half to death for disobeying him. He retrieved his pistols from his cabin and returned to the deck to confront Thorn, threatening to blow the captain's brains out unless he put about immediately, a threat he later said he fully intended to carry out had Thorn not complied. "I was young, imprudent and destitute of religious principle," Stuart said of his actions.

With Stuart's cocked pistols pressed hard against the side of the captain's head, he and Thorn railed furiously at each other as the remaining passengers and the ship's crew and officers looked on, none of them raising a hand in Thorn's defense. A few days earlier, Thorn had threatened to kill a sailor who hadn't returned to the ship on time and viciously abused his mates when they came to the sailor's defense. Thorn's first mate, Ben Fox, was still smarting from the punishment Thorn had imposed on him after the target practice incident. Perhaps Stuart would be doing them all a favor by disposing of the *Tonquin*'s dangerously ill-tempered captain.

Finally, Thorn relented, though in a letter to Astor he would claim that it was the changing direction of the wind and not Robert Stuart's brace of pistols that caused him to wait for the stragglers. "Had the wind (unfortunately) not hauled ahead soon after leaving the harbor's mouth, I should positively have left them; and, indeed, I cannot but think it an unfortunate circumstance for you that it so happened, for the first loss in this instance would, in my opinion, have proved the best, as they seem to have no idea of the value of property, nor any apparent regard for your interest, although interwoven with their own."

With the wind mounting to near-hurricane force, it was another five or six hours before David Stuart and the others rejoined the *Tonquin*. They had lost an oar as well as the bailing bucket and could barely make out the ship in the darkness. Finally coming aside the *Tonquin* in violent seas, the canoe and its passengers were nearly dashed to pieces by the waves and by the rolling of the ship. As exhausted as they were, any one of them would have gladly torn Thorn to pieces given the chance. "All the former feuds and squabbles between the Captain and the passengers sank into insignificance compared to the recent one," Ross wrote. "Sullen and silent, both parties passed and re-passed each other in their promenades on deck without uttering a word; but their looks bespoke the hatred that burned within." McKay had a similarly alarming assessment. "I fear we are in the hands of a lunatic," he confided to the other partners.

CHAPTER 8

PARADISE

ON FEBRUARY 13, SIX DAYS BEFORE ROBERT STUART'S twenty-sixth birthday, the *Tonquin* dropped anchor in Kealakekua Bay off the western coast of one of the Sandwich Islands—today's Hawaii. On deck, Stuart and the others drank in the balmy tropical air as they surveyed the island's pristine white beaches. The shoreline was dotted with clusters of coconut and banana palms and the huts of the islanders. In the distant background were cultivated valleys and verdant volcanic peaks that extended into the clouds. This was the first land the passengers and crew had seen since the *Tonquin* doubled Cape Horn on a cold, wet Christmas morning under a slate-colored sky.

For the *Tonquin*'s passengers and crew, the Sandwich Islands were probably the closest thing to paradise they would find in life or death. Hundreds of islanders, men as well as women, canoed and swam out to meet the ship. Their bare, copper-colored bodies were tattooed, and they frolicked in the blue Pacific like dolphins, diving for coins and trinkets that Stuart and the others threw from the decks. The women, many of them no more than teenagers, were overtly flirtatious and vied for the visitors' attention. "The women are handsome in person, engaging in their manners, well-featured and have countenances full of joy and tranquility, but chastity is not their virtue," Ross noted.

After five months at sea, it was all Thorn could do to keep his randy crew from stripping down and jumping overboard to frolic with the female swimmers. He restricted his men to the ship, but the Astorians were under no such restraints. On February 19, Stuart and the other partners went ashore with Franchere, Ross, and some of the other clerks. Guests of John Young, the flamboyant English sailor who ably governed the island of Hawaii on behalf of Kamehameha the Great, king of all the Sandwich Islands, Stuart's party was entertained by nineteen female dancers, the men likely pairing off with the island women at the end of the festivities. "They are very amorous which is to be expected in this climate," Franchere noted in his journal.

The following day, an elderly islander took Stuart and the others on a tour of the island, showing them where Captain Cook, the first westerner to visit Hawaii, had been killed on the same date thirty-two years earlier in a dispute with the islanders over a stolen boat. Naturally, Thorn disapproved of this little excursion, even more so of the bacchanal the previous evening. His passengers were acting as if they were on holiday. To his chagrin, they even brought back souvenirs from their outing, including bark from the trees marked by musket balls and stones from the site where Cook had died.

Since the incident in the Falklands, the captain and Astor's men had continued their feud. Thorn seemed hell-bent on asserting his authority. For much of the voyage, he imposed "man-of-war" discipline, at one point ordering all hands to empty the contents of their trunks on deck, then demanding that each of the passengers and crew members inspect the belongings of the other men to determine what items had been stolen. After hours of this tedious, demeaning drill, only a spoon, a pamphlet, and a clasp knife had been claimed, and there was no conclusive proof that these items had actually been pilfered. Nonetheless, Thorn placed the three men in whose possession these objects had been found on what was called a "rogue's mess," the dregs from the kitchen, for a month and condemned them as thieves.

More and more, Thorn took his anger out on his own crew and officers, singling out Stuart's friend Ben Fox for punishment. Just before the *Tonquin* reached Hawaii, Thorn even put his own younger brother, James, the ship's fourth mate, in irons. In this, at least, he won the approval of his passengers for, by all accounts, the younger Thorn was as moody and bellicose as his brother.

Embittered and eager to consort with the island women, Thorn's crew began deserting in droves soon after the *Tonquin* made port. One sailor slipped ashore at night and disappeared entirely, as did the boatswain John Anderson, with whom Thorn had exchanged angry words. After the islanders returned the two would-be deserters to the ship, the captain awarded the Hawaiians with a bounty and had the sailor flogged and put in irons. Thorn would not allow Anderson back on ship even though, in McDougall's estimation, he was perhaps the best of the sailors on the *Tonquin*. Pacing angrily on deck before the assembled crew, Thorn warned that future deserters would be dealt with even more harshly.

With the crew's ranks diminishing daily, Astor's men put aside their differences with the captain, temporarily at least, and pitched in to help maintain some degree of order aboard ship. Otherwise, they would never reach their destination. The clerks were assigned to assist the officers while the voyageurs and mechanics took the place of sailors in standing watch and performing other duties onshore. Meanwhile, the partners aided the captain in providing for the wants of the *Tonquin*.

Along with Thorn, they traded for provisions, obtaining yams, breadfruit, sugarcane, and other fruits and vegetables from the Hawaiians. But what Astor's representatives really needed was an abundance of fresh water and livestock. The partners intended to stock the Columbia settlement with a herd of pigs to ensure a supply of fresh pork. John Young informed them that fresh water was in short supply since no rain had fallen in the immediate region for several years. He noted, as well, that King Kamehameha had a monopoly on the islands' swine trade. If the PFC partners wanted pigs, they would have to sail to the island of Oahu and deal directly with Kamehameha at the royal court.

The partners recognized that such a visit was critical to their mission here. The islands figured prominently in Astor's plans to establish a global trading empire. He had given Thorn orders to stop here en route to the Columbia, a considerable detour, and had instructed McKay, McDougall, and the Stuarts to establish cordial relations with the islands' rulers with an eye toward creating a possible trading post there. Astor was also interested in possibly adding one of the islands to his real-estate portfolio at a later date. Clearly, the partners needed to meet with Kamehameha.

By any measure, Kamehameha was a formidable figure. Originally, local chiefs had ruled the twenty or so islands and islets that make up the Hawaiian chain, but Kamehameha had conquered them one by one. By 1810, he had united the entire archipelago. He had also acquired and built a fleet consisting of a brig and several dozen schooners, which he used to transport the goods paid him in tribute by the inhabitants of the islands.

Smart and ambitious, Kamehameha was quick to learn the ways of visiting Europeans. He'd persuaded a number of them over the years, including John Young, to stay on to help him rule, develop foreign trade, and acquire western technology. At the time of the *Tonquin*'s arrival, Kamehameha was in his fifties and at the peak of his power.

After leaving Young, the *Tonquin* sailed northwest, bound for Oahu and the royal court. On February 21, under brilliant blue skies, the ship anchored in Waikiki Bay, where she was met by several of the king's emissaries as well as Kamehameha himself. He was a physically imposing, robustly virile figure, tall and dark skinned. Flanked by his three wives and a prime minister named Kraimaker— whom the British had nicknamed William Pitt after England's secretary of state because of his negotiating skills—the king arrived with great fanfare aboard a brilliantly decorated catamaran. It was paddled by twenty-four chiefs and accompanied by a flotilla of canoes.

The *Tonquin* fired four guns in honor of its royal visitor and displayed the American flag. Outfitted in a beaver hat, a long blue coat with a velvet collar, corduroy trousers, and sturdy military shoes, and armed with an elegant sword he claimed had been a gift from his brother, the king of England, Kamehameha was greeted warmly by Thorn and the partners. For the occasion, Robert Stuart and the other partners had donned scarlet coats to signal their rank as the grand seigneurs of the PFC.

Followed closely by a valet who carried a spitting box, Kamehameha toured the decks of the *Tonquin*, asking for an explanation of equipment he hadn't seen before on other ships. Of particular interest was a small distilling apparatus with which the *Tonquin*'s crew could convert seawater to fresh water. Such a device could prove invaluable on his drought-ridden islands, the king noted.

Quickly bored by the tour, Kamehameha's corpulent wives scandalized their hosts by unceremoniously shedding their clothing, which amounted to no more than strips of bark cloth wrapped around their abundant waists. They then plunged into the water, where they swam and sported noisily as an embarrassed Thorn and the partners led their royal guest below to the cabin.

With the wine flowing copiously, the bargaining began. The partners explained they were chiefs of a great company, which would bring Kamehameha all the trade he could handle. In the future the PFC intended to send many ships to the islands, each of them weighed down with valuable goods for trade with the king. For now, though, the partners needed pork, goats, poultry, fruit, vegetables, and water for the long voyage to the Columbia. To this wish list, Thorn added his request that the king return any sailors who deserted. Otherwise, the *Tonquin* was going to be without a crew.

Joined by his wives, who crowded into the cabin after their swim to make quick work of several bottles of wine, the king conferred with his prime minister. In exchange for coffee, tea, chocolate, other commodities, and a substantial cash payment, the chiefs of the PFC could have their livestock and supplies. Moreover, the king gave Thorn his assurance that deserters would be returned to the ship. As part of the bargain, he would loan his hosts some of his islanders, who were renowned for their nautical skills, to help sail the *Tonquin* to its destination and man the outpost the partners planned to establish at the mouth of the Columbia. But Kamehameha wanted a substantial portion of the payment upfront, in piastres, pieces of eight.

The price was steep, but the partners and Thorn agreed to Kamehameha's demands. They had little choice. "We soon came to terms with the King, kept him on board for dinner and sent them all ashore towards evening well pleased with their visit," Franchere recalled.

The next morning, the partners and clerks went into the royal city of Honolulu, a cosmopolitan metropolis with several thousand residents, a number of them British, American, Spanish, Chinese, and French. For the excursion, the Stuarts and their fellow Scots dressed in their finest Highland regalia, much to the delight of the islanders, who apparently had never seen kilts before. This display was more than Thorn could stomach. In high dudgeon, he wrote Astor complaining that the partners were putting on intolerable airs and acting foolishly. These "great eares of the north-west," as the captain derisively described them, strutted about in their Highland plaids and kilts, Thorn claimed, bragging about the enormous hardships they could endure and how they could face all weather, put up with all kinds of fare, and even eat dogs if necessary.

"It would be difficult to imagine the frantic gambols that are daily played off here," he continued, barely able to restrain himself. "Sometimes dressing in red coats, and otherwise very fantastically, and collecting a number of ignorant natives around them, telling them that they are the great eares of the north-west, and making arrangements for sending three or four vessels yearly to them from the coast . . . while those very natives cannot even furnish a hog to the ship. Then dressing in Highland plaids and kilts, and making similar arrangements with presents of rum, wine or anything at hand. . . . Then setting down with some white man or native who can be little understood, and collecting the history of these islands, of [Kamehameha's] wars, the curiosities of the islands . . . [it] is indeed ridiculously contemptible."

Stuart and the others were blithely indifferent to Thorn's criticism. For the next few days, they had the time of their lives. Ashore they encountered two of the queens. Their majesties were out for a stroll, accompanied by one of their pages, who walked between them carrying a splendid silk parasol measuring nearly seven feet in diameter. Kamehameha's wives greeted the Scots like old friends and chatted gaily with their visitors, then brought them to see the king, who was equally effusive in his greeting.

His majesty offered his guests arrack, potent liquor distilled from the fermented sap of toddy palms, and ordered fifty of his warriors to parade. For his guests' benefit, Kamehameha had his men put on a display of their skill in throwing and parrying the pahooa, a twelve-foot long, barbed spear. Three of the best marksmen lined up some sixty yards from another warrior, and in quick succession each hurled a dozen pahooas at their comrade, all of which he nimbly parried with his own spear or somehow managed to catch in midair, seizing his opponent's pahooa the instant it came into contact with his own. On this occasion the human target received only a slight wound on the arm, but as Kamehameha—a dexterous pahooa man himself—told his visitors, frequently his warriors weren't so lucky.

Next on the itinerary was the royal shipyard, where artisans fashioned tackle, blocks, and rope for the royal fleet and built magnificent canoes and schooners. "The tools used by the different workmen were very simple, slender and ill made, and yet the work done by them surprised us," Ross reported.

From the shipyards, the king led his guests to the Royal Palace, a complex that was secured by some forty bodyguards armed with muskets and bayonets. It consisted of some thirteen houses constructed, like all of Honolulu's residences, of wicker. Each residence, the visitors noted, was remarkable for its neatness and regularity. The king occupied three of these abodes—one for eating, another for sleeping, and a third for business and receiving visitors. In turn, each of Kamehameha's queens was accorded three houses—a sleeping house, an eating house, and a dressing house. The king never intruded on his wives' privacy by entering their dwellings, and they never entered his houses. A thirteenth dwelling served for those occasions when Kamehameha wanted to bed down with one of his spouses.

Kamehameha proved an affable and generous host. He plied his visitors with more arrack and served them a banquet of roast pork, yams, taro, coconuts, and breadfruit. To cap off the evening, the by now thoroughly inebriated party followed Kamehameha to a large stone building that housed the royal treasures. The treasury, the king bragged, had cost him two thousand dollars to build.

The tour over, the *Tonquin*'s passengers drunkenly thanked their royal host for his hospitality and ambled off into the night to seek the favors of island women and savor this last brief respite from the tyranny of Captain Thorn. In a few days, the *Tonquin* would be off for Oregon on the last and most dangerous leg of its journey.

CHAPTER 9

ARRIVAL

FOR SIX DAYS, THE *TONQUIN* RAN BEFORE A VIOLENT gale, bound for the coast of the Pacific Northwest and the mouth of the Columbia. On the morning of March 22, 1811, cries of "Land! Land!" brought Stuart and the passengers to the storm-damaged deck. Despite the rain and patches of fog, Stuart could make out the distant outline of the lofty coastal mountains. Captain Thorn had not been able to make a celestial observation for almost a week because of the storm, but he was confident that the *Tonquin* was in immediate proximity to the Columbia's mouth. His judgment was borne out as the three-masted bark came within a few miles of the coast, and Thorn, reading from his charts, identified Cape Disappointment. Named by Lewis and Clark, the rugged promontory marked the north side of the Columbia's four-and-a-half-mile-wide entrance. To the south was Point Adams, a low, sandy point that jutted out several hundred yards into the river. After five months at sea, the passengers and crew exuberantly congratulated one another on surviving the harrowing voyage. Only a few miles ahead was the gateway to the fur-rich territory of the Pacific Northwest. "The sight filled every heart with gladness," one of Stuart's shipmates noted.

But the exhilaration was short-lived. The *Tonquin* still had to cross the Columbia's treacherous bar. Ever since Captain Robert Gray had made the first recorded trip up the river aboard the *Columbia Rediviva* on May 11, 1792, the Columbia's bar had acquired a reputation for being among the most dangerous in the world. Stuart was no navigator, but he recognized the danger that lay ahead. Under ideal conditions, the crossing could be perilous, and on March 22, conditions were anything but ideal. Still at near-gale force, the wind, Stuart noted, blew in from the sea, creating enormous waves that broke over the mouth of the river and made it almost impossible to find a channel.

Thorn proposed entering immediately. Both Stuarts, McKay, and McDougall objected, advising the captain to "lie off and on" a day or two until the wind abated and the weather cleared. The last thing the contentious Thorn wanted was advice from the Scots. In Hawaii, he had somehow become convinced that the partners had become privy to new information regarding the possibility of war between the United States and Britain. Certain they intended to seize the ship and cargo for their own purposes, he refused to let them open the bales and boxes in which the traders' winter clothes were stored even though the weather had turned frigid.

The result was a near mutiny, with David Stuart once again acting as peacemaker. Were a few items of warm clothing really worth an all-out battle? Reluctantly, his nephew, McKay, and McDougall gave in and retreated to their cabins, where they spent much of the remainder of the voyage shivering in their hammocks.

If anything, the partners' qualms made Thorn even more determined to make the crossing right away. "He was told it would be certain death for anyone to attempt entering in a boat—that a boat could not 'live' in such a sea," Stuart later recalled. "All the entreaties and advice of the passengers, however, availed nothing."

Thorn ordered his first mate, Ben Fox, to take a whaleboat out to sound for channel, and he commanded an old sailor; two of the Lapense brothers, Ignace and Bazil; and a former Montreal barber, who had never before been to sea, to accompany him. Fox asked for more experienced hands, but Thorn insisted he had none to spare. Again, the partners, all of whom liked Fox, interceded, pressing Thorn to wait until the weather cleared but to no avail. When Fox protested that, even with the best seamen, the small boat couldn't survive in such rough seas, Thorn responded sharply, "Mr. Fox, if you are afraid of water, you should have remained in Boston." Stung by this rebuke, Fox immediately ordered the boat into the water. "My uncle was drowned here not many years ago, and now I am going to

Entrance of the Columbia River. Ship Tonquin *crossing
the bar, March, 25, 1811.*

lay my bones with his," Ross reported Fox as saying. "Farewell, my friends. We will perhaps meet in the next world."

In the violent seas, the boat was thrown and spun about wildly by the enormous waves. Within a few minutes, Fox hoisted a distress flag. Again, the passengers and crew implored Thorn to try to save the boat, but in an angry voice the captain ordered "about ship." In an instant, Fox and his men were lost. "When the boat had got about half a mile from the ship, she upset and all on board perished," Stuart later recalled.

After several more unsuccessful attempts to locate a channel, Thorn on the afternoon of March 25 ordered the rigger, the Scot Job Aitken, accompanied by a crew of four, to sound along the northern banks of the Columbia's mouth near the rocky outcroppings of Cape Disappointment in a jolly boat that, McDougall noted, "was without a rudder and only a broken oar to steer her."

The channel here was deep but narrow and intricate. Accompanied by the armorer, Stephen Weeks; the sail maker, Aaron Slaight; and two of the islanders, Harry and Peter, who had joined the *Tonquin* in Hawaii, Aitken was successful. As soon as he hoisted a flag, the prearranged signal that he had found water at least three and a half fathoms deep, the *Tonquin* weighed anchor and headed directly for the channel. At the same time, Aitken and his men pulled away from the bar to meet the oncoming ship.

To the horror of the crew and passengers, Thorn sailed right by Aitken's boat, passing within twenty yards of Aitken and the others as they waited to be taken aboard. "The boat! The boat!" several of the crewmembers shouted. Astonished at the captain's callousness, the partners, joined in this instance by John Mumford, the second officer, implored Thorn to stop, but he refused, claiming he might endanger the *Tonquin*. As the *Tonquin* moved away, a member of the crew threw ropes to Aitken's boat. "A man caught hold of one of the ropes, but the swiftness of the vessel's motion, caused him to let go," Stuart recalled. Aitken and the others were left to try to follow the *Tonquin* across the bar in their fragile craft, a sentence of almost certain death.

With Aitken's boat fading from view, the *Tonquin* entered the breakers, "the sight of which was appalling," Ross noted. The captain ordered Mumford to the masthead to point out the channel, which decreased abruptly to a depth of two and a half fathoms. The *Tonquin* struck a succession of shoals, tossing wildly as waves ten feet high broke across her decks. Crew and passengers alike climbed aloft and clung for their lives to the rigging.

By dark the ship had progressed a mile or so into the breakers and was drifting dangerously close to Cape Disappointment. Stuart could hear the surf crashing against the rocks and see the dark, foreboding outline of the cape with its scattering of wind-stunted pines looming directly ahead. In desperation, Thorn dropped both the ship's anchors, but they failed to hold, and the *Tonquin* drifted closer and closer to destruction. "We are all lost!" one of the crew cried out. "The ship is among the rocks!"

The flood tide saved them. It swept in providentially from the Pacific, carrying the *Tonquin* beyond the Cape into the relative calm of Baker Bay and safety. It was near midnight. At first light, the exhausted crew and passengers would begin the search for survivors and the bodies of the men who had drowned.

CHAPTER 10

GETTING SETTLED

THE FIRST FEW DAYS ON THE COLUMBIA, ROBERT STUART and his shipmates were visited by Indians: Chinooks from the north shore of the river, the largest and most prosperous tribe in the region, and Clatsops from Point Adams to the south. They paddled out to greet the whites, pulling alongside the *Tonquin* in their great flat-bottomed canoes.

They were diminutive people, these coastal Indians, many not much more than five feet tall, with round faces, small animated eyes, broad flat noses, and thick black hair. The men wore small robes of deer or muskrat skins thrown loosely over their shoulders; the women nothing more than a fringe of cedar bark tied around their waists. "All go lightly dressed with nothing below the waist in the coldest weather; a piece of fur around their bodies and a short rope composes the sum total of their dress, except a few hats and beads about their necks, arms and legs," William Clark characterized their attire.

From the *Tonquin*'s deck Stuart admired their adroit seamanship and their brightly painted, handsomely crafted canoes, the largest nearly a third of the *Tonquin*'s length and five feet in width. "The natives of this river . . . are the most expert paddle men any of us had ever seen," he would later note. "Their canoes for the most part are made of cedar . . . If perfect symmetry, smoothness and proportion constitute beauty, they surpass anything I ever beheld."

The Chinooks and their neighbors to the south greeted these new-comers warmly. Several spoke rudimentary English salted with pro-fanities learned from visiting sailors. They had come to barter and brandished pelts. Led by their one-eyed chief, Comcomly, who was known as a great warrior and savvy in the laws of supply and demand, the Chinooks had been dealing with whites for nearly twenty years, exchanging sea otter and beaver pelts for the European-manufactured goods that now pervaded native life. "Great hagglers in trade," Meriwether Lewis had called them. In their transactions, the Chinookan women did much of the negotiating, sometimes offering their sexual favors to seal the bargain.

"They informed us that Captain [Robert] Gray of the Ship Columbia, from Boston, was the first white who entered the river," Stuart noted.

> On the vessels first appearance . . . they were all seized with such consternation as to abandon their village, leaving only a few old people who could not follow; some imagined that the ship must be some overgrown monster, come to devour them, while others supposed her to be a floating island, inhabited by cannibals, sent by the great spirit to destroy them and ravage their country. However, a boat's crew soon came ashore, who by their mild behavior and distributing a few trinkets, succeeded in assuring the old people of their friendly intentions, which they soon found means to communicate to the fugitives; thus a friendly intercourse was immediately entered into, which has never since been interrupted.

Fearful that the Nor'Westers might have beaten them to the Columbia, Astor's men were concerned with more recent visitors. Had the natives done business with British traders of late?

No, the Indians informed them. Theirs was the first ship in many months.

Assured by this news, the partners told their visitors that trade would have to wait. First, they had to search for their missing comrades, Job Aitken and his crew, and select a site on which to build a trading post that would command the entrance to the Columbia.

THE INDIANS APPEARED eager to help with both tasks. Soon after the *Tonquin*'s arrival, Stephen Weeks, the armorer who'd gone out with Aitken, was discovered at the base of Cape Disappointment,

Three Chinook men by George Catlin.
COLLECTION OF THE NEW-YORK HISTORICAL SOCIETY.

semidelirious and half dead. "The armorer made his appearance on the beach opposite to where the ship lay at anchor; this for the moment gave hopes of their all having been saved but how sadly we were disappointed," McDougall said.

Aitken and Aaron Slaight, the sail maker, had drowned after a huge wave broke over the stern of the boat, turning over their craft, Weeks reported. Cold, wet, and miserable, he and the two Hawaiians clung to the upturned craft after an ebb tide carried it back to sea. One of the islanders, Peter, died during the night, but Weeks and the other islander, Harry, managed to get to shore by morning a few miles to the north. Weeks's companion was so weak Weeks had to leave him on the beach.

On the morning of March 27, Chinooks found the nearly lifeless islander. "They got him aboard [their canoe] and before next morning he was considerable recovered, but his feet were much swollen and torn by the cold and walking through the bushes," McDougall said. Of the ten men Thorn had sent out, only two—Weeks and the islander Harry—had survived, although Harry, McDougall later reported, had been crippled by the boat wreck.

The casualty list could easily have mounted. Twice in the first few days after their arrival, the traders capsized as they were negotiating the choppy waters of Baker Bay in the *Tonquin*'s remaining lifeboats. On both occasions, Comcomly and his Chinooks plucked them from the water, saving a number of lives including those of a sputtering Duncan McDougall, who couldn't swim, and David Stuart, at forty-five the old man of the expedition. Comcomly entertained Stuart and McDougall for three days in his village, where they were detained because of bad weather, and then brought them back to the shores of Baker Bay where their colleagues had established an interim camp.

With the search for survivors concluded, the traders began to look for a building site. Like Lewis and Clark on their visit here five years earlier, the partners initially reconnoitered the north shore of the wide inner bay but found no suitable break in the thick, swampy forest. With a naturalist's eye, Stuart marveled at the region's profuse and varied vegetation, observing in his journals:

> The principal trees are the hemlock, spruce, white and red cedar (all of which are an enormous size) and incredible as it may appear we found some . . . 7 to 9 fathoms in circumference and 250 to 300 feet long. . . . Of aromatic scrubs, and other undergrowth, there is an endless variety, as also of berries, gooseberries, strawberries, raspberries (of the two kinds, red and yellow and very large having an exceedingly fine flavor). . . . Climbing plants or creepers are found in great abundance in all the thickets; among others is a species of vine that deserves to be noticed; its flowers, each of which is composed of six petals or leaves, about 3 inches in length, are of the most beautiful crimson, spotted within, with white; its leaves are disposed by threes, of a handsome green and oval shape, this plant climbs upon the trees like the ivy, but without attaching itself to them. When it reaches the top of the tree, it descends perpendicular . . . and extends from tree to tree until at length it exhibits some resemblance to the rigging of a ship.

From a distance the rain forest on the southern shore seemed equally impenetrable. Discouraged, on March 27, McKay, Thorn, and David Stuart hired one of the Clatsop headmen, Daitshowan, to take them upriver on a reconnaissance.

In the captain's absence, a holiday atmosphere prevailed. The weather cleared and the *Tonquin*'s crew and Stuart and the other passengers who remained onboard the ship bathed and washed their clothes in Baker Bay, splashing about and joking boisterously. To the relief of all, the livestock that had been acquired in Hawaii—a ram, a ewe, four goats, and fourteen hogs—was brought ashore on March 28. Once on land, a sow and a boar escaped into the woods. In the ensuing months, the traders would glimpse the elusive pair in the distance accompanied by half a dozen piglets.

David Stuart, Thorn, and the others returned on April 4, having still not found a site. As a last resort the Stuarts and McDougall decided to explore the south shore, leaving on April 5. While they were away, an impatient Thorn began unloading the trade goods and cargo on the shores of Baker Bay. When the partners returned on the evening of the 8th, they were outraged at Thorn's action. Not only was Baker Bay ill-suited for their outpost, but with his usual arrogance, Thorn had not bothered to consult them regarding his decision. "This morning Captain Thorn without consulting any of us on board went ashore and pitched upon a place to build a shed to receive the rigging, etc.," McDougall complained in his log.

The partners convened a hasty meeting and agreed to build on the south coast about seven miles north of Fort Clatsop, Lewis and Clark's winter post, which was now in ruins. The site Astor's men had chosen, Stuart reported, "is delightfully situated on the southeast extremity of Point George, which is a commanding as well as in every respect a commodious station, having an excellent harbor within fifty yards of the shore for vessels not exceeding two hundred tons."

On April 12, the *Tonquin*'s passengers left the ship and encamped onshore. Franchere recorded the moment. "The weather was magnificent and all nature smiled. Spring was already well advanced and we, having reached our journey's end and being freed from the ship, found everything wonderful. The forests looked like pleasant groves and the leaves like flowers."

But the newcomers' optimism was stayed by the daunting task of clearing away the dense underbrush and felling the closely clustered trees, some as tall as a twenty-story building. Few of the inept loggers had handled an axe before. Working from sunrise to after dusk six days a week, often with an audience of bemused Chinook and Clatsop onlookers, this unlikely pioneer corps built scaffolds around the giant trees and hacked away, Lilliputians in Gulliver's forest, sometimes for several days until the tree was finally ready to fall.

None of the group knew the art of making a tree topple in a pre-ordained direction, and they would spend hours trying to calculate the path of downward trajectory, only to have a giant spruce or cedar topple toward the cutters and send them scattering as it crashed thunderously to earth. So dense was the forest that often a tree would be held partially upright by other trees after it was cut, and sometimes a cluster of trees would hang together, keeping the workers in terrible suspense.

Once a tree had been felled, Stuart and the others had to remove the giant stump, tear up the roots and blow both the stump and tree to pieces with gunpowder before either could be removed from the site. Two of the party were injured by falling trees; another had his hand blown off in an explosion.

The frustrations of clearing the site—and transporting the supplies Thorn had left at Baker Bay to this new site with a launch from the *Tonquin*—were compounded by frequent periods of rain and sleet and the dense, damp fog that rolled in frequently from the sea. The traders had neglected to bring an adequate supply of tents, and everyone except for the partners and clerks had to sleep out in the open.

The dampness and chill caused many of the men, particularly the Sandwich Islanders, who were used to the dry, warm climate of their homeland, to fall ill. Soon, half the party was on the sick list—several with venereal disease contracted on the Sandwich Islands. Morale was so low that six of the men deserted, only to be brought back to camp three days later by Comcomly. The traders were still not ready to trust the Chinook leader, but thus far he had proven a valuable friend.

Among the newcomers themselves, however, there was considerable bickering. Thorn forbade the partners from trading with the Indians aboard his ship and soon wouldn't allow any of his former passengers to board except the American clerk James Lewis, whom he apparently trusted. Before long, Thorn and the traders were communicating exclusively in writing with Lewis acting as the intermediary.

Ashore, some of the men faulted Astor for not having sent a medical man along to care for the sick, while Ross complained that McDougall hoarded delicacies for himself while others subsisted solely on boiled fish and wild roots. "He [McDougall] was a man of but ordinary capacity with an irritable peevish temper; the most unfit man in the world to head an expedition or command men." The view was one that a number of others, including Astor himself, would ultimately share.

WITH THE CLEARING progressing at a ponderous pace, the *Tonquin* anchored off Point George, and the partners began trading with the Clatsops and Chinooks as well as the Chehalis, who lived about forty miles up the coast, and the Tillamooks, a Salish-speaking tribe whose village lay approximately the same distance to the south. "These four nations generally come directly to the Establishment with what furs they have to trade," Stuart observed, "but the Chinooks are more especially the intermediate traders between the whites and the more inland tribes, particularly those to the northward."

On April 30, work was interrupted when a native reported that farther up the Columbia, above the Great Cascades, white men had established a trading post. "An Indian from the Rapids informed us of having seen a party of almost 30 men building homes, etc.," McDougall noted in the headquarters log. Certain that the traders must be Nor'Westers, Robert Stuart, McKay, Franchere, and several others engaged a Clatsop headman named Coalpo as a guide, and set out to investigate on a rainy May 2 in a large canoe provided by the Indians.

For the two partners and Franchere, the expedition was a welcome respite from the backbreaking work at Point George. McKay in particular had been growing increasingly restless since the *Tonquin*'s arrival. A few weeks earlier, he'd suffered a bad fall and had been confined to bed. He hadn't come all this way to lie around camp or chop wood and blow up tree stumps. Delighted as schoolboys who'd been assigned some chore that took precedence over their lessons, the veteran trader, Stuart, and Franchere traveled up the Columbia as far as the Great Cascades, an extended stretch of wild rapids. En route they encountered a blind Spanish castaway, known as Soto, and Cowlitz Indians who had never seen whites before. They examined the visitors intently, pulling up their trousers and opening their shirts to see if the skin of their bodies matched in color that of their faces and hands.

Beyond the Great Cascades, however, the Indians they encountered assured them there were no white people in the region, but the rumors were nonetheless disturbing. Shortly before the *Tonquin* had left New York, Astor had heard that the NWC was mounting an overland expedition. Its arrival, the traders feared, was imminent.

When Stuart and the others got back to camp on May 15, they found that several acres had been cleared and all hands were busy building a shed to store the goods and supplies the group was to receive from the *Tonquin*. By May 18, the foundations for a capacious storehouse had been laid and the plans for the rest of the station had been drawn up. The post was projected to be "120 yards in extent," Stuart noted, and "well stockaded with pickets 17 feet long and 18 inches in diameter, having two strong bastions, at opposite angles, so as to rake two sides each." It was to include "a framed store two stories high, 60 feet by 30 feet, with good cellars and a powder magazine; a dwelling house, one story high and 60 feet by 25; a blacksmith shop, and a large shade for carpenters and coopers."

The traders named the outpost, the first American settlement on the Pacific Coast, Astoria, in honor of their patron, and celebrated the event with drams of rum and the firing of muskets. With Stuart, Ross, and some of the others looking on, McKay ordered one of the engages, the French Canadian laborers, to climb a tree and dress it like a maypole to commemorate the inauguration of the post. The man willingly undertook the job, expecting an extra dram as his reward, but he had no sooner reached the top when McKay, who had a penchant for practical jokes, lit a fire at the base of the tree. At first, the prank seem harmless, but the flames leapt quickly up the gummy pine, and the water the Astorians bucketed to douse the blaze created so much smoke that McKay's hapless victim finally had to leap like a squirrel to a nearby tree, where he hung precariously until another of the Astorians climbed up to rescue him.

With a disapproving eye, Thorn watched these antics from the deck of the nearby *Tonquin*. The partners' protracted search for a building site, their boisterous drinking and smoking parties, and the ongoing delays in completing Astoria drove him to repeated rages and caused him to lash out against those who remained under his command. On May 4, after a quarrel, he'd kicked his last remaining officer, John Mumford, off the ship. Mumford subsequently asked to join the Astorians' enterprise, and the sympathetic partners readily welcomed him to the company's ranks.

THORN WAS EAGER to depart Astoria. His orders called for him to sail up the coast to trade, returning to the Columbia in late summer before heading out for Canton and finally returning to New York. Since the captain knew nothing of the Indian trade, the partners wanted someone to go along as supercargo and represent the company in all its commercial dealings with the coastal tribes. Robert Stuart was chosen.

Stuart bridled at the assignment, but in deference to his uncle and the others, he adhered to their bidding. He and the other partners had a financial interest in the *Tonquin*'s trade, and Stuart resolved to put aside his differences with Thorn for the duration of the voyage north. When the captain came ashore on May 30, the day before the *Tonquin*'s scheduled departure, Stuart went down to meet him. The two men had scarcely spoken since Stuart had threatened him at the Falklands. Stuart approached the captain warily, explaining that he had been asked to serve as the *Tonquin*'s supercargo. When Stuart asked Thorn if he could transport his trunk to the *Tonquin* aboard the captain's boat, Thorn scornfully told Stuart he would have to find some other way to get his trunk aboard.

Stuart reacted as if Thorn had struck him in the face. He turned abruptly on his heels and stalked back to the post, where he angrily told his uncle, McKay, and McDougall that he would not sail with Thorn under any circumstances. If his fellow partners wanted Stuart's advice, they should put the captain in irons.

McKay agreed to go in Stuart's place. He didn't like Thorn much better than the Stuarts and McDougall did, but there was no one else. McDougall was in command of the enterprise, at least until the Astorians were joined by Wilson Price Hunt's overland expedition. He had to remain at the post, and David Stuart would soon be off to establish an ancillary trading post in the interior.

The *Tonquin* left as scheduled on a gray, gloomy June 1 for Vancouver Island, carrying Thorn, what was left of his officers and crew, McKay, and clerk James Lewis as well as the majority of Astoria's provisions. These the truculent captain, Astor's ever-vigilant watchdog, refused to unload until the ship returned.

The previous evening, as he was packing to leave, McKay confided to the others that he had ominous forebodings about the upcoming trip. He asked Alexander Ross, an old friend, to care for his son Tom, one of Astoria's young clerks, in case he didn't return. "If you ever see us safe back, it will be a miracle," he told Ross.

CHAPTER 11

THE OVERLANDERS

From Montreal to the Missouri

ON APRIL 2, 1811, WHILE MCDOUGALL, THE STUARTS, and McKay were still selecting a site for their trading establishment, the overland expedition led by Wilson Price Hunt finally departed its winter headquarters on the Nodaway River and started up the Missouri. Following the same route blazed seven years earlier by Lewis and Clark, Hunt was headed for the mouth of the Columbia, where he planned to be reunited within five or six months with his colleagues who had the made the journey by sea—a projection that would prove well off the mark.

From the outset, bad luck, bad timing, dissension, delays, and ineffectual leadership plagued Hunt's expedition. In part, the problem was Hunt himself. Though he was intelligent, indefatigable on Astor's behalf, and resourceful, Hunt's background consisted largely of having run a general store in St. Louis with his partner John Hankinson and serving briefly as a lieutenant of the Missouri militia. He had no special leadership skills—or at least none that had yet come to the fore—and no firsthand knowledge of the wilderness. Certainly, he was out of his element in Indian country and ill-equipped to lead a large, unruly cadre of adventurers and misfits across several thousand miles of some of the roughest and most dangerous terrain in the world. In naming Hunt his field general, Astor had overestimated Hunt's capabilities and vastly underestimated the challenges in leading this, the second overland crossing within the borders of the United States after Lewis and Clark.

On trips to Montreal in July 1810 and Mackinac Island later that month, Hunt had some success in recruiting additional partners, among them the twenty-three-year-old Ramsay Crooks. Like Robert Stuart, Crooks was a Scot who'd learned the fur trade as a clerk first in Montreal and later on Mackinac. He had been trading on the Missouri since 1807, and perhaps earlier, and had known Hunt for several years. Hunt had such a high regard for Crooks's expertise and judgment that he gave him five shares of PFC stock—the same equity allotted the more senior Canadian partners.

Later, Crooks's former partner, Robert McClellan, whom Hunt had also known in St. Louis, joined up as well. A tough, wiry, impetuous American in his early forties, McClellan had been one of "Mad Anthony" Wayne's most daring scouts in the campaign against hostile natives in northwest Ohio, before moving to Missouri and teaming up with Crooks. His prowess with firearms was legendary. "This gentleman is one of the first shots in America," Ross said of him. "Nothing could escape his keen eye and steady hand."

Both Crooks and McClellan would prove valuable additions to the company, as would—at the outset, at least—Joseph Miller, a former second lieutenant in the U.S. infantry, who'd resigned from the army in a huff after being denied a furlough. Miller, too, had been trading on the Missouri and was well acquainted with Hunt as well as Crooks and McClellan. Irving described him as "a gentleman well educated and well informed, and of a respectable family. . . . He was easily induced by Mr. Hunt to join as a partner, and was considered by him, on account of his education and his acquaintances, and his experience in the Indian trade, a valuable addition to the company." Hunt brought both Miller and McClellan in as junior partners with two and one half shares of PFC stock—a sum both thought too low but nevertheless agreed to.

In mounting the expedition, Hunt didn't receive much cooperation from his second in command, Donald "Fat" Mackenzie. Mackenzie remained embittered that Astor hadn't appointed him expedition leader and repeatedly groused that his rival was dawdling in making preparations for the journey. The rift between the two widened late in 1810 when Astor sent Hunt a letter confirming that he wanted the St. Louis merchant to be in sole charge of the expedition.

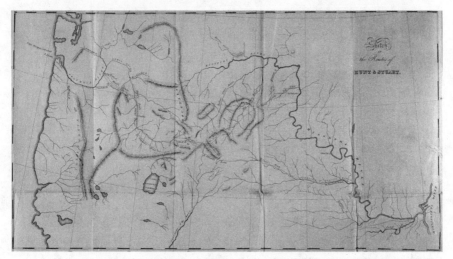

Sketch made in 1836 of the routes taken by Hunt and Stuart.
PUBLIC DOMAIN.

Hunt's biggest problem, at first, was recruiting the hunters and voyageurs needed for the trip. When Hunt and Mackenzie visited Montreal in early July 1810 to acquire trade goods and to hire men, the Nor'Westers, concerned that Astor wasn't going to include them in his Columbia River venture, secretly interdicted the best hands from signing on with this new company, according to Irving.

Worse, Mackenzie and Hunt were continually quarreling over personnel. At Astor's urging, Hunt wanted to sign on as many Americans as possible. Mackenzie, who had gained a firsthand respect for the ability of the French Canadians in the wilderness, thought him biased against the voyageurs, as did Alexander Ross. In Ross's view, Hunt, the somber, conservative shopkeeper, "detested the volatile gaiety and ever changing character of the Canadian voyageurs and gave decided preference to Americans." With Hunt nixing a number of Mackenzie's choices, the two partners left Montreal with only fourteen hires. "No more Canadian voyageurs were taken than were barely sufficient to man one canoe," Ross wrote.

Hunt got his first taste of the demanding, often frustrating task of managing the exuberant, willful, and independently minded French Canadians—many of whom didn't like taking orders from an Ameri-

Wilson Price Hunt by O. L. Erickson.
COURTESY OF MISSOURI HISTORICAL SOCIETY.

can half their age—on the nine-hundred-mile canoe trip from Montreal to Mackinac. The experience was a far cry from supervising docile clerks in a general store and harbingered some of the difficulties that lay ahead.

Hunt, MacKenzie, and their party arrived in Mackinac on July 22. Here, at this island trading center, Hunt had even less luck, initially, in finding recruits than he'd experienced in Montreal. This was the time of year—summer rendezvous—when the fur hunters and traders came in from their remote winter posts to sell their furs and to whore and drink until their money ran out and they had to return to the wilderness. "Every nook and cranny on the whole island swarmed, at all hours of the day, with motley groups of uproarious tipplers and whiskey hunters," Ross said. Plenty of men were on the island, including a number of Americans who traded on the Great Lakes. None, however, showed any enthusiasm for joining the PFC.

According to Irving, who drew much of his information from later discussions with Crooks, the Mackinac voyageurs that Hunt approached were reluctant to commit to this new trading enterprise on two counts: It was an unproven operation, and Hunt was headed into remote, unknown, and potentially dangerous territory. "It was objected that the expedition would have to navigate unknown rivers, and pass through howling wilderness infested by savage tribes, who had already cut off the unfortunate voyageurs that ventured among them," Irving wrote. There was a third, overriding consideration as well. As long as the voyageurs and engages had enough money left in their pockets to buy whiskey, they had no interest in working for anyone.

Eventually, Hunt managed to hire one man whom James Ronda identified as Francois Landry. With Landry acting as a "stalking horse," talking up the PFC and its can't-miss prospects to his colleagues in the grog shops along the bay, Hunt recruited a handful of additional men including one American—but only after they'd blown all their earnings and begun to sober up. At that point, Hunt, Mackenzie, and Crooks, who had joined the party soon after Hunt's arrival here, agreed to advance their wages and pay off some of their debts, including what was owed the local publicans. In one instance, Hunt even covered the court fine and damages for a voyageur named Joseph Perrault, who had smashed a tavern table or two in a drunken rage shortly after Hunt's arrival.

The newcomers were hardly first-class canoe men and traders, however. In fact, a good many were burnt-out cases or greenhorns who hadn't ventured much beyond Mackinac Island. By the time he left Mackinac, even Hunt conceded he should have done far more hiring in Montreal.

TRAVELING ON TWO barges—Hunt had sold the canoe at Mackinac—Hunt; Mackenzie; Crooks; a new clerk, the Irishman John Reed; and the Montreal and Mackinac hires departed Mackinac around August 12, proceeding to St. Louis by way of Green Bay and the Fox, Wisconsin, and Mississippi rivers. They arrived September 3, 1810, a week before the *Tonquin* sailed from New York.

By now, it was much too late in the year to set off across the Great Plains and the Rocky Mountains. Besides, Hunt still had some unfinished business in St. Louis. Always tight with a dollar, Astor had wanted to limit the overland expedition to thirty men. Crooks thought this number too low by half. He was the only one in the present party who had actually traded on the upper Missouri and had experienced the perils of dealing with the Sioux.

In the summer of 1809, Crooks and his then-partner, Robert McClellan, and a trading party of about forty men heading up the Missouri were confronted by some six hundred Sioux who appeared on a high bank above the traders and ordered them to turn around and land downriver. There, the Sioux chiefs made it clear they did not want the white traders proceeding any farther and dealing with their enemies to the north, the Mandans and Aricaras. If Crooks and McClellan wanted to trade, they would establish a post at the landing site and trade exclusively with the Sioux. Crooks and McClellan agreed. With six hundred Sioux braves ready to launch a shower of arrows down on them, they didn't have much of a choice.

Now, if Hunt realistically expected to get by the Sioux, Crooks insisted, he needed to take on an additional two or three dozen men, American frontiersmen, who could handle a rifle with the same facility the French Canadians wielded a canoe paddle.

HUNT AND THE OTHERS spent a little more than six weeks in St. Louis trying to hire the additional riflemen Crooks said were needed, but pickings were slim. By early autumn most of the traders and trappers had already returned to their wintering posts. Additionally, a rival St. Louis trading outfit, the Missouri Fur Company (MFC), planned to send an expedition of its own up the Missouri the following spring. Once he got wind of the Hunt party, the St. Louis–based company's cofounder and guiding spirit, Manuel Lisa, was determined not to let this new enterprise poach any of his people. "He was also deeply suspicious of Astor's true intent," David Lavender wrote. "Although Hunt protested that the party had no intention of pausing on the rich beaver grounds of the upper Missouri where the local company was struggling to get established, Lisa did not believe him."

Born of Spanish parents in New Orleans in 1772, Lisa was a formidable rival. "A person better qualified for this arduous undertaking could not have been better chosen," said an English writer and adventurer named Henry Brackenridge, who joined Lisa's Missouri expedition. "Mr. Lisa is not surpassed by any one, in the requisite experience in the Indian trade and manners, and has few equals in perseverance and indefatigable energy."

Lisa and Crooks had already experienced one run-in that had left Crooks and McClellan embittered. When the traders had been blocked by the Sioux from continuing up the Missouri, they'd been following Lisa upriver. Both were certain Lisa had convinced the Sioux to prevent them from going farther north so that the MFC could have the upper Missouri to itself.

With Lisa undercutting their recruiting efforts, Hunt had to offer American hunters various perquisites for signing, including tea, coffee, and whiskey allowances. When the Canadians learned of this, they wanted the same treatment. Hunt resolved the dilemma by denying both groups these niceties, thereby alienating Canadians and Americans alike, many of whom quit on the spot, taking their advances with them.

When the story got out that Hunt was such a tightwad—and, naturally, Lisa did everything he could to spread the word in every tavern on the waterfront—hiring came to an abrupt halt, at least until Miller joined the company in late September. Miller was immensely popular in the St. Louis trading community, and his participation in Astor's venture made it possible for Hunt to hire most of the trappers, hunters, and interpreters he needed.

The overlanders spent forty-eight days in St. Louis buying tools; clothing; food, including almost one thousand pounds of biscuit mix; weapons—muskets, bayonets, and even a pair of howitzers; medicines such as castor oil and opium; and a keelboat and another barge. On October 18, they started off again, proceeding 450 miles up the Missouri to its juncture with the Nodaway River in today's Andrew County in northwest Missouri.

Here, Hunt intended to establish a winter camp, his thinking being that his sixty overlanders could winter here far more inexpensively than in St. Louis—a move he hoped would make his addition of thirty extra men more palatable to Astor. Moreover, by leaving from this spot rather than St. Louis the following spring, the expedition would save considerable time. Lewis and Clark had taken the same approach, wintering with the Mandans during the winter of 1804–1805.

With Mackenzie muttering that they should have been on the Columbia by now, the expedition arrived at the Nodaway on November 16. While the traders were building the storehouse and huts that would shelter them over the winter, Robert McClellan appeared in camp. He had already verbally committed to joining Hunt's party, though he'd expected to be given five shares—the same equity as his former partner Ramsay Crooks. Angered when Hunt showed him the contract granting him only half that sum, McClellan, having recently been robbed by the Sioux of all his trading goods, begrudgingly decided to accept after several days of intense wrangling. The Hunt offer, niggardly as it was, at least provided a fresh beginning. "I intend to begin the world anew tomorrow," he wrote his brother from the Nodaway camp.

HUNT HEADED BACK to St. Louis from the Nodaway camp with eight men on January 1, 1811, the same day his colleagues on the Columbia were celebrating their first New Year's at Astoria. He had some remaining business to conduct in the city and certainly a St. Louis boarding house was preferable to a drafty hut in the dead of winter.

Arriving on January 20, Hunt remained in St. Louis until March 12. Sometime during his stay, according to Alexander Ross, he received the aforementioned letter from Astor putting him entirely in command of the expedition, a ruling that Hunt knew would further strain his already tense relations with Mackenzie.

In St. Louis, Hunt asked two young English naturalists, John Bradbury and Thomas Nuttall, to travel with the expedition to the upper Missouri. Bradbury had met Crooks and Mackenzie earlier in St. Louis, and on learning of their plans, Bradbury and Nuttall expressed an interest in making the trip themselves. Hunt graciously extended an invitation.

During the later weeks of his stay, he also hired eight more frontiersmen and scored a costly but important coup by signing on the half-breed Sioux interpreter Pierre Dorion Jr. The son of Lewis and Clark's interpreter, "Old" Dorion, the younger man agreed to join the expedition on the condition that his strong-willed, pregnant Iowa Indian wife, Marie, and their two small children come along as well. He also demanded a salary of three hundred dollars a year, two hundred of it in advance.

Dorion's presence was critical if Hunt's party was going to get past the Sioux. Determined to block Hunt's expedition—much as he had stymied Crooks and McClellan earlier—Manuel Lisa came up with a last-minute ploy to have Dorion arrested, issuing a writ of debt for an unpaid bar bill Lisa claimed Dorion had run up while working for the MFC at the company's Mandan post.

At the time (March 12) Hunt and sixteen men had already started back up the Missouri, while Bradbury and Nuttall had stayed behind awaiting important letters from England. They planned to catch up in a few days, but their plans changed abruptly when Bradbury learned Lisa planned to have the writ served at St. Charles upriver. "Knowing that the detention of Dorion would be of serious consequence to the party, I left St. Louis at two o'clock the flowing morning [March 13] in company with a young English man named Nuttall, determined to meet the boat [carrying Dorion] previous to its arrival at St. Charles, which I effected," Bradbury later wrote.

On learning of Lisa's scheme, a grateful Hunt instructed Dorion, his spouse, and his children to hide in the woods and continue by foot on past St. Charles, where he would pick them up. But nothing came easy for Hunt. North of St. Charles, the expedition met up with Dorion on March 14, but there was no sign of Marie Dorion or the children. "They had quarreled and he had beaten her, in consequence of which she had run away from him into the woods, with a child in her arms and a large bundle on her back," Bradbury recalled. The following morning the bedraggled and bruised Marie Dorion hailed the expedition from the riverbank. She had been searching for her husband and the others the entire night.

Hunt finally reached the Nodaway camp on April 17, only to be greeted with some bad news. In the three and a half months he'd been away, he'd lost a number of men. Joseph Perrault, the Mackinac tavern brawler, had died under mysterious circumstances in December, while a number of other recruits, all but one of them Americans, had deserted. Still, with the new hires, Hunt had the requisite number of men in the party, plus the Englishmen and Marie Dorion and her two small children. After four days of loading supplies and checking their equipment, the overlanders were finally off. "We . . . embarked in four boats," Bradbury reported. "Our party amounted to nearly sixty persons: forty were Canadian boatmen, such as are employed by the North West Company, and are termed in Canada *Engages* or *Voyageurs*. Our boats were all furnished with masts and sails, and as the wind blew pretty strong from the south-east, we availed ourselves of it during the greater part of the day."

CHAPTER 12

VISITORS

TWO WEEKS AFTER THE DEPARTURE OF THORN AND the *Tonquin*, a pair of Cree-speaking natives, seemingly man and wife, arrived at the camp, brought there in a canoe by half a dozen Clatsops. Dressed handsomely in buckskin, the man, Ko-come-ne-pe-ca, impressed Robert Stuart and his fellow Astorians as being keenly intelligent. He carried a letter dated April 15, 1811, and addressed to John Stuart, a partner in the NWC and a distant cousin of the Stuarts'.

Ko-come-ne-pe-ca told Benjamin Pillet, who served as the post's translator and who was conversant in Cree, he had been given the letter by a fur trader, one Finnan McDonald, at Spokane House, the NWC post in present-day eastern Washington, with instructions to deliver it to John Stuart at Fort Estekakadme. En route down the Columbia, the pair had become lost and, learning of Astoria, had delivered the letter there, after wandering into a nearby Clatsop village.

The contents of the letter were vague and inconsequential, McDougall reported in the post journal, but in questioning Ko-come-ne-pe-ca, it became evident that Fort Estekakadme was situated somewhere on the upper Columbia in present-day north central Washington. This meant that the NWC under John Stuart had established a new post in the region. If so, it directly challenged the PFC's plans for expansion.

To McDougall and the Stuarts, this was alarming, if not entirely unexpected, news. The traders had planned to extend their operations into the interior once the overland party under Hunt arrived, but with word of this new NWC post, it was clear they needed to establish a presence of their own in the upper Columbia to check the NWC's influence there. To this end, David Stuart volunteered to set out for the region as soon as possible with Alexander Ross and several engages. They would select a site not too far from Fort Estekakadme, build their own outpost there, and spend the winter trading with the local natives.

For the next few weeks, the Astorians busied themselves making preparations for the elder Stuart's expedition. Robert Stuart, who thought the Indian canoes vastly superior to those produced by the company's shipbuilders, commissioned the Chinooks to build three canoes for his uncle's journey up the Columbia.

On July 15, just a few days before David Stuart's scheduled departure, both Stuarts and Duncan McDougall were completing an inventory of the eighteen hundred pounds of merchandise and supplies the elder Stuart intended to take with him when they heard an outcry from Franchere. He and some of the other men were working a few hundred yards upriver from the post. Rushing immediately down to the riverbank to see what the commotion was about, they spotted a big canoe coming downstream, a Union Jack flying conspicuously from the prow.

As the vessel neared, David Stuart and McDougall recognized the short stocky man with shoulder-length black hair standing in the bow. A well-educated, teetotaling Englishman who revered the Indians and was thoroughly versed in the use of astronomical instruments, David Thompson was a legend in the fur trade, an NWC partner and its chief geographer. McDougall and David Stuart knew him from their NWC days, while Robert had heard countless tales of his exploits. Working first for the HBC, which he joined in 1784 at age fourteen as an apprentice, and in 1797 signing on with its rival NWC, Thompson had hiked and canoed more than fifty-five thousand miles—the equivalent of nearly twice around the globe— through the Northwest, making observations of latitude and longitude wherever he went and recording his prodigious travels in his journals.

In his career as a Nor'Wester, he'd pinpointed the headwaters of the Mississippi, explored the upper reaches of the Missouri and the southeastern corner of British Columbia, and was presently mapping

Astoria as it was in 1813.

COURTESY OREGON HISTORICAL SOCIETY, NEGATIVE # ORHI 21681.

out the Columbia River system, opening these vast tracts of previously uncharted territory to the NWC traders who followed in his footsteps. Many thought him to be the greatest geographer of his day.

Attired in fine European clothing donned for the occasion, the visitor exuded a robust energy and confidence. Accompanied by French Canadian voyageurs in bright caps and sashes, two Indian interpreters and an imposing pair of Iroquois hunters, he bounded energetically from the canoe as soon as it came aside Astoria's little quay.

Even though Thompson was a rival, McDougall and David Stuart greeted their fellow trader and former colleague warmly and, with Robert Stuart and several of the clerks in tow, proudly gave the Nor'Wester a tour of their fledgling operation. Privately, Thompson wasn't impressed. "The fur trading post of Mr. J. J. Astor of the city of New York . . . was four low log huts, this far-famed Fort Astoria of the United States," he later noted in his journals. "The place was in charge of Messrs. McDougall and [David] Stuart who had been clerks of the North West Company and by whom we were politely received."

The Astorians entertained their guest as lavishly as their meager larder would allow and listened intently as Thompson recounted the details of his harrowing midwinter crossing of the Rockies. Despite the desertion of many of his men, the loss of all his supplies, and 30-degree-below-zero temperatures during his January crossing of the Athabaska Pass, the hard-driving forty-one-year-old Thompson had been the first to travel the entire length of the Columbia, beginning from its source high in the Canadian Rockies.

Robert Stuart and some of the younger men, like Ross, had little doubt that Thompson was less interested in exploration than in beating the PFC to the mouth of the Columbia and securing the Pacific Northwest for the NWC. This clearly was the expedition that Astor had warned them was coming; yet to the annoyance of the younger men, especially Ross, McDougall treated Thompson like a brother. "Nothing was too good for Mr. Thompson," Ross said. "He had access everywhere, saw and examined everything, and whatever he asked for got, as if he had been one of ourselves."

Ross charged that his visit had no purpose other than to discourage the PFC men—"a maneuver of the North West policy to extend their own trade at the expenses of ours." There's some evidence to suggest that Robert Stuart agreed with this assessment, yet none of the Astorians were about to challenge their guest's motives openly, especially after the Nor'Wester astonished them with two completely unexpected revelations.

The first involved the two Indians who had come to Astoria with the letter for John Stuart. Thompson had immediately recognized Ko-come-ne-pe-ca. In actuality, he explained, this was not a man but a woman—the one-time former wife of his servant, a Canadian named Boisvard. She had left Boisvard three years earlier, proclaimed herself a prophetess, declared her sex changed, and had taken a young woman as a wife. Hadn't the Stuarts, McDougall, and the others recognized there was something unusual about this visitor and his companion of whom he seemed so jealous?, Thompson asked with some amusement.

The second bit of news was even more startling. Thompson handed Astor's partners another letter, this one addressed to Messrs. McDougall, Stuart & Stuart and dated July 15, 1811. It read:

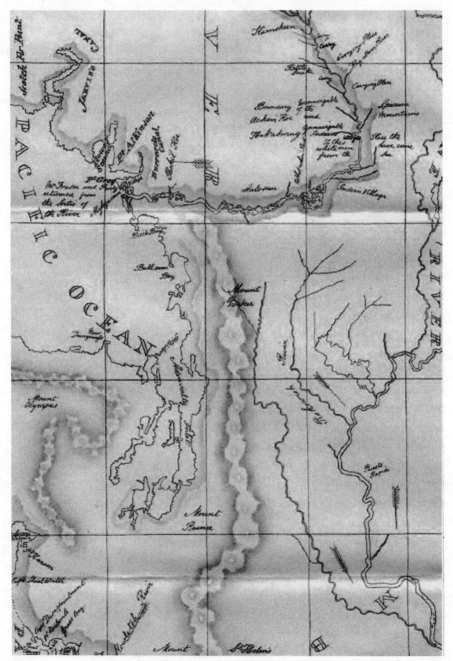

David Thompson's map of the Columbia River, 1813 and 1814.

Gentlemen,

Permit me to congratulate you on your safe arrival & building in the mouth of the Columbia River. Your situation is such as to enable you with the aid of good Providence to command an extensive commerce and humanize numerous Indians in which I wish you success.—

With pleasure I acquaint you that the Wintering Partners have acceded to the offer of Mr. Astor, accepting one-third share of the business you are engaged in, their share of the Capital not to exceed 10,000 pounds without further permission. I have only to hope that the respective parties at Montreal may finally settle the arrangements between the two Companies which in my opinion will be to our mutual interest.—

Accept of my best wishes for your health and that of the young Gentlemen with you.—

I am with Esteem, Your Humble Servant.

David Thompson

According to this letter, Astor had sold the Nor'Westers, his rivals, a one-third share in his Columbia River enterprise. The partners were nonplussed. The transaction simply didn't make sense, particularly since Astor had avowed to secure the Pacific Northwest for the United States. Once their guest had retired for the night, McDougall and the Stuarts gathered in Astoria's modest meeting room. Perhaps the letter was simply a ruse. Yet, Astor had in fact been negotiating to sell the Montreal traders equity in the PFC at one point, McDougall reminded them. Perhaps David Thompson was telling the truth.

With Astor on the other side of the continent, there was no way the partners could determine if the information in the letter was accurate. To protect themselves, the Stuarts and McDougall decided to respond with a letter of their own, making it clear they welcomed this supposed arrangement with the NWC. At the same time, they'd use their response to indicate they were dealing from strength rather than weakness. It was important to emphasize that they had established a firm alliance with the area's natives and that reinforcements—Hunt's expedition—were expected any day now. Never mind that Hunt wasn't due for several months. Thompson didn't know that. In the letter, the Astorians would claim David Stuart was on his way upriver to greet them—thus, the expedition to the interior. They could play this duplicitous game as well as Thompson.

Late into the night they drafted their response, presenting it to their guest at breakfast.

> Fort Astoria 16th. July
> David Thompson Esq.
>
> Sir,
>
> We have the pleasure to acknowledge the receipt of your note of yesterday, communicating the pleasant intelligence of the Wintering Partners . . . having accepted of Mr. Astor's offer of the business we are engaged in, and with you sincerely wish that final arrangements may take place to the mutual satisfaction of both parties.
>
> We have been on the most friendly terms with the Natives around us ever since our arrival on the 25th. March last, [and] have explored the interior of the river for a considerable difference, where we also found the Natives peaceably inclined & on your arrival were on the point of setting off to facilitate the passage of Our Friends whom we expect across the Continent by the Missouri and Lewis' river.
>
> Sir,
>
> > Your most obedient servants
> > Duncan McDougall
> > David Stuart
> > Robert Stuart

Thompson remained at Astoria for a week. He was given the run of the place and used his access to make a thorough study of the Astorians' trade operations and talked to the Indians with whom they were trading, all the while surreptitiously recording their short-comings in his journal: "They had been unable to settle any steady rate of barter, either for furs or provisions," he noted. "Every sturgeon or salmon had to be again valued in barter; a great part of this fault lay in the very low quality of the goods, especially the cotton goods, and all their tobacco was in leaf of the lowest price. The natives were displeased with several of their articles."

By the end of Thompson's stay, even McDougall was convinced that he'd come to spy on them, but since none of the Astorians had proof, the charade continued with David Thompson doing his best to convince his new "partners" not to extend their operations inland, emphasizing that furs were scarce beyond the Great Cascades and the danger great. In turn, David Stuart insisted he was going off to meet Hunt's overlanders. For mutual protection, Stuart proposed that the two parties travel together at least part of the way upriver.

Seeing Stuart's three Chinook canoes loaded down with trading goods and enough supplies to last for months, Thompson was not fooled for a moment, yet he couldn't very well leave his new business associates behind. On July 22, the two parties, sixteen men in all, left Astoria, "offering a prayer," Thompson noted, "to all powerful Providence to grant us a safe journey."

From the quay, Robert Stuart watched his uncle gradually disappear from view. The elder Stuart had rigged his party's canoes with small sails. A brisk eastwardly breeze helped him and his men keep pace with the great David Thompson.

CHAPTER 13

THE DIPLOMAT

WITH BOTH MCKAY AND HIS UNCLE AWAY AND MCDOUGALL
in charge of the day-to-day operations at Astoria, Robert Stuart had
become the company's emissary to the coastal tribes. It was a task
for which he proved well suited.

Stuart hadn't come West with any deep-seated romantic notions
regarding Indians. But the Scottish trader was intrigued by these
natives who lived in harmony with the bountiful environment of the
Columbia, and he became friendly with a number of them.

The Chinooks and their Chinookan-speaking neighbors, the Clatsops, thrived as fishermen and traders, fashioned canoes that would
have been the envy of the master shipbuilders of Great Britain, crafted
beautiful wooden bowls and baskets, and constructed large, comfortable split-cedar homes that kept them dry and warm throughout the
chilly, wet coastal winters.

During the spring and summer of 1811, Stuart often visited the
Clatsop village at Port Adams and the Chinook settlement on the
north side of Baker Bay. Using the French Canadian clerk and interpreter Benjamin Pillet as well as sign language and a pidgin trading
language that had evolved among the coastal tribes, Stuart questioned the natives about their way of life. In his journals, he wrote
detailed descriptions of everything from native religion and war-
making techniques to burial rituals and architecture.

In the Chinook settlement, Comcomly, the "one-eyed potentate,"
as Washington Irving dubbed him, never failed to extend a generous
welcome to the headmen of the PFC. As Comcomly's guest, Stuart

was entertained in the banquet hall and fed a copious dinner. Afterward, there was music and dancing in Stuart's honor. Stuart gave this entertainment a mixed review. "Their manner of singing has something in it harsh and disagreeable to the ear, their songs being almost all extempore . . . They have several kinds of dance, some of which are lively, pleasing, and possess some variety."

The women, he noted, "are rarely permitted to dance with the men, but form companies apart, and dance to the sound of the same instrument and song." Had he desired, Stuart later could have readily paired off with one of the Chinook women for the night. Chinook women often were sleepover guests at Astoria and were, by Anglo conventions, highly promiscuous. Patrick Gass, a member of the Lewis and Clark expedition, said that an aged Chinook madam used to visit the Corps of Discovery encampment regularly with a string of nine prostitutes in tow. Of course, had there been no market for her services, the Chinook madam would not have bothered to cross the bay.

Noted Stuart, "The women are very inconstant to their husbands and the worst of disorders is deeply rooted among them, having been first introduced by some of our countrymen, probably from the Sandwich Islands, where it has been known since time immemorial. The effects, however, are not as destructive as might be expected."

During these visits, Stuart made a study of the well-built Chinook dwellings, which were warm and dry in winter and cool in the heat of July and August:

Their lodges are constructed of cedar boards, a little sunk in the ground, and leaning against strong poles set erect, [with cross spars] which serve likewise as a support to the roof; those dwellings are generally large enough for the accommodation of 3 or 4 families, have a door in the gable end, made of a square piece of board, or framed seal skin, a fire place (or places) in the middle, & a hole over it, in the roof of the house which serves at once for the discharge of smoke and the admission of light. The sides are partitioned off for sitting and sleeping places, and covered with neat grass mats; the principal houses have a small apartment attached to them which serves as a vapor bath to prepare which

*Chief Comcomly. Drawing from Duncan
McDougall's Astoria Journal.*

COURTESY OF THE ROSENBACH MUSEUM AND LIBRARY.

stones must be heated and placed in a large hole dug in the middle
of the bath, or sweating house, where the heat may be increased to
any degree by the steam of the water which is poured on them.

He was struck by the native custom of flattening the crown and
forehead of their infants with a small piece of board shaped and
bound to the child's head shortly after birth, a practice Meriwether
Lewis thought barbarous. "This in their opinion is a great acquisition to personal beauty," Stuart observed. "Consequently whoever
has the broadest and flattest head is esteemed by far the handsomest
person."

These Indians, who called whites "long beards" by way of

reproach, viewed beards and body hair as uncouth and aesthetically displeasing. They plucked hair from their chins and removed it from their bodies, yet prided themselves in letting the hair from their heads grow to great length; often, Stuart noted, they wore it pleated and wound fancifully around the head in tresses.

Their religion, Stuart determined, centered on a supreme being, an enormous bird known as "Uth-lath-Gla-gla." This omnipotent deity, the Chinooks maintained, was responsible for the earth's creation. It was viewed as benevolent, yet in righteous wrath it often soared through "the aerial regions . . . hurling down thunder and lightning" upon guilty mortals.

The Chinooks told Stuart that another deity, a creature of fire that was possessed by the power of good and evil, acted as the intermediary between them and their winged protector. To this god, the Indians offered annual sacrifices including the first salmon of the season in hopes of procuring such desirable things as male children, a plentiful fishery, and an abundance of game.

When any of the headmen of the village were ill, Stuart observed, "all the literati of the nation are immediately convened. The high priest and physician, or medicine man, consults his deity (i.e. the . . . spirit of the air and that of fire), which are made of wood and ingeniously carved, with a number of bear and eagle claws suspended from them, they are capriciously formed in [the] shape of a horse, bear, deer, beaver, swan, fish, etc." These idols were placed in the chief's lodge by the various medicine men in attendance. If there was a dispute about which diagnosis to pursue, the contending physicians, who were invariably rivals for fame, power, and influence, violently beat their figurines together until a tooth or claw fell off one—proof that the medicine man whose idol remained intact had the more potent medicine. His prescriptions "are implicitly tended to," Stuart noted.

If the sick person recovered, a sacrifice was immediately made, but if the patient died, no compensation was offered and the demise was attributed to the displeasure of the deity rather than faulty practice on the part of the medicine men. Stuart detailed the burial ceremony:

A day or two after his death, a few of the nearest relatives carry off the corpse, which, with his most valuable movables, they deposit in a canoe, prepared for the purpose, and neatly covered with handsome mats made of straw; they then lay it on a scaffold, or suspend it between two trees, in a retired part of the woods.

After the funeral, the mourners cut off their hair in a token of grief and for several days neither ate nor drank but wandered the village shrilly lamenting the departed. When the mourning season was over, after perhaps a month, the dead man's slaves and property were divided up in accordance with the deceased's request at his deathbed.

Stuart, who may have been reflecting upon his engagement to Betsy Sullivan, was especially intrigued by the native courtship and marriage practices, finding them sensible, if not entirely in accord with the strict Presbyterian morality of his homeland.

Their manner of courtship and marriage is somewhat singular; when a fair one has the good fortune to kindle a flame in the bosom of a hero, he watches for a private conference and if favorably received, repairs soon after to her father's lodge with a considerable present . . . The sire then inquires whether the proposal is agreeable to his daughter, and on being answered in the affirmative, demands so many slaves, horses and canoes according to her beauty and accomplishments and promises a certain return on her going into housekeeping; preliminaries thus settled, the remainder of the day is devoted to festivity and mirth. At a late hour the party breaks up and all retire to rest except the lover, who steals to her ladyship's couch where he remains until morning, when, if they are fully satisfied with each other's company, the match is finally settled; but should either be inclined to retract, they are at liberty to do so, as the present the lover had made his intended father-in-law, is thought the full equivalent for his breach of the maid's virtue.

AS ASTORIA'S ROVING ambassador, Stuart visited the native villages in hopes of creating trading alliances with as many of the region's tribes as possible. He was on the lookout for potential problems as well.

In early June he led an exploratory probe up the coast to determine why the number of Indians appearing at the post with pelts to trade had dropped off so sharply. Initially after the Astorians' arrival, native traders from up and down the coast overwhelmed the whites in their eagerness to do business, but after the departure of the *Tonquin*, the Chinooks were Astoria's only visitors.

From the Clatsops, he'd heard that the Chinook headman was spreading rumors that the whites were dangerous and not to be trusted. With these tales, Stuart suspected, Comcomly hoped to keep both the Quinault traders from the Olympic Peninsula and the Chehalis to the immediate north at bay, thereby controlling access to trade at Astoria. As the middleman between the whites and the northern traders, Comcomly could earn a profit on every pelt the Astorians acquired, an advantage he was surely determined to retain.

Accompanied by Coalpo, Ross, and five other men, Stuart soon discovered that his suspicions regarding Comcomly were justified. The first Indians he encountered during the June expedition, the Chehalis, were a Salish-speaking tribe of seafaring fishermen, seal hunters, and traders, who lived about forty miles north of the Columbia's mouth. They seemed terrified of the Astorians, a fear that no doubt the Chinook chief had fueled. At the sight of Stuart's small party, they seized their weapons and made signs for the whites to keep their distance. Even after Stuart and Ross displayed gifts, they would have nothing to do with the visitors and might well have attacked had the Astorians not moved on.

Farther north, Stuart encountered less timorous Indians, probably Quinaults, another Salish-speaking tribe. The Quinaults showed the whites several piles of furs they were preparing to deliver to the Chinooks. These coastal traders "put their hands on their mouths in astonishment" when they learned the Astorians were offering a far more generous price for furs than Comcomly, Ross reported, "and strongly urged us to return again, saying they would never more trade with the one-eyed chief."

Despite these assurances, the Quinaults threatened Stuart as he and his party were crossing a river on their way north and later killed one of the traders. They clearly viewed the whites as enemies, probably as the result of what the Chinooks had told them about the "long beards."

Stuart continued north as far as Gray's Harbor, where he encountered Kodiak Indians from Alaska, who controlled much of the fur trading along the entire north coast. On his return, he related the disquieting news about Comcomly and reported that the coastal region teemed with beaver, otter, sea otter, elk, deer, bear, and wolf. Stuart recommended establishing a depot on Gray's Harbor that would be affiliated with the Kodiaks' and would extend the reach of the PFC to the far north, one of Astor's chief goals in establishing the Columbia River base. "It is his [Stuart's] opinion that an establishment in that quarter [with a few good Kodiak Indians] would turn out well as they would not only make a good hunt themselves, particularly in sea otter, but secure the most of the furs this side of Neweetie or the Straits of Juan De Fuca," McDougall noted upon Stuart's return on June 24.

STUART'S ENCOUNTERS with the Chehalis and Quinaults underscored how firmly Comcomly controlled the flow of pelts from the north. If Astor's endeavor was to succeed, Stuart believed, he and his fellow traders would have to come to terms with the Chinook leader, on whom they already relied for much of their food—the salmon, sturgeon, and game the Chinooks brought to the post. They needed to win him over. Consequently, Stuart and McDougall decided to invite Comcomly to Astoria and present to the chief and his two sons gifts including suits of clothing befitting great chiefs. These were to be made in recognition of Comcomly's role as their trade broker and benefactor.

The tribute, which they presented to Comcomly in late June with requisite ceremony, had the hoped-for result. The chief—"the Great Mufti" as Ross called him—seemed as much delighted with the warm reception he'd received at Astoria as the gifts. Almost immediately trading parties from the north once again began appearing at Astoria eager to bargain. But this honeymoon was short-lived. Soon after, during another of Comcomly's visits, McDougall was showing off the inner workings of a blunderbuss. The weapon went off, just missing Comcomly. This was not McDougall's first mishap with a weapon. On June 5, McDougall had been holding a blunderbuss in his lap. The gun went off, injuring him in the genitals and just missing David Stuart, who was standing a few feet away. On this occasion, Astoria's supervising partner almost started a war. Certain McDougall meant to kill him, the chief fled from the trading house without his cap, robe, or gun and began frantically calling to his warriors, many of whom had accompanied him to the post. Sounding war cries, they immediately armed themselves and seemed prepared to attack the garrison.

Ater hearing the report and seeing smoke emanating from the cabin, the Astorians supposed Comcomly had murdered McDougall and drew their own weapons, calling out "Treason! Murder!" Before the confrontation could escalate into bloodshed, McDougall inserted himself between the two angry factions, frantically making signs of peace and explaining what had happened.

Then, in late July, the Chinooks warned the whites that Indians from the north, perhaps the Chehalis, whom Stuart and Ross had encountered in the spring, were planning to attack the post. If so, the whites would be badly outnumbered. More than a third of the Astorians had either sailed with the *Tonquin* or gone off to the interior with David Stuart. Robert Stuart estimated that the Chehalis could muster a force of more than two hundred men. Still, he was confident that the Indians were no match for the Astorians, even with their ranks depleted. "Their arms are principally bows and arrows, iron and bone bludgeons, with a few muskets they are extremely fond of," he said of the coastal natives. "Their military power is an undisciplined rabble, unfit to contend with 1/5 the numbers of whites."

During his travels in late July, a friendly chief warned Stuart—he didn't reveal the Indian's identity—that an attack on Astoria was imminent. Stuart rushed back to the post with the news. "According to information received from an Indian who had become friendly with Mr. R. Stuart, we discovered that they planned to take us by surprise in view of our reduced numbers," Franchere said.

In the meantime, several other Chinooks came to Astoria with stories that forty or fifty canoes were expected soon from both the north and south to wage war on the traders. Alarmed, McDougall and Stuart ordered all hands to hurry the cutting and setting of sharply pointed palisade pickets and begin construction of two elevated bastions on which small cannons and swivel guns were to be mounted. Guards were posted every night. On the last day of July, McDougall reported: "All hands employed raising the pickets, putting the great guns, swivels, etc., in order."

If an attack was imminent, the Astorians at least would not be taken by surprise.

THROUGHOUT THE SUMMER, the Astorians heard seemingly confused stories from the Indians that those aboard the *Tonquin* had been massacred. Initially, the traders dismissed these reports as unfounded. Since their arrival, a number of rumors had reached the fort via the native grapevine, many of them without substance. Reports about an attack on the *Tonquin*'s crew were simply more of the same, the Astorians believed.

On August 11, though, an Indian visitor to the post—McDougall identifies him only as a friendly Chinook—said he'd heard a report regarding the *Tonquin*'s fate from Indians who had recently arrived from the northwest end of Vancouver Island, where Thorn and McKay had gone to trade. According to the visitor's grisly account, in the course of bartering with the natives, the ship's captain slapped the tribal chief in the face with an otter skin after the native had spoken to him in what Thorn viewed as an insolent tone. The following day, these same natives returned and murdered almost everyone aboard. Faced with certain death, several of the crew had descended to the powder magazine, where they lit a fire, blowing up the ship, themselves, and a hundred or so Indians on deck.

If true, the news was devastating on several counts. All twenty-three of the men aboard the *Tonquin* had lost their lives, including McKay, the group's most experienced trader. Moreover, when the *Tonquin* sailed, Thorn had allowed only a small portion of the cargo to be set ashore. He intended to off-load the remainder upon his return. This meant the Astorians were confronted with a severe shortage of food going into the fall and winter—four to five months of almost constant rain, sleet, and strong, mostly southerly gales that made travel difficult and living conditions miserable. It also meant that McDougall, Stuart, and the others were left with limited goods to trade for furs and food.

McDougall now decided that Comcomly had known the details of the *Tonquin*'s destruction all along, even though the Chinook chief disclaimed any knowledge of the event. "His sole purpose in not telling us the news had been to inspire us with a false sense of security so that, in not keeping up our guard, we could be more easily attacked when the opportunity presented itself," he noted. McDougall redoubled his efforts to secure the post, drilling the men relentlessly and making sure firearms were in proper order.

Stuart had become equally guarded. On August 19, Comcomly sent a messenger asking Stuart and Franchere to come to his village as he was ill and needed treatment that only the whites could provide. "Old Comcomly sent to Astoria for Mr. Stuart and me to come and cure him of a swelled throat, which, he said, afflicted him sorely," Franchere wrote in his journal. "As it was late in the day, we postponed till tomorrow going to cure the chief of the Chinooks; and it was well we did for the same evening the wife of the Indian [Daitshowan] who had accompanied us in our voyage to the Falls, sent us word that Comcomly was perfectly well, the pretended tonsillitis being only a pretext to get us in his power. This timely advice kept us at home."

The summer passed and no attack came; the northern tribes returned to their homeland without incident. Still, the Astorians couldn't relax their guard. Nor could they risk alienating Comcomly, who was now complaining openly about the hostile, militarylike environment that now prevailed at the trading post. Stuart and McDougall sought to convince him that the pickets were only temporary. He and his people were always welcome, they assured him. Indeed, they would soon discover that without the assistance of Comcomly and the Chinooks, they wouldn't be able to survive the coming months.

CHAPTER 14

THE RAINY SEASON

THE BY-NOW SEEMINGLY CERTAIN LOSS OF THE *TONQUIN* cast a pall over Astoria. Though Stuart related the story of the massacre in later years, blaming Thorn for initiating the dispute, he made no mention of the ship's destruction or the death of his friend and mentor Alexander McKay in his journals.

Provisions were in short supply. The traders had stepped up their efforts to replenish the fort's larders before the rainy season set in at the end of September 1811 but without much success. Some of the men tried to fish in the Indian manner using scoop nets, but the midsummer run of what would later become known as Chinook salmon had ended in August. Only the dogtooth salmon, or dog salmon, which Stuart pronounced "a very inferior species of that fish," remained in the river.

The Astorians didn't prove any more proficient as hunters, a failing Stuart attributed to the dense junglelike nature of the surrounding forest. "The country is . . . so very broken and heavily timbered that it is seldom possible to distinguish an object more than 40 yards, which when added to the impenetrable underbrush affords such a secure retreat that the utmost efforts of the hunter are seldom crowned with success," he wrote, adding that the advent of the rainy season "made it impossible for a man to keep his arms in order."

Food and grog rations were reduced sharply, much to the chagrin of the already disgruntled men, many of whom were talking openly of deserting and in several instances had already made attempts to do so. In hopes of bettering the situation, Stuart led a seven-man party on September 29 into the rain forest to find the family of hogs that had escaped from Fort Astoria back in April. An Indian had spotted them gallivanting through the forest. Stuart's party returned a day later, soaked through and disheartened, having seen nothing of the elusive sow and boar and their six offspring.

Fortunately for Stuart, there was a means of escape. By early October the post's mechanics and carpenters had assembled a small schooner from the timber and frames the traders had brought with them from New York. In a move he knew would gain favor with his employer, McDougall had christened the schooner *Dolly*, the nickname of Astor's daughter Dorothea. Now that the *Dolly* was ready for its maiden voyage, Stuart intended to sail it up the Columbia to obtain much-needed provisions as well as oaken staves to serve as building timber.

AS HE WAS PREPARING to leave, Stuart got word that his uncle was safe and well. The elder Stuart had sent two of his men, Benjamin Pillet and Donald McLennan, one of the clerks, back to Astoria, accompanied by an independent trader, Regis Bruguier, as well as an Iroquois hunter and his family. They arrived at Astoria on October 5 with news that David Stuart had established a post on the Okanogan River in what today is north central Washington near the present Canadian border. The Indians in this region were hospitable and honest, the furs abundant, and the Indians there willing to hunt for them, Pillet and McLennan reported.

A week later, Stuart left on his river trip, taking with him John Mumford, the former second officer of the *Tonquin*, the clerk Russell Farnham, and two of the islanders whom the fur traders had recruited on their visit to the Hawaiian Islands, Paul Poar and William Karimoo. The Hawaiians, like most of their countrymen, were superb sailors, but Mumford quickly proved a problem. As a partner, Stuart held rank over him, even though Mumford was acting as master of the *Dolly*. Mumford, who had a dangerous temper—in a drunken brawl earlier in the year he'd badly cut one of the islanders with the sharp point of an elk or deer horn—had problems accepting orders from a lubber.

When he challenged Stuart's authority, Stuart promptly cashiered him, sending him back to the post.

"At the end of five days Mr. Mumford returned [to Astoria] in a canoe of Indians," Franchere wrote in his journal. "This man having wished to assume the command . . . had been sent back in consequence to Astoria." At the post, the American seaman complained that the younger Stuart was every bit as autocratic and overbearing as Thorn. Stuart, Farnham, and the islanders, who had witnessed Mumford's attack on their countryman, thought themselves well rid of him.

During this same trip, Stuart helped capture three deserters: the Canadian voyageur P. D. Jeremie and the Belleau brothers, Jean Baptiste and Antoine. The moody Jeremie had been one of the boatmen under McKay who canoed from Montreal to New York. After McKay departed Astoria, the Stuarts and McDougall accused Jeremie of faking various illnesses. On June 29, he wrote a letter repenting his conduct and promising to do better. Not quite a month later, he tried to desert. "In the morning we were informed that Jeremy had packed up his clothes, etc. and hid them in the wood some days ago, with the intention of deserting tomorrow evening, having made an arrangement with four of the natives to conduct him some distance up the river," McDougall reported the same day.

The voyageur was put in irons until he agreed to serve out his time in Astoria, but he was determined to make his way back to Canada as soon as possible. In early November, Jeremie and Antoine and Jean Baptiste Belleau, the latter both engages, had been given leave to go out hunting for several days, taking with them firearms, ammunition, and a handsome light Indian canoe. They hadn't come back.

Franchere, whom the Stuarts and McDougall had appointed Astoria's constable, and the English-born clerk William Matthews, went after them in a large Indian canoe, leaving November 10. A day later, at Oak Point on the south bank of the river, they met up with Stuart, who was taking on a cargo of timber. With him was the American clerk Russell Farnham, whom Stuart had come to admire for his intelligence and grit.

Indians with whom Stuart had become friendly told the Astorians they had seen footprints of white men in the sand heading east, and for the next ten days the Astorians pursued the runaway engages, finally tracing them to what today is Sauvie Island on the Columbia, where the deserters were being held captive by the Cathlapotle tribe.

There, after being set ashore by Stuart, Franchere and Matthews along with Farnham, whom Stuart told to accompany them, found the three hapless deserters in the chief's house. They were being kept as slaves and pleaded with Franchere to be taken back. After a sleepless night, during which the Indians sang and made medicine over a dying man, Franchere ransomed them for a copper kettle, an axe, an old pistol, a powder horn, shot, and all the group's blankets, and brought them back as prisoners to Astoria.

In the meantime, Stuart continued on to explore the Willamette River valley as a possible site for another trading post. From the Indians, he'd heard that beaver proliferated in the region—reports that proved conservative. "The incredible number of beaver who inhabit its banks . . . exceed from all accounts anything yet discovered on either side of the continent of America," he reported.

Stuart and his little crew survived a mild pillaging of the *Dolly* by natives and two nights of rough weather on Gray's Bay but otherwise completed their mission without incident, returning to Astoria on November 22 with a bounty of geese, ducks, venison, and dried fish obtained from the Indians upriver as well as an ample quantity of oak for use by the company's carpenters.

STUART SET OFF again on December 5 with Russell Farnham and five others for an extended probe of the Cowlitz River, which, he later said, "I navigated with six men for 260 miles, partly for the purpose of diminishing the number of months at the Fort, and partly to explore the interior and trade with the natives."

Stuart and his party didn't return to the post in time to celebrate the New Year, an event McDougall described in his journal, providing us with a glimpse of a rare festive moment during that bleak winter:

Jan. 1st, Wednesday. Ushered in a pleasant sunshine with white frost. . . . At sunrise, the drum beat to arms and the colors were hoisted. Three rounds of small arms and three discharges from the great guns were fired, after which all hands were treated to grog, bread, cheese and butter ... At sundown 3 guns were fired and the colors taken down, after which we had a dance, and retired about three A.M.

In his journal, McDougall always seemed determined to put the best face on things, but a few days later when the weather took a turn for the worse, he noted ominously, "The sudden change from frost to rain has affected most of our people in a very serious manner, particularly the Sandwich Islanders." Disease—gonorrhea, dysentery, and pneumonia—was rampant. Even more worrisome, there was still no word of the Hunt expedition, now months overdue.

CHAPTER 15

THE OVERLANDERS

From the Missouri to Astoria

ON JANUARY 18, 1812, TWO CANOES CARRYING THE first of the overlanders—Donald Mackenzie, Robert McClellan, the clerk John Reed, and eight voyageurs—arrived at Astoria. McDougall, Franchere, and the others who were there to greet them—Stuart was still away, exploring the Cowlitz River—noted that these members of Hunt's party seemed, as Franchere put it, "safe and sound but in a pathetic state with their clothes in rags."

On the following day, a Sunday, the post was the scene of wild rejoicing. McDougall and the rest of their little troop joined with "Fat" Mackenzie's group in celebrating the safe passage of these overlanders and the news that the remaining men—most of them anyway—were not far behind.

Not quite a month later, on the afternoon of February 15, just as a dense fog was lifting, Wilson Price Hunt, thirty of his men, plus Marie Dorion and her two children—all in six canoes—reached the Columbia post. "It had rained all night," Hunt wrote in the journal he began keeping on the upper Missouri. "The fog was so thick we could see only the lowlands and some small island; all was covered by it. It disappeared in the afternoon at high tide. I found that we were navigating along a large bay and shortly afterward I saw the Fort of Astoria on the southerly bank."

Stuart, who'd returned to the post on January 27, and the others had listened intently to Mackenzie and McClellan's account of their

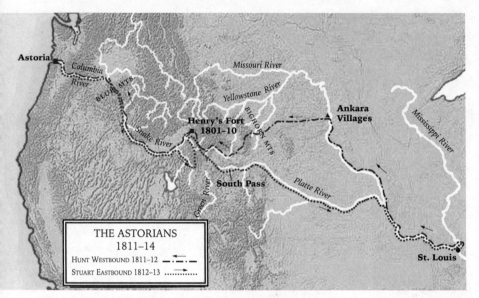

The Astorians, 1811–1814.

COURTESY AMERICAN STUDIES AT THE UNIVERSITY OF VIRGINIA.

arduous journey to Astoria, with Stuart noting many of the details in his own journal. Now, it was Hunt's turn to recount the narrative of his trouble-plagued expedition.

STARTING UP THE Missouri on March 12, Hunt's overlanders proceeded as if they had all the time in the world to reach their destination. With Hunt's permission, and often encouragement, the English naturalists Bradbury and Nuttall frequently went ashore to sightsee or to collect plant specimens, while Crooks departed the expedition for days on end to deal with loose ends from his fur-trading ventures.

On March 17, the overlanders reached the last white settlement on the river, the French village of La Charette. Just beyond, Hunt took Bradbury aside and pointed out an old man standing on the bank. "Mr. Hunt . . . informed me [that the man] was Daniel Boone, the discoverer of Kentucky," Bradbury wrote. "As I had a letter of introduction to him, from his nephew Colonel Grant, I went ashore to speak to him, and requested that the boat might go on, as I intended to walk until evening. I remained for some time in conversation with him. He informed me, that he was eighty-four years of age; that he had spent a considerable portion of his time alone in the back woods, and had lately returned from his spring hunt, with nearly sixty beaver skins."

The following day, Bradbury, Crooks, Hunt, and the other partners spent several hours visiting with one of Boone's upriver neighbors, John Colter. The former Corps of Discovery hunter had recently returned from a trading expedition that had taken him deep into Yellowstone country. Presumably, Colter provided the overlanders with advice on their projected route and the dangers presented by the Blackfoot Indians, who had twice tried to kill him. "He seemed to have a great inclination to accompany the expedition; but having been lately married, he reluctantly took leave of us," Bradbury reported.

In early May, Crooks and Bradbury left the expedition for almost a week so that Crooks could travel to the Oto village on the Platte to retrieve some pelts that were owed him. They finally rejoined Hunt on May 10 at an Omaha Indian village near today's Homer, Nebraska. There, Hunt became involved in a tribal dispute that took another five days to resolve.

Hunt's biggest concern was getting by the Sioux, who by now knew of the expedition and had, they would tell the whites, been awaiting them for eleven days with the intention of opposing their progress. On the morning of May 31, they appeared, some six hundred warriors on horseback, a sight that gave pause to even the most fearless of the traders. Bradbury recorded the scene. "We had a view of the bluffs, and saw the Indians—Brules, Tetons and Yankstons—pouring down in great numbers, some on horseback, and others on foot. They soon took possession of a point a little above us, and arranged themselves along the bank of the river. By the help of our glasses, we could perceive that they were all armed and painted for war. Their arms consisted chiefly of bows and arrows, but a few had short carbines that were provided with round shells."

The confrontation with the Sioux had come sooner than Hunt had expected. Nonetheless, he was prepared to deal with it. He ordered a display of force—the overlanders fired their howitzers and swivel gun, both of which were loaded only with powder, into the air. Next, the traders rose to fire, at which point the Sioux spread their buffalo robes before them as an indication they wanted to parlay rather than fight.

The partners, accompanied by Dorion and Bradbury, went ashore, joining a solemn half-completed circle of Sioux chiefs. The requisite peace pipe was then passed from hand to hand, its stem at least six feet in length and decorated, Bradbury said, with tufts of horsehair, dyed a brilliant red.

The Sioux seemed pleased when the traders passed out gifts of fifteen carrottes of tobacco and an equal number of bags of corn, but it was Hunt's speech, translated by Dorion, that saved the day. "The purport of the speech," said Bradbury, "was to state that the object of our voyage up the Missouri was not to trade, [but] that several of our brothers had gone to the great salt lake in the West [the Pacific], [and we were] on our way to see our brothers, for whom we had been crying ever since they left us. . . . We would rather die than not go to them, and would kill every man that should oppose our passage."

Hunt was so convincing that the Sioux leaders believed this story. The head chief rose, explaining that his people were at war with the Aricaras, Mandans, and Minnetarees to the north and would suffer if the whites furnished their enemies with arms or ammunition. Since Hunt and his companions were only going to see their brothers, however, the Sioux would not attempt to stop them. He, too, had brothers far to the north, whom he had not seen for many moons and for whom he had also been crying. The whites could continue their journey with his blessing.

THE OVERLANDERS MOVED so ponderously up the Missouri that Manuel Lisa and a group of MFC traders managed to overtake them on June 2, even though Lisa had initially been three weeks behind them. Ostensibly, Lisa had raced upriver to join forces with Hunt so that their united party would be better able to confront the Sioux, but the St. Louis trader was still intent on disrupting the PFC by whatever means he could.

From the moment Lisa arrived, camping on the opposite side of the river, relations between the two camps were tense. Still bitter that Lisa had used the Sioux to thwart his trading efforts, McClellan had vowed to shoot his rival if they ever met up in Indian country. Now, they were thirteen hundred miles from the nearest civil authority.

The ill feelings erupted into violence on June 5 after Lisa had been needling Dorion extensively for having run out on his whiskey bills. That evening, in Hunt's camp after Lisa started in again, Dorion snapped, striking Lisa several times before seizing a pair of Hunt's pistols. After crying out, "O mon Dieu!" Lisa ran back to his boat. "I found Mr. Lisa furious with rage, buckling on his knife and preparing to return," Henry Brackenridge, the Englishman who was a member of Lisa's expedition, reported. "Finding that I could not dissuade, I resolved to accompany him."

When Lisa returned, Brackenridge at his side, Dorion was awaiting him, pistols in both hands. Hunt's entire party had gathered to witness the confrontation, including McClellan and Crooks, who were pressing to take on Lisa themselves. Hunt restrained them, but when Lisa insulted him, Hunt challenged the rival commander to a duel. "He told Lisa that the matter should be settled by themselves, and desired him to fetch his pistols," Bradbury said. He and Brackenridge followed Lisa to his boat and somehow managed to restrain him. "We with great difficulty prevented a meeting, which, in the present temper of the parties, would have certainly been a bloody one," Bradbury said.

With the Englishmen, one from each party, acting as mediators, the two expeditions reached an uneasy accord as they continued upriver, both bound for the Aricara village a week's travel to the north.

HUNT HAD INTENDED to follow the Lewis and Clark route up the Missouri and across the Bitterroots at Lemhi Pass, but a few days before the confrontation with Lisa, he had met John Hoback, Jacob Reznor, and Edward Robinson coming downriver. In 1809, these three grizzled trappers had accompanied Andrew Henry, another MFC founder, to the upper Yellowstone region and across the Wind

River to the Tetons and beyond. They recommended that Hunt follow a more direct and southerly route across the Rockies than that taken by Captains Lewis and Clark, one that would circumvent the dangerous Blackfoot Indians and afford an abundant source of game, a suggestion Hunt and the other partners agreed to almost immediately. "The gentlemen of the expedition at once abandoned their former ideas of passing by the Falls of the Missouri and made the necessary arrangement for commencing their journey over land from this place," Ramsay Crooks later told the Missouri *Gazette*.

Hoback and his companions were on their way back to their homes in Kentucky, but when Hunt asked them to join the expedition as hunters and guides, they agreed. With these three frontiersmen pointing the way, Hunt planned to abandon the Missouri for this new overland route. First, though, he needed horses. These he hoped to obtain at the Aricara villages on Ashley Island, where the Corps of Discovery had stopped seven years earlier.

Arriving on June 12 at the Aricara settlement—some 160 lodges fortified by a ditch and nine-foot-high pickets—Hunt wanted to obtain 150 horses, but as the Indians were hard-pressed to come up with so many mounts, the trading dragged on for weeks. In the meantime, the Aricaras, whose sexual morals were notoriously liberal, flocked to the traders' camp each night with their wives, sisters, and daughters, bartering the women's sexual favors for prized strings of blue beads, vermilion fur scrapers, and items of clothing and personal possessions. These Hunt dispensed like a parent supervising a children's birthday party.

IT WAS NOT until July 18 that the Hunt expedition—minus Bradbury, who had started back to St. Louis, and Lisa, who went on to the Mandan post—started out again. Instead of continuing on up the Missouri, the overlanders, guided now by Robinson and the other Kentuckians, set out by foot and horseback across the northwest corner of present-day South Dakota, cutting briefly across the southeastern corner of Montana and on across northern Wyoming. While this route skirted the dangerous reach of the Blackfoot and was well populated with herds of buffalo and other game, it presented a number of harrowing challenges. These Hunt only became aware of after making the decision to abandon the Lewis and Clark trace.

For starters, voyageurs may have been the argonauts of the wilderness waters, but afoot they were at best disgruntled plodders. Unlike Lewis and Clark's men, many of whom had military backgrounds, the overlanders had no experience with packhorses and, in many instances, had never seen real mountains before nor had ever scaled a dangerous switchback trail or descended a steep slope leading half-wild horses loaded with thousands of pounds of trade goods and supplies. To get to the Snake River, a tributary of the Columbia, using Hoback's directions, they would have to negotiate the Black Hills, the Powder River range, the Bighorns, the Winds, and the Tetons.

And that was the easiest leg of the passage to Astoria.

From the Aricaras, Hunt ended up with only eighty-two horses, most of which were needed as pack animals. As a result, the entire party—except for the partners and Marie Dorian and her children—had to walk across the hot, treeless Dakota plains, dense with knee-deep prairie grass. "The country was bare," Hunt reported. "Only a few cottonwoods grew along the rivers."

By the time the disorganized caravan reached Firesteel Creek in today's Corson County, South Dakota, a number of the travelers, including Ramsay Crooks, had become ill. Hunt called a halt to travel and went off to trade for more horses at a nearby Cheyenne camp. "I there bought thirty-six horses, at a much better price than at the Aricaras' village," he boasted.

On August 6, as the overlanders resumed travel following the Grand River, Hunt observed proudly that "we now had horses enough to permit every two men to ride alternately, and six were allotted to the hunters whose duty it was to pursue bison."

With the Cheyenne horses, the expedition was now averaging better than twenty miles a day—twice its earlier pace—but soon had to slow down so that the hunters, who lagged the main caravan, could catch up. For the first time, the overlanders encountered rugged terrain: a progression of steep hills. "The road was irksome because of the steepness and the great number of stones," Hunt complained. He thought he was crossing a range of mountains, but he had yet to see the Rockies. They would dwarf these little hills and cause Hunt to wonder why he had ever left St. Louis.

On August 13, the overlanders forded the Little Missouri into present-day Montana. Turning southwest, they rode across Wyoming's red hills, living on buffalo meat and an occasional bighorn sheep, which Hunt said much resembled mutton in taste. It was a hard march. "The great heat, the bad road and the lack of water caused much suffering," he wrote. "Several persons were on the verge of losing courage."

Hunt's own courage was shaky as well. One of his hunters, Edward Rose, was a powerful, moody man, the son of a white Indian trader and a mother who was half Cherokee, half black. Rose's nickname was Nes Coup, or "Cut Nose Rose," a moniker that had been bestowed upon him because of an ugly scar on the bridge of his nose. By one account, Rose was a celebrated outlaw who had escaped to the frontier in chains. Irving claimed he had been a Mississippi river pirate, though there doesn't seem to be any evidence for such an assertion. Hunt described him as "a very bad fellow full of daring," and was clearly intimidated by him, though Rose had given the expedition leader no cause for concern.

On August 30, after Hunt pitched camp at the base of the Bighorn Mountains, he learned that a large band of Absaroka, or Crow Indians, were summering nearby. Invited to their camp, the overlanders traded knives, powder, and tobacco for fresh horses. That night, Hunt and his lieutenants kept a close watch on Rose. They had heard, from whom Hunt doesn't say, that Rose planned to desert as soon as the overlanders reached Crow country and take many of Hunt's men with him. Hunt feared his expedition would be crippled.

On September 2, Hunt decided to get rid of Rose. Instead of simply firing him or worse—the old Indian fighter McClellan wanted simply to shoot the man—Hunt offered Rose half a year's pay, a horse, and three beaver traps if he would stay with the Crows. "He accepted these terms and immediately quit his confederates, who no longer having a leader, continued the journey," Hunt asserted.

Before his departure, the Crows had given Hunt directions to a pass across the crest of the Bighorns, but by September 3 the overlanders were lost and "desperately trying to get out of the precipices and arid mountains." At the behest of the Crow chief, who saw that Hunt had taken the wrong road, Rose had to ride up and direct his embarrassed former employer to the proper path.

Soon after, the expedition met up with several Flathead and Snake, or Shoshone, Indians, who led the whites through Powder River Pass, along an Indian trail already aflame with aspens and red fireweed, and down the western slopes of the range past Tensleep Creek. The march continued with the travelers looping northwest along the banks of the Bighorn and then Wind rivers, supping on gooseberries—the best Hunt had ever tasted, he enthused—strawberries, elk, and black-tailed deer along the way. By the second week in September, they were ascending into the narrowing upper Wind River valley, headed due west along the cottonwood-lined banks of the Wind, the leaves already a bright autumnal yellow. To the south, they were flanked by the Winds, to the north the Absarokas. "The mountains drew nearer to each other," Hunt reported. "Consequently, the country was very rugged, the trail very winding between the heights."

Hunt's intent was to cross the Winds in order to reach the Snake or Mad River, which he knew to be a tributary of the Columbia. To accomplish this, he had two choices. Due west at the head of the valley was Togwotee Pass. Had the overlanders taken this, they would have come down into present-day Jackson Hole at the base of the Teton Pass. That, in turn, would have led them to the now abandoned fort of Andrew Henry at its juncture with what is now known as Henry's Fork of the Snake.

Instead, on September 15, the expedition followed an Indian trail, now Union Pass, southwest over the Winds into the Green River basin. During the crossing, "one of the hunters who had been on the shores of the Columbia, showed us three immensely high and snow covered peaks [the Tetons] which, he said, were situated on the banks of a tributary of that river."

Running low on provisions, the overlanders found ample game in the Green River basin, as Hunt had hoped, but it was another two weeks before they finally reached the Columbia tributary, the Snake, at its juncture with the river Hunt named after one of his guides,

John Hoback. Here, Hunt made two discoveries, one more devastating than the other: There were no trees in the area that were suitable for producing the canoes needed to travel the river. Moreover, the river, which cascades south in a series of rapids before rushing through the Tetons at present Alpine Canyon, was far too dangerous to canoe. It now dawned on Hunt that the expedition was in trouble. "We should have continued at that time to cross one of the mountains [over Togwotee Pass] because we would have reached the headwaters of this river," he noted in his diary.

HUNT HAD FAILED to grasp that there was both a north and south fork of the Snake. The north fork, also known as Henry's Fork, was west of the Tetons, the south—the waterway Hunter encountered at its confluence with the Hoback—east of the mountains. Disoriented and increasingly demoralized—Hunt's voyageurs had been counting heavily on continuing by canoes—the party, guided now by two friendly Snake Indians they'd met en route, headed north to Jackson Hole, crossed the Teton Pass, and on a cold, snowy October 8, finally reached Henry's Fort, which consisted of several abandoned little cabins. Hunt could have reached this destination almost three weeks earlier had he continued by way of Togwotee instead of Union Pass.

Here, though, Hunt was encouraged to note that this river, which he failed to recognize as another branch of the feared Snake, was seemingly navigable. There were also plenty of logs for canoes. In an optimistic moment, he named this the Canoe River and ordered his men to hollow out logs for fifteen dugouts. So confident was Hunt that the Canoe River would provide a rapid and relatively smooth passage to Astoria that he decided to leave the horses behind with his Indian guides. "On the 17th, all being ready for embarking, we cached our saddles in a spot which we showed to the two young Snakes who promised to care for them, and also for our seventy-seven horses, until one of us should return," he wrote.

Mackenzie and McClellan, both of whom had dealt extensively with Indians, may have well believed Hunt was being naive entrusting this large herd of prized mounts to the Snakes. If so, they let the matter slide. With winter closing in, there was little time left for bickering.

ON OCTOBER 19, the party pushed off in their just-completed canoes in an early snowstorm and, as Hunt had hoped, initially made good time. "The force of the current made us travel rapidly," he reported. But the next day, the Columbia-bound traders began to realize that this river, now nearly half a mile wide by Hunt's estimates, was more than they could handle. "On the 20th, we traveled forty miles, but during the last twenty of them, the bed of the river was intersected by rapids," Hunt wrote. "In passing there, two canoes were filled with water. It was necessary to stop forthwith. I set my canoe and one other to their assistance. The men were rescued. Many goods and provisions were lost."

The Snake was proving treacherous, unforgiving, and ultimately deadly as Hunt's party over the next week canoed past more rapids, waterfalls, whirlpools, and fearsome boulders, one so large it dammed the river from one bank to the other. On October 28, near a dangerous whirlpool the overlanders named Cauldron Linn after a similar gorge in Scotland, a boulder dashed Ramsay Crooks's canoe. Crooks saved himself "only by an extreme exertion in swimming," he later explained. The Canadian Antoine Clappine, one of the most valued of the voyageurs, drowned.

After the accident, Hunt led a small scouting party thirty-five miles downstream to determine if the northerly side of the broad Snake was passable by canoe. It wasn't. Another group of sixteen men tried to bring four canoes through the rapids on the south side of river. They lost one and got the remaining three stuck in the rocks. "Our situation had become critical," Hunt wrote. "We had food for not more than five days."

It was at this juncture that the remaining bonds holding the expedition together began to unravel at an alarming rate. Hunt sent the Irishman Reed and two other men downriver to try to find Indians from whom they might acquire food and horses. With four men, Mackenzie headed north. McClellan went off on his own as well, while Crooks and several others started the 200 miles back to retrieve the horses the overlanders now realized should never have been abandoned. Crooks returned to camp on November 4. In the midst of his ponderously slow two-hundred-mile march back to Fort Henry, Crooks realized that the journey was going to take far longer than anticipated and turned back before reaching the horses. If he had continued on, he wouldn't be able to get back to Hunt that winter, even if the horses were still where the overlanders had left them.

At the base camp, Hunt lingered still, his hunters catching a few beaver and netting a single fish from the river and awaiting Reed's return. On November 6, Reed's two companions arrived to report they'd had no luck. Most of the Indians in this region were root eaters—Digger Shoshone and Bannocks—who had nothing to contribute to the overlanders' fast-dwindling food supplies.

Two days later, Hunt cached the party's trade goods and distributed the remaining provisions—roughly 125 pounds of meat, 40 pounds of corn, 20 pounds of fat and some bouillon tabs—and set off by foot with what remained of his party, having wasted the last nine days in what he conceded was a "fruitless effort."

EVEN BEFORE CLAPPINE'S drowning, the expedition had begun to splinter off into separate groups. At Henry's Fort, one of the partners, Joseph Miller, quit the party, insisting he wanted out despite Hunt's efforts to dissuade him from leaving. Hunt's Kentuckians, Hoback and the others, went off as well, saying they wanted to stay behind and trap beaver. Miller ended up joining them.

Then, after the incident at Cauldron Linn, Mackenzie, his fellow frontiersman McClellan, and Reed, each with three to four men, had gone off on separate reconnoitering missions. If Hunt was counting on them returning to the base camp Hunt had set up near Cauldron Linn, he was sadly mistaken. Instead, they struck out for Astoria, ascending the Snake through what would later be aptly called Hells Canyon, one of the deepest and least accessible major river valleys in North America, the Grand Canyon of the Snake.

As Mackenzie and McClellan later described it to Stuart, the 150-mile-long canyon was "confined between precipices of astonishing height . . . Cascades and rapids succeeded each other almost without intermissions . . . Mountain here appears as if piled on mountain, and after ascending incessantly for half a day, you seem as if no nearer the attainment of the object in view at the outset." The party stayed as close to the riverbank as possible but frequently found the way blocked by massive piles of rock and had to backtrack, scaling icy gray cliffs. Of their ordeal, Stuart wrote: "They were in all twelve persons, took 21 days [of] constant traveling and subsisted during the time on an allowance [of] . . . not more than two Ibex [mountain goats] and 5 beaver, the skins of which they preserved and subsisted on for the last five days."

Hunt and Crooks followed the river as well. It now flowed north. Hunt was on the east side, Crooks on the west, each accompanied by eighteen men. Hunt's group was the more fortunate. He encountered Indians with an abundance of salmon and some horses they were willing to trade. Crooks met only a few Digger Indians generally too miserably poor to afford his party assistance.

While Hunt was trading with the natives, Crooks forged ahead, entering Hells Canyon on November 23. Several days into the journey, he spotted Mackenzie, who'd joined now with Reed and their small party moving north on the opposite side of the river, their little caravan a ghostly mirage in the early winter mists. Over the roar of the rapids they shouted to him that McClellan had crossed the mountains in hopes of falling in with friendly Flatheads.

For Crooks and his relatively large party, the going was torturously slow and dangerous. Crooks later described climbing over rocky ridges projecting into the stream that ran with incredible velocity, scaling nearly impassable precipices of immense heights, and enduring "a series of hardships and privations which the most hardy and determined of the human race must have found themselves inadequate." On the evening of December 3 he and his men gave up hope of continuing on up this canyon and turned back. In the past nine days, they'd subsisted on a single beaver, a dog, some cherries, and old moccasin soles.

Regaining the riverbank as they retraced their steps up out of the canyon, Crooks and his men spotted Hunt and his followers proceeding toward them on the opposite side of the river. Hunt immediately ordered a canoe to be made from the hide of a horse killed and eaten the previous night, and sent food over. "What was my aston-ishment and distress!" he noted in his diary. "I beheld Mr. Crooks and his party on the other side of the river."

Crooks and Francis LeClair took the canoe back across the Snake. "Poor man!" Hunt exclaimed on seeing Crooks's emaciated features. "He was well nigh spent from fatigue and want." When Crooks had regained some measure of strength and lucidity, he debriefed Hunt regarding the deplorable conditions ahead and his encounter with Mackenzie. Hunt now had to decide whether to continue on or turn back. "I spent the night in considering my situation," he reported. "I had to provide for the needs of more than twenty starving people and in addition give my utmost aid to Mr. Crooks and his party. Notwith-standing all the discouraging reports to me concerning the region below here, I would have continued my journey . . . [but] the depth of snow would make the undertaking impractical."

At first light, Hunt informed Crooks and the others they would be turning back, in hopes of encountering Indians encamped on three small rivers (the Payette, Weiser, and Boise) they'd crossed several days earlier. "I counted on buying from them a sufficient quantity of horses to feed up until we should reach the Big River," Hunt explained.

In opting to return, Hunt could not have foreseen the nightmar-ish events that would ensue. As the horsehide canoe had been lost in the violent current, Crooks and Francis LeClair had been unable to rejoin the men on the other side of river. The enfeebled Crooks had great difficulty keeping up with Hunt and his men. On December 7, Hunt slowed his pace for Crooks's benefit. "Whereupon, my men grumbled, saying we would all die of hunger; and importuned me in every way to go on," Hunt wrote. Desperate now, most of Hunt's men went on ahead.

On December 8, Crooks had a raft made but was still unable to rejoin his party on the other side of the river because of the danger-ous current. That night, Crooks grew quite ill and was unable to travel at all. Leaving three men with him, Hunt pressed on in hopes of rejoining his men, in particular Dorion, who possessed the group's remaining horse. This bag of bones Hunt fully intended to kill and eat, but Dorion was deeply attached to the animal and wouldn't let Hunt anywhere near it. Fortunately, Hunt came upon a Shoshone village and walked off with five of their horses after the Indians fled in fear. After one the animals was slaughtered, Hunt sent a man—probably Dorion, because he traveled by horseback—with a portion of meat for Crooks. Even after devouring the horseflesh, Crooks and his companions were so famished they barely restrained themselves from killing Dorion's mount.

Early on the morning of December 11, Crooks, who'd regained some of his strength, caught up with Hunt's party with the assistance of Dorion. From Dorion, he knew about Hunt's success in obtaining horses, and in Irving's words, "was shocked to find that, while the people on [Hunt's] side of the river, were amply supplied with provisions, none had been sent to his own forlorn and famishing men on the opposite bank."

Worse, despite Crooks's entreaties, and those of his men on the far bank, none of Hunt's followers was willing to ferry the meat across. According to Irving, Hunt's followers were simply too fearful to help their starving companions. "Vague, almost superstitious terrors had infected the minds of Hunt's men"—terror apparently inspired by the "desperate, forlorn cries of the haggard souls lining the opposite bank of the river." More likely, having been near starvation themselves, they simply were unwilling to share their limited provisions with the others.

What part exactly did Hunt play in this macabre scene? We know he was present. Irving reports—information he almost surely got from Crooks many years later—that Crooks's men called out Hunt's name, pleading with him for at least some of the meat. Did he simply ignore them as well as Crooks's entreaties to send meat across?

Frantic now, Crooks had another canoe built but was too weak to risk the narrow but still turbulent Snake himself. Eventually, the Virginian Benjamin Jones crossed over from the Hunt camp with some uncooked meat. Delirious, one of Crook's voyageurs, who had been tortured by the smell of meat stewing in the Hunt camp and who'd been pleading with Hunt to send a canoe for him, jumped into Jones's canoe as soon as it landed and started back across. "Starvation had bereft J. B. Provost of his senses entirely, and on seeing the horseflesh on the opposite side of the river, he was so agitated in crossing in a skin canoe, that he upset it," Crooks told the *Gazette*. Provost drowned. The Snake had claimed another victim. Hunt briefly describes the same incident, saying only "one of Mr. Crooks's men was drowned while crossing the canoe which capsized with many goods."

IN HIS DIARIES, Hunt—perhaps concerned how history, or more immediately, Mr. Astor, would judge him—is careful to spell out the rationale for his actions, but on December 12 he reached a decision for which he offered no explanation. That evening, he brought the skeletal John Day, a Kentuckian, over to be with his old friend and former employer Crooks. Day was in even worse shape than Crooks, so weak he couldn't even sit up without assistance. With Crooks and Day was the engage J. B. Dubreuil, who was also too frail to continue.

Crooks himself was unable to travel. Nor had he any intention of abandoning Day, his old trading companion from the Missouri. But Hunt, perhaps with Crooks's assurances that he, Day, and Dubreuil would be all right—after all, there were some friendly Indians encamped nearby who hopefully would share some of their food with the stragglers—had made up his mind to press on. He left Crooks with what food he could. "I had another horse killed," he says in his diary. "I left two of them for Mr. Crooks with part of the flesh of another, hoping that with this help he would be able to proceed to the encampment of the Indians above us."

The following morning Hunt departed with what remained of his party—thirty-two men, two children, and an eight-month-pregnant Marie Dorion—leaving his partner Crooks, Day, and Dubreuil to the mercies of the winter wilderness.

CHAPTER 16

DANGEROUS PASSAGE, REUNION, AND RESCUE

AT THE DALLES, SEVERAL HUNDRED MILES UPRIVER from Astoria, the Columbia, in its rush to the sea, cascaded over Celilo Falls with a thunderous roar, then entered a narrow, prolonged channel between two high basalt walls. Robert Stuart arrived here in early April 1812 when the snows had to begun to melt and the rapids descended in what naturalist John Muir later described as "huge, roaring torrents."

On this trip, Stuart's mission was to search for the lost overlanders and transport two canoes filled with supplies to his uncle, whose inland post was situated at the confluence of the Columbia and Okanogan rivers some six hundred miles northeast of Astoria. With Stuart were two other parties, one bound cross-country for New York, the other destined for Cauldron Linn on the Snake, where Hunt's overland party had cached some of its supplies the previous autumn.

Described by one of his companions as "a rough, warm-hearted, brave old Irishman," John Reed had been chosen to bring important dispatches back to Astor. These he carried in a bright tin box strapped to his back. Traveling with him were two Canadians as well as the hunter Benjamin Jones and Robert McClellan. Apparently dissatisfied at the small number of shares he'd been given, the volatile McClellan had resigned from the company soon after his arrival at Astoria.

The third small group, under the clerk Russell Farnham, had been sent to retrieve the goods Hunt had left behind. Stuart was in command of the entire group, some sixteen men, until the three parties went their separate ways at the Walla Walla River in what is now eastern Oregon.

The Dalles was the most formidable obstacle along their route, one requiring a long and rigorous portage. The Wishram Indians, an upper Chinookan people, had a permanent village here and jealously controlled the commerce that flowed through their domain, extracting a toll from all who passed by. With daggers drawn they had insisted, the previous summer, that David Stuart let them help carry his goods and canoes and then demanded excessive payment. "He had to distribute leaf tobacco to ten times the value of their services," wrote David Thompson, who somehow was allowed to pass without offering up tribute. "It appeared . . . they were determined to pick a quarrel for the sake of plunder."

"To say there is not a worse path under the sun would perhaps be going a step too far, but to say that, for difficulty and danger, few could equal it, would be saying the truth," Alexander Ross noted.

The Wishrams were waiting for Robert Stuart and his men when they arrived at The Dalles. Being short-handed, Stuart had no choice but to engage them to help portage the party's goods and heavy canoes along the south bank of the rapids. Stuart sent Reed ahead with five men and a number of Indians carrying bales of supplies and the canoes. As Reed's party proceeded along a steep, rocky ledge, several of the mounted natives turned their horses up a narrow path and made off with two bales of goods. At the same time, other Indians who had accompanied the party on foot began pillaging knives, blankets, and even pocket handkerchiefs from the Astorians while their tribesmen hurled large rocks down on the "long beards" from above, damaging one of the canoes.

It was several hours before a shaken Reed was able to rejoin Stuart. "Being dusk before we succeeded in getting all together, it was impossible at such a late hour to better our forlorn situation before morning, so we passed the entire night under arms without one of us closing an eye," Stuart reported after the attack.

The next day, emboldened by their earlier success and armed

with bows and arrows and war clubs, upwards of four hundred natives, by Stuart's estimate, escorted the Astorians to Celilo Falls, where they insisted on making the portage on behalf of the whites. Stuart reluctantly engaged them to carry the canoes but insisted that it was too late in the day to transport the remaining cargo. If the Indians "behaved well," he would accept their offer in the morning, he told them. Satisfied, the Wishrams returned to their village on the opposite side of the river, leaving some thirty men to keep watch on the Astorians' camp.

Having lost two bales of supplies already, Stuart had no intention of entrusting the Indians with what remained. Stuart and his men waited until 1 A.M., when the Indians were asleep, and by moonlight began carrying their goods to the head of the falls. "Two loads were only remaining at daybreak," Stuart noted, "when those spies who had remained to watch our motions perceived what had been going on and, thinking themselves too weak for an attack, gave the alarm to those on the opposite side."

When the alarm went up, only Reed and McClellan remained at the base of the falls. They looked on in alarm as a dozen or so canoes, filled with angry Wishram warriors, started for their side of the river. "No sooner did the canoes touch the shore than their cargoes leaped on the rocks and without the least hesitation made directly for the goods, beginning an indiscriminate pillage," Stuart said.

Vastly outnumbered, McClellan prudently backed away from the targeted supplies, calling for Reed to follow. But one of the Wishram was already grappling with Reed for his gun. Another warrior threw a buffalo robe over McClellan's head, but McClellan managed to disengage himself. "[He] had just enough time to draw up his piece when the villain made a lunge at him with his knife and received the content of his rifle in the breast, which laid him lifeless on the spot," Stuart reported.

McClellan rushed over to assist Reed, who was still struggling with his assailant. As he was trying to reload his pistol, fumbling with the cap, one of the Wishram swung at him with an axe handle. The athletic McClellan eluded the blow by jumping over a canoe. Reed, who'd been standing directly behind him, caught the blow full force on the side of his head and went sprawling, at which point

McClellan shot Reed's attacker with a small pocket pistol he'd had in reserve. Still clutching the axe handle, the Indian fell to the ground beside Reed, who was unconscious.

Normally, Stuart later noted, Indians who were unaccustomed to firearms fled after an initial round had been fired. Not the Wishram. They pressed forward, several of them striking the supine Reed with tomahawks. His gun empty, McClellan shouted like a madman and charged the attackers, momentarily driving the Indians back.

Stuart had heard the gunfire and rushed to the base of the falls with eight men. According to Franchere's account, McClellan thought Reed had been killed and urged Stuart and the others to flee. "Mr. Stuart, however, was unwilling to go until he was convinced that Mr. Reed was dead and, in spite of Mr. McClellan's protests, went back towards the spot where the latter had left him," Franchere said. "He had scarcely gone 200 paces when he met Mr. Reed coming towards him holding his head with both hands." Several Wishrams were still striking him as he stumbled forth.

Stuart said nothing of McClellan's urging him to run, stating only: "We found Mr. Reed weltering in his blood, having received five tomahawk wounds on the head. Notwithstanding our sudden appearance with present arms, not one of [the Indians] seemed in the least alarmed; nor did they make any disposition to attack us until I called to the fellow who was mauling Mr. Reed to desist or he should be shot instantly; this seemed to rouse them all and some began to advance on us in a very menacing manner."

Stuart had his men fall into a column two deep and ordered the twosome at the head of the formation to fire at a brave who continued to assault Reed. "This was executed in a twinkling, when we gave a cheer and charged, which so disconcerted our assailants as to produce an instant and universal flight," Stuart reported.

Reed was still alive but unconscious. The Astorians carried him to the canoes, which proved too leaky to put in the water. Moreover, the oars had been left at the lower end of the portage, so Stuart and his men could go nowhere. This discovery so alarmed two of the young Canadians that both fainted. The moment they recovered, Stuart reverted to an unorthodox courage-building technique he'd learned from the Indians. He ordered the others in his party to strip the Canadians and dress them like squaws with pieces of cloth tied around their waists. They were then stowed away among the goods in one of the canoes. "This ludicrous affair, in spite of the perilous situation we were placed in, excited considerable mirth, and seemed to reassure a few who were wavering between fear and determination," Stuart later reflected.

Once the canoes were caulked and the oars retrieved, the Astorians continued upriver, only to discover several days later that a mounted and well-armed war party of more than one hundred men had followed them from The Dalles. When one of Stuart's men, acting as a scout, discovered that the Indians were waiting in ambush on the southern bank of the Columbia just above its confluence with the Deschutes River, Stuart ordered all the canoes tied together and retreated to a little island nearby. There, the Astorians made a fire and treated Reed's wounds.

Soon the war chief and three of his tribesmen approached in a canoe. After a long preamble, the Indian leader explained apologetically that relatives of the deceased had compelled him to take command of the war party against his will and demand satisfaction of the long beards. They thought Reed dead and wanted his body, which they intended to cut in pieces. If he was still alive, all the better.

By Stuart's account, the Astorians responded emphatically: "Our answer was *NO*, the man you had wounded is our brother and you must destroy all of us before you get him. We are prepared and ready for your warriors. Bring them on and we will teach you a more serious lesson than you learned this morning."

Confronted with this resolve and the sobering realization that the mysterious weapons the whites carried were far deadlier than their own bows and arrows, the Indians lost heart. After consulting with his tribesmen, the chief promised that the entire war party would return peaceably to their village if the long beards gave them three blankets to cover their dead and some tobacco.

Stuart agreed without hesitation, and once the transaction was completed, the Astorians saw no more of the war party. Yet with Reed wounded, the dispatches lost—thinking it contained valuables, the Indians had made off with the tin box—and the men badly shaken by the attack, it made no sense to continue on to Cauldron

Linn or attempt to reach St. Louis. Stuart decided to lead the entire party north to his uncle's establishment on the Okanogan.

In this his first battle with natives, Stuart had handled himself superbly. Stuart's behavior, Franchere reported, was that of a "self-possessed and fearless man."

THE OKANOGAN VALLEY, with its gentle, heavily timbered hills and shimmering lakes, was David Stuart's little kingdom. Here, far from the intrigues of Astoria and the melancholy coastal rains, the elder Stuart held sway, a benign monarch who reaped the rewards of a region no other Europeans, not even the far ranging Nor'Westers, yet had laid eyes on.

David Stuart and his eight companions had arrived at the Okanogan the previous September and quickly won over the local Indians, thanks to the appearance of a comet in the western sky, which the natives read as a favorable omen, and Stuart's own diplomacy. "He saw everything and his mild and insinuating manners won their [the Indians'] affection," the elder Stuart's companion on the Okanogan expedition, Alexander Ross, later wrote of him. "He was a good old soul."

At the Okanogan, Stuart and his men built a crude dwelling out of driftwood, christening it Fort Okanogan. Fearing he hadn't adequate supplies to last out the winter, Stuart sent several of his men back to Astoria, left Ross to man Fort Okanogan, and with two French Canadians, Ovide de Montigny and Michel Boullard, and another unidentified engage, set out to explore the Kamloops region in what is now British Columbia.

He started north on September 16 after telling Ross he'd be gone no more than a month, an estimate that did not take into account the severity of the north country winters. Later, he recounted his journey to Ross and his nephew.

After leaving this place [Fort Okanogan], we bent our course up the Okanogan, due north, for upwards of 250 miles, till we reached its source. We then crossed a height of land and fell upon Thompson's river, or rather the south branch of Frazer's river, after traveling for some time amongst a powerful nation called the She Waps [the Shuswap Indians]. The snow fell while we were in the mountains and precluded our immediate return; and after waiting for fine weather, the snow got so deep that we considered it hopeless to attempt getting back, and therefore passed our time with the She Waps and other tribes in that quarter. The Indians were numerous and well-disposed and the country throughout abounds in beaver and all other kinds of furs; and I have made arrangements to establish a trading post there the ensuing winter. On the twenty sixth day of February we began our homeward journey and spent just twenty-five days on our way back.

The long winter in the north had taken its toll, however. When Robert Stuart, fresh from his encounter at The Dalles, arrived at Fort Okanogan on April 19, he found his uncle in frail health but ebullient as ever. The winters trade, the elder Stuart announced proudly, had yielded twenty-five hundred prime beaver pelts, a bounty that no doubt would gladden the heart of Mr. Astor in New York. For five days, Robert Stuart remained at Fort Okanogan, resting and enjoying the reunion with his uncle. The old man was not eager to return to Astoria, but Stuart, concerned about his uncle's well-being, insisted. Once his health had improved, the elder Stuart could return to the Okanogan with the reinforcements he needed to open a second post to the north, his nephew assured him.

WITH THEIR CANOES laden with bales of furs, the Stuarts started back on April 24, leaving only Ross and two engages behind to continue trading. Several days later, near the Umatilla River, not far from their earlier encounter with the Wishrams, Stuart's party heard someone cry out in English, "Come on shore." Fearing that the summons might be a ruse by natives to lure them into a trap, Robert Stuart ordered the canoes closed together, but again the call sounded. To the Astorians' amazement, two nearly naked men, both severely emaciated and burned brown by the sun, gestured frantically to them from the riverbank.

At first, Stuart and the others thought the two were Indians, but as the Astorians approached, McClellan and Reed recognized them as two of the missing overlanders, the Virginian John Day and Ramsay Crooks. After Stuart found them some warm clothes and they had a chance to eat—their first food since some friendly Indians gave them dried horsemeat several days before—Crooks took the lead in relating their ordeal.

They had last seen Hunt and his men on the north bank of the Snake River on December 12. At the time, Day was too ill to travel, and Hunt had gone on, leaving Crooks to stay with Day and the engage Jean Baptiste Dubreuil. They had two live horses and the partial carcass of another as their only food.

It was another three weeks before Day was well enough to travel. In the meantime, they lived on the horsemeat and on food provided by a small band of Indians who had joined their camp. When the natives departed, apparently taking the overlanders' two horses with them, the three men nearly starved to death. Crooks and Dubreuil dug up roots, intending to cook them, but when they returned to camp, their fire had extinguished. Neither man had the energy to relight it. Delirious, Day was too weak to sit up.

As the overlanders lay in a torpor, passing in and out of consciousness, two Indians appeared, built a fire, and gave Crooks and the others food and water. For two days, they nursed the whites back to health. Crooks was not religious, but he had come to believe in miracles. Not only had the Indians saved the whites, but they'd informed them that the roots they'd collected were poisonous. Had he and Dubreuil managed to restart the fire, all three probably would have died.

After their saviors departed, a rejuvenated Day shot a wolf that been prowling near camp, providing an immediate meal. The bones were pounded, mixed with nontoxic roots and made into a nourishing broth. The wayfarers dried the remaining flesh for future use.

In mid-January, they were joined by three earlier castoffs from Hunt's expedition, Jean Baptiste Turcotte, Andre LeChapelier, and Francois Landry. Together, the six stragglers set out in the snow to try to follow Hunt's trail. When a blizzard erased any trace of the now month-old trail, the three engages went off on their own, leaving Crooks, Day, and Dubreuil to wander in the mountains, subsisting mainly on the beaver they killed and roots they were able to extract from the frozen earth.

Sometime near the end of March—the overlanders had lost track of time—Dubreuil became ill. Crooks and Day left him behind with friendly Indians and several days later reached the Columbia.

After resting in the camp of hospitable natives, they proceeded west along the river's south bank by foot. En route they had the bad luck to fall in with a band of natives just above Celilo Falls who robbed them of everything, including all their clothing, and drove them out of camp. After four days with nothing to eat, they wandered into another native village where they were given shelter for the night, skins for raiment and enough dried horseflesh to last several days. It was the second time that winter their lives had been saved by Indians.

They'd just set out again for Astoria when they'd seen Stuart's canoes come around a bend in the river. It had been thirteen and a half months, Crooks calculated, since he and Day had begun their journey to the Columbia. Now, Crooks wanted nothing more than to return east as soon as possible and escape this dreadful wilderness that had almost killed him. Like the two partners Hunt had recruited, McClellan and Miller, Crooks planned to resign from the PFC at the first possible opportunity

With two new passengers crowded into the canoes, neither strong enough to lift an oar, Stuart started for Astoria early the next morning. On Monday, May 11, as they rounded Tongue Point and their destination came into view, the returning Astorians saw a sailing ship anchored in Baker Bay. Even from a distance, Stuart could tell it was not the *Tonquin*.

CHAPTER 17

BEARERS OF BAD NEWS

LIKE THE *TONQUIN*, THE SHIP ANCHORED IN BAKER BAY was owned by Astor. The 480-ton *Beaver* had sailed from New York in October 1811, arriving at Astoria only a few days before the return of the Stuarts.

To the Astorians, the appearance of the *Beaver* was a godsend. The ship's hold was filled with much-needed supplies and trading goods, and it was carrying reinforcements, including a new partner, John Clarke, as well as six clerks, fifteen American mechanics, half a dozen French Canadian voyageurs, and several more islanders who had been recruited during a stopover in Hawaii.

Equally important, the *Beaver* brought news of the outside world, the first the Astorians had received in more than a year. Unfortunately, most of it was bad. The *Beaver*'s amiable captain, Cornelius Sowle, told the traders that in Hawaii he'd found a letter waiting for him from another of Astor's pilots, John Ebbets of the *Enterprise*. Sailing the Northwest coast the previous summer, Ebbets had learned of the terrible fate that had befallen the *Tonquin*.

According to Ebbets's account, which agreed with much of what the Indians had already reported regarding the incident, the ship had sailed north after leaving Astoria, anchoring in Clayoquot Sound, on the west coast of Vancouver Island, in mid-June. This was the same area where in 1792 Captain Robert Gray had his crew burn a native village in punishment for the Indians' attempt to capture his ship, the *Columbia*, and massacre his men.

On arrival, McKay went ashore to the village of Newiti to confer with the local chiefs. In the meantime, a group of Indians came aboard to trade, and Thorn, who held the natives in "sovereign contempt," decided to deal with them himself rather than wait for the return of the ship's supercargo. Unaccustomed to the spirited exchange of coastal bartering, Thorn had quickly gotten into a heated dispute with an old chief about the price of a certain article. In a display of temper that was all too familiar to those who had sailed with him from New York, the choleric captain physically ejected the old man from the ship, adding insult to injury by rubbing the chief's face in one of the sea-otter pelts the Indian had brought aboard to trade. Enraged, the old man and his followers railed at the captain, vowing to have their revenge.

Several days later, a large dugout canoe approached the *Tonquin*. It was early morning. Thorn and McKay, back from Newiti, were apparently still below in their cabins. Pulling alongside the American ship, the nearly two dozen Indians in the dugout were quick to assure the sailors on watch of their intentions. They seemed friendly and appeared unarmed. Each held up packets of sea-otter pelts and other furs to indicate they had come to trade.

Confronted with an abundance of pelts that would bring a small fortune in the fur markets of Canton, the officer of the watch ignored Thorn's standing order to allow no more than a few Indians on the ship at a time and gave the natives permission to board. Almost immediately additional dugouts arrived, their occupants following the first group's lead in boarding the *Tonquin*. By the time Thorn and McKay arrived on deck, the ship was swarming with natives who, rather than haggling as was their custom, traded briskly at the prices Thorn had set earlier. Each pelt brought its owner a blanket and a knife.

Suddenly the Indians blocked the passages, pressing around the captain, McKay, and James Lewis, the ship's clerk, with their furs, crying "Trade! Trade!" Thorn was sufficiently alarmed to order the anchor raised and the sails unfurled, but his command came too late. At a predetermined signal, the Indians rushed upon the crew with the knives they had just secured in trade as well as bludgeons and additional daggers that had been concealed amidst the furs.

McKay was struck on the head with a potamagene, a crude saber, and knocked to the deck. His attackers hurled him into the water, where the women waiting in the canoes finished him off, clubbing McKay to death with canoe paddles as he floundered in the water.

Lewis had been leaning over a bale of blankets trading with the visitors when he was struck by a dagger in the neck.

Thorn, the principal target of the onslaught, had come on deck armed only with a jackknife, which he used to keep his attackers briefly at bay. Stabbed repeatedly, he collapsed on the tiller, where, like McKay, he was clubbed to death. Meanwhile, several of the sailors who'd gone aloft to unfurl the sails managed to slide down the rigging into the hatchway. From the cabin where the ship's armaments were stored, they'd fired out at close range with pistols and muskets, driving the Indians from the ship. The following day they'd tried to escape aboard one of the *Tonquin*'s longboats, only to be captured and later tortured to death.

As soon as the sailors rowed off, the Indians on shore set out to plunder the *Tonquin*, believing the ship deserted. While as many as four hundred natives swarmed over the decks, someone below, perhaps Stephen Weeks, the armorer, or a wounded sailor who had been left behind by his colleagues, ignited the large store of gunpowder aboard. In what must have been an enormous explosion, the *Tonquin* was blown to pieces as were those on deck, the blast sending a ghastly shower of bodies, limbs, and heads in all directions.

Only George Ramsay, a half-breed interpreter the *Tonquin* had taken on before it left Baker Bay, survived to tell the tale.

THE NEWCOMER JOHN CLARKE, a Montrealer who was distantly related to Astor, brought some additional bad news from the PFC's home office in New York. Just before the *Beaver* had sailed from New York, Astor, Clarke reported, had learned that having been beaten to the Columbia, the Nor'Westers were determined to throttle the Astorians' trade efforts. Toward this end, they'd dispatched several new overland expeditions and a ship, the *Prince*, to the Columbia.

No doubt David Thompson had known of this all along.

The Astorians, naturally, bristled at Clarke's report that the Nor'Westers intended to challenge them. David Stuart's success in the Okanogan valley underscored the richness of the fur harvest that was there for the taking. Throughout the Pacific Northwest, Stuart and other Astorians had pinpointed at least a dozen other sites that looked equally promising. Now, with the arrival of Hunt's overlanders and the *Beaver*, the Astorians had the men and resources they needed to seize the initiative and stay the Nor'Westers' long reach. But they needed to act promptly and decisively.

For the next few weeks, the partners, in a series of meetings, carefully charted their strategy for expansion. At one of these gatherings, it was unanimously resolved that Hunt should sail aboard the *Beaver* to make a detailed study of the coastal trade and visit the Russian settlement of Sitka in what is now Alaska. Astor had earlier initiated an alliance with the Russians in hopes of undercutting the NWC's influence in the Northwest. Hunt's visit would reinforce this partnership and provide the Astorians with a firsthand assessment of its commercial potential.

In Hunt's absence, Duncan McDougall would continue in command at Astoria. This directly contradicted Astor's mandate that Hunt take charge of the post upon his arrival, but Astor was three thousand miles away. After a rocky start, McDougall had proven himself a competent leader. The other partners, all of whom—including the newcomer John Clarke—were Scots, wanted their man running the day-to-day operations. Hunt apparently accepted their judgment without complaint.

To check the Nor'Westers' ambitions in the territories west of the Great Divide, the partners also voted to establish a series of new trading posts. Clarke was charged with building a depot on the Spokane River in direct competition with the already existing NWC post, Fort Spokane, and opening up trade in the Coeur d'Alene region. The clerks Russell Farnham and the newcomer Ross Cox were directed to open up trade in Flathead country in western Montana. Donald Mackenzie opted to reconnoiter the Snake River region with an eye toward later establishing a post there among the Nez Perce, who had helped him survive the previous winter. And at the recommendation of Robert Stuart, the partners decided to open a post on the Willamette under William Wallace, another of the company clerks.

As important as it was for Astor's traders to stake out as much of the Northwest as they could, the partners recognized that one of their number had to lead an overland expedition—what the Nor'Westers referred to as an "Express"—back to New York by way of St. Louis. Its leader was to apprise Astor of the loss of the *Tonquin* and update him as to the status of his Columbia River venture. The PFC's president had received no word from the Astorians since their arrival the previous spring. Reed's expedition had been the first attempt to send dispatches back, and that had ended in near disaster. It was critical, the partners believed, that this next Express must get through so that Astor would send the additional men and provisions needed to compete with the oncoming Nor'Westers.

Initially, the partners nominated David Stuart to lead the expedition, but Robert Stuart objected to his uncle's going due to the older man's still feeble health and the great fatigue and danger he would encounter. "I offered myself to go in his place," he later recalled. "This was finally agreed to." Presumably, he was also eager to reunite with Betsy Sullivan, though he mentions nothing of this in his journals.

His mission was spelled out in a resolution drawn up by the partners at a meeting on June 27:

> Resolved, that it, being necessary to send an Express to New York, and all papers, and other things being prepared, Mr. Robert Stuart is hereby instructed to have and take charge of them, with which he is to go directly to New York as circumstances will admit—and there to be governed by the directions of Mr. Astor as to the time of his returning to the Northwest Coast. It is also resolved that John Day, Benjamin Jones, Francois Le Clerc [Francis LeClair], [and] Andre Valle accompany Mr. Stuart as far as St. Louis where he is to pay them the balances due each by means of drafts drawn by our W. P. Hunt on John Jacob Astor on account of the Pacific Fur Company.

"The mission was one of peril and hardship, and required a man of nerve and vigor," Washington Irving noted. "It was confided to Robert Stuart, who, though he had never been across the mountains, and a very young man, had given proofs of his competency to the task." Stuart's fellow partners estimated that with any luck he'd reach New York by Christmas.

CHAPTER 18

TAKING STOCK

AS THE LEADER OF THE SO-CALLED EXPRESS, ROBERT Stuart was about to attempt the first crossing of the western half of the continent by a small expedition. The earlier crossings within U.S. boundaries—those of Lewis and Clark and Wilson Price Hunt—had been carried out by parties whose numbers and firepower were sufficient to keep even the troublesome Sioux and the dangerous Blackfoot at bay.

Hunt's company consisted of sixty-two men, while the government-backed Corps of Discovery set out from St. Louis with fifty-one men—two army captains, three sergeants, eight corporals, twenty-four privates, a slave, and a dozen or so engages. They'd traveled up the Missouri with a swivel gun mounted on their keelboat, which could kill or maim half a dozen Indians with a single blast, and also carried blunderbusses, the early nineteenth-century version of a shotgun.

By comparison, Stuart's party wasn't likely to intimidate anyone. Once he and his six companions broke off from the main body of traders at the forks of the Columbia, just about any war party or band of hostile natives they encountered would likely outnumber them. Still, there was at least one important advantage in sending a small, mounted party across the western wilderness—namely, speed. A larger expedition, even one that was as well organized and well disciplined as the Corps of Discovery had been, often required several hours getting started for the day. The cumulative tasks of rounding up and saddling dozens of horses, stowing sleeping gear, repacking the pack animals, making breakfast for fifty or sixty men (and, in Hunt's case, a woman—Marie Dorion—and her two children), and mounting up could consume a good part of the morning, particularly at the outset of the journey when travelers were still growing accustomed to the routine. And, of course, it was far easier to hunt for six than for sixty.

Stuart was well qualified to lead such an expedition. Granted, he couldn't match Lewis and Clark's experience as frontiersmen or Lewis's training in areas such as medical cures, botany and wildlife, and the use of a sextant or compass—not that Stuart was fortunate enough to have either instrument to help guide him across the Rockies. In the fourteen months since the *Tonquin*'s arrival, however, he'd headed up a number of small exploratory expeditions throughout the Pacific Northwest, much of it territory through which no other white man had yet traveled. He had gotten to know the tribes in the region, for the most part gaining their friendship and respect. Certainly, the former clerk had proven his courage and leadership abilities, most recently during the skirmish at The Dalles. He was quick-tempered— a shortcoming he shared with Meriwether Lewis—and on occasion high-handed, but on the whole the Astorians could not have chosen a better man to take on such a dangerous and demanding challenge.

His six companions were also seemingly up to the challenge. All six had been part of Hunt's group. They knew the terrain through which the expedition planned to travel, knew the various tribes they would encounter, and were well aware of the mistakes made by the Hunt expedition. Among Stuart's party were two Canadian engages: Francis LeClair, who had traveled in Crooks's contingent the previous winter, and the half-breed Andre Valle. Both were seasoned woodsmen who knew how to handle a canoe and a rifle, knew sign language, and knew a smattering of a variety of tribal languages.

Traveling with Stuart as well were two hunters: John Day and Benjamin Jones. Born in Virginia, Jones ran away from home at sixteen and made a beeline for the Western frontier. By 1800 or so, he was in St. Louis, where he began trading on the Upper Missouri. On his way back to St. Louis from one such excursion, he and his partner Alexander Carson decided to join Hunt's party after meeting up with the overlanders below the mouth of the Niobrara River.

Jones had been one of several members of Hunt's party who had discovered and reconnoitered the Cheyenne camp at which the expedition had obtained many of its horses. The previous winter, when Crooks had been too sickly and enfeebled to ferry horsemeat to his men across the turbulent Snake, it had been Jones who had volunteered to take his place. In April, Jones had traveled with Stuart to The Dalles, there shooting the Wishram warrior who was about to murder Reed. Stuart had the utmost confidence in Jones.

John Day was also a Virginian, though he had apparently lived in Kentucky for a time as well. Born about 1770, he migrated to St. Louis, where, by 1798, he'd secured a small plantation, but he seemingly much preferred trapping and fur trading to plowing cornfields. As a result, he hired a man to run his plantation and signed on with Ramsay Crooks and Robert McClellan to trade on the Missouri. Day joined up with Hunt's overlanders at the same time McClellan enlisted. He was an excellent woodsman, a crack shot, and an imposing figure. Washington Irving described him as "six feet two inches high, straight as an Indian; with an elastic step as if he trod on springs and a handsome, open, manly countenance."

As a young man, Day boasted that he was all but invincible, able to dodge Indian arrows, outwrestle grizzlies, and outshoot the best marksmen on the frontier. Truly, he'd been a larger-than-life figure in the mold of Daniel Boone, but now in his early forties, his health had been impaired by years of hard living, and more recently, the horrendous exertions of the previous winter and spring when he and Crooks had made their way to the Columbia. As Stuart, who'd rescued Crooks and Day as they wandered nearly naked and semidelirious along the banks of the Columbia, would soon discover, Day's recent near-death experiences had extracted a greater toll on the Virginian than anyone knew.

HAVING BOTH RESIGNED from the PFC, Ramsay Crooks and Robert McClellan were, officially at least, simply along for the ride. They'd joined Stuart's Express as passengers bound for St. Louis. Nevertheless, both were welcome additions to the expedition. And passengers or no, both were expected to pull their own weight.

Crooks, with whom Stuart had formed what would prove a lasting friendship, had been born northwest of Glasgow in 1787, the son of a shoemaker, William Crooks, and Margaret Ramsay. In 1803, after her husband died, Margaret Ramsay migrated to Montreal with young Ramsay and her three other children.

Crooks was ambitious, resourceful, and blessed with a good head for business and the entrepreneurial spirit that characterized many of the independent traders. He was prone to illness, however. During the latter part of July and early August 1811, while Hunt's party made its way across the high plains of today's South Dakota and Wyoming, Crooks had been so ill he'd been forced to travel strapped to a travois, poles that were bound together and pulled by a horse. In December, he'd been near death when Hunt left him. On reaching Astoria, still frail and thoroughly dispirited, he'd quit Astor's enterprise. Stuart could only hope that his fellow countryman would prove strong enough to make the return trip.

Robert McClellan was made of far tougher stuff. Born near Mercersburg, Pennsylvania, about the same time as Day, in 1770, he had, said Philip Rollins, a slight but powerful build; dark, deep-set eyes; and an impetuous, reckless temperament. In his youth he had been an extraordinary athlete, winning any number of wagers through his prowess as a high jumper. Reportedly, he had once even cleared a pair of draft oxen who'd strayed across his path in Lexington, Kentucky.

McClellan's first lessons in frontier survival, according to historian James Ronda, had come as a teenager, helping his brother take pack trains across the Alleghenies. When the Indian wars erupted in Ohio country in 1790, McClellan joined Major General "Mad Anthony" Wayne's campaign as a scout under the famed William Wells. His daring exploits brought him to the attention of both young Meriwether Lewis and William Clark, with whom he developed a friendship that lasted until McClellan died in 1815. Clark described him as "brave, honest and sincere: an intrepid warrior."

According to one biographer, in August 1794, McClellan, Wells, and three other scouts, all disguised as Indians, rode into the enemy camp several days before the Battle of Fallen Timbers as if they were warriors coming to join the fight. They remained long enough to gather useful intelligence, seize two hostages, and start back to report to Wayne. En route they came across a second Indian camp and, in a spur-of-the-moment decision, tied up their prisoners and rode in, planning to kill an Indian apiece and escape in the ensuing confusion.

The Indians, likely members of the Wyandot tribe, hadn't been fooled and opened fire on them. Both Wells and McClellan were wounded, McClellan by a ball which entered his scapula and emerged at the top of his shoulder. Nonetheless, they retrieved their prisoners and hid in the woods until another of the scouts returned with help. A less fortunate member of their party had been captured, tied to a tree, and used for target practice.

When the Ohio wars ended in 1795 with the Treaty of Greenville, McClellan, a lieutenant, left the army, spent several years with his brother in Ohio, mostly hunting, then moved on by flatboat to New Orleans, where he contracted yellow fever and nearly died.

Still suffering the ill effects of his war wounds, McClellan made a trip back east to seek a pension from the secretary of war. The examining surgeon ruled that McClellan was entitled to one-third of a full pension, nothing more. Greatly offended, McClellan, according to Rollins, at first refused any funds at all but eventually he acceded to the government's ruling and also took a position in the quartermaster's bureau, winding up in St. Louis as a captain. Soon after, he retired to try his hand at the fur trade, eventually partnering with young Ramsay Crooks.

McClellan had been among the first to greet Lewis and Clark on their return, meeting up with the Corps of Discovery on September 12, 1806, about four hundred miles above the Missouri's mouth, where McClellan had been sent on orders from Jefferson to inquire after the overdue Lewis and Clark party. McClellan spent the day updating his old friends as to the events that had transpired during their long absence. In turn, they undoubtedly briefed McClellan on the highlights of their journey, providing valuable information that he added to his already extensive knowledge of frontier geography and its native peoples.

McClellan had a short fuse, a long memory—he never forgave those, like Manuel Lisa, who had wronged him—and a propensity for violence that hadn't been tempered by advancing middle age. Hunt had to contend with McClellan's violent streak on more than one occasion. It was all he could do to keep McClellan from killing Lisa when the rival traders shadowed the Astorians as they made their way up the Missouri. McClellan had also threatened to shoot the half-breed Edward Rose. On reaching Astoria, McClellan had resigned from the company, supposedly angry that he had been given only two and a half shares in Astor's enterprise. More likely, however, he was embittered at Hunt's inept leadership and the resulting loss of life and near deaths of Crooks and others. He planned to return to St. Louis and try his hand at something new.

Stuart was well aware of McClellan's volatile nature, but the former army scout had been of valuable service to him at The Dalles. "I was much aided by that advice which Mr. McClellan's long intercourse and residence among Indians enabled him to give," Stuart acknowledged. Should the Express encounter hostile natives on this trip, Stuart wanted McClellan at his side, no matter the cost.

CHAPTER 19

SEND-OFF

THE DAY OF DEPARTURE, JUNE 29, 1812, WAS CLEAR
and warm. Unaware that five days earlier the first shots had been
fired in a new war against Great Britain—an attack by the U.S. frigate
President on British ship *Belvidera*—the normally sleepy garrison at
Point George was alive with activity and excitement as the Astorians
made hurried last-minute preparations to leave. "All hands were stirring early, preparing for the general departure," McDougall noted in
the headquarters log.

Some sixty-two men, more than half the PFC's ranks, were about
to set off to the interior. They would travel together as far as the
forks of the Columbia and there disperse, most to lonely outposts in
present-day Washington, British Columbia, Idaho, and western Montana. A handful of men under Robert Stuart would continue on to St.
Louis.

On that final morning in Astoria, Stuart made sure that all the
necessary equipment and supplies had been loaded into his party's
canoe. The Astorians' entire flotilla consisted of ten canoes and two
bateaux, or light barges. All the vessels except Stuart's carried several dozen bales and barrels of trade goods that had been brought by
the *Beaver*: spears, hatchets, knives, beaver traps, copper and brass
kettles, white and green blankets, calicoes, beads, rings, thimbles,
hawk bells, and blue, green, and red cloths—items necessary for
commerce with the Indians.

Stuart was traveling light, however. He was bringing only a few
trade items, while reserving the rest of the space in the cedar canoe for

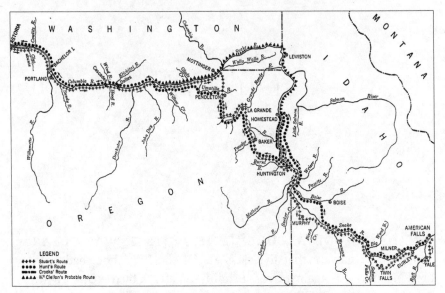

Routes of Stuart and Hunt in Oregon and Western Idaho.

PHILIP ASHTON ROLLINS, *THE DISCOVERY OF THE OREGON TRAIL*
(NEW YORK: EDWARD EBERSTADT, 1935).

the six other members of his expedition and the supplies and provisions that would be needed to sustain a cross-country expedition. His lading consisted of ammunition, pistols and muskets, flint and steel for creating fires, pork, flour, rice, biscuits, tea, sugar, and quantities of rum and wine. The soft and hard goods were secured in bales and boxes and the liquids in kegs, holding an average of nine gallons; the firearms were stored in long cases. As with the other vessels, the lading was covered by a tarpaulin to protect it from rain and dampness.

In addition, Stuart carried dispatches for Astor carefully secured in a pouch—there would be no shiny tin box to attract attention on this trip—letters from his fellow Astorians to their loved ones in New York and Montreal; and his journals, two ordinary white-page blank books bound in checkered brown paper boards. With him, too, he brought a supply of black ink, which, as the expedition progressed, Stuart would infuse with berry juice thickened occasionally with drops of his own blood.

By noon, the canoes and barges were fully loaded. The departing clerks took them to the embarkation site—Tongue Point, a few miles upriver—while the partners and their guests—Captain Sowle, his officers, and young George Ehninger, Astor's nephew, who'd arrived on the *Beaver*—stayed behind to enjoy a farewell luncheon.

After more than a year of frustrations and setbacks, the PFC was finally ready to assert itself as a trading entity throughout the Pacific Northwest. In the brief history of the enterprise, this was a grand day, a cause for celebration. And celebrate the Astorians did. "Every man was nearly drunk on quitting the fort," reported Ross Cox, a clerk who'd come with the *Beaver*.

The festivities continued aboard the *Beaver* as Captain Sowle insisted on ferrying the partners to their canoes upriver. Wrote Stuart:

> In the afternoon of Monday the 29th day of June 1812 we sailed from Astoria under a salute of cannon from the fort. Mr. Hunt, the agent, Mr. McDougall, Mr. Ehninger and Captain Sowle of the company ship Beaver accompanied us as far as Tongue Point where we found two barges and ten canoes, which had been sent out from the establishment this morning, destined for the interior posts of the country above the forks of the Columbia. Messrs. Mackenzie, [David] Stuart, and Clarke had charge of the [two] boats and nine canoes with seven clerks, 32 Canadians and 12 Sandwich Islanders under them. The other contained R. McClellan, R. Crooks, John Day, Benjamin Jones, Andre Valle, Francois LeClerc [Francis LeClair] and myself with the necessaries for the prosecution of this voyage.

Joining their companies at Tongue Point late that afternoon, the fuzzy-headed partners as well as Captain Sowle decided to camp for the night on the site of a deserted Indian village. There, they discovered that the campsite was infested by legions of fleas that hadn't tasted human blood since the last inhabitants had moved on. "We had not been on shore five minutes when we were obliged to strip, get a change of clothes, and drown the invaders . . . by dipping them in water," Ross Cox recalled.

The entire party moved to a nearby beach to escape the blood-suckers, but this site proved even more hazardous than the first. Near midnight, Robert Stuart and his companions were awakened by the noise of water beating on the canoes and the baggage. So close to the garrison—and no doubt suffering the consequences of the afternoon's imbibing—the Astorians had neglected to post a watch and had forgotten entirely about the tide, which had crested several hours after they'd gone to sleep. Knee-deep in water, they frantically retrieved their gear and had no choice but to return to the grassy, flea-infested riverbank, where they passed what remained of the night sleeping fitfully and cursing their relentless tormentors.

It was not an auspicious beginning for the journey that lay ahead.

CHAPTER 20

JEOPARDY

BY THE EARLY SPRING OF 1812, ASTOR HADN'T LEARNED of the loss of the *Tonquin,* the deaths of Thorn and McKay, or Hunt's difficulties in reaching the Columbia. His last word from the Astorians, a July 17, 1811, letter from Hunt, indicated that all was well. At the time, the overlanders had progressed to within 180 miles of the Mandan settlement on the Missouri.

At this juncture, Hunt reported, he had decided to abandon the Lewis and Clark course for a more southerly route to the Columbia. Having just procured nearly one hundred horses, he was confident he and his overlanders would be united with their seagoing counterparts within a few months.

Astor had heard nothing since. In the meantime, relations between Great Britain and the United States were rapidly worsening. Locked in a prolonged and costly war with Napoleonic France, the English increasingly were stopping American commercial vessels and impressing American sailors to serve in the British navy. In his *Naval History of the United States,* James Fenimore Cooper estimated that, by 1812, there were as many American sailors serving unwillingly on British warships as there were seamen in the entire American navy.

Along the northern Great Lakes, where Astor still had hopes of competing successfully against the Nor'Westers, and in the eastern Mississippi valley, the Shawnee Chief Tecumseh and his older brother Tenskwatawa, "the Shawnee Prophet," had mounted a formidable threat to American interests—a grand alliance of tribes dedicated to blocking further expansion by American settlers. In 1810,

British leaders in Canada pledged to support Tecumseh and began sending him supplies.

Seizing upon mounting anti-British sentiment, the young hawks in Congress, led by the Kentuckian Henry Clay and South Carolina's John C. Calhoun, orchestrated a renewed embargo against British imports that severely curtailed the ability of the AFC to trade in the Old Northwest.

Just before Congress passed this new embargo, Astor had ordered a big shipment of goods for the Indian trade from England. With the new restrictions, he was unable to bring these goods into the United States. Instead, they had been unloaded and stored in Montreal and on the Canadian island of St. Joseph's near Mackinac, where they were inaccessible to Astor and his traders. Astor had extended himself financially nearly to the limit in backing the PFC. To have his trade on the northern Great Lakes put on hold indefinitely could drive him out of business.

Seeking an exemption from the new embargo, he wrote to Jefferson's successor, President James Madison, in August 1811, only to be told by the White House that the U.S. Congress hadn't given the president permission to grant such an exemption.

After additional efforts failed, Astor, in a letter dated March 14, 1812, appealed to Thomas Jefferson, retired now to Monticello. Astor apprised the former president of his progress in establishing trade with the Indians in the Great Lakes and Columbia River regions—endeavors he reminded Jefferson that, "at its commencement was favored by your approbation." These efforts, especially the upper Great Lakes business, he went on, were in real jeopardy because of the embargo. "This dead expanse is a serious loss to us," Astor complained, stressing how concerned he was that the Indians of the region would be deprived of their goods—an argument he no doubt believed would resonate with a man who prided himself on his benevolent paternalism in dealing with the native peoples.

Astor hoped that Jefferson might be of some assistance in gaining Madison's support or, at least, provide some guidance how best to deal with his administration. After all, Madison had been Jefferson's secretary of state and a loyal lieutenant. "Perhaps, sir, you will condescend to give advice to me to proceed," he ventured.

It wasn't until May 24 that Jefferson responded. It had been three years since he and Astor had last corresponded, yet Jefferson hadn't forgotten the New Yorker or his attempt to extend the commercial reach of the United Ststes to the Pacific coast.

"I am sorry your enterprise for establishing a factor on the Columbia River, and commerce through the line of that river and the Missouri, should meet with the difficulties you stated in your letter," Jefferson wrote. "I remember well having invited your proposition on this subject and encouraged it with the assurance of every facility and protection which the Government could properly afford.

"I considered as a great public acquisition the commencement of a settlement on that point of the Western coast of America, and looked forward with gratification to the time when its descendents should have spread themselves thro' the whole length of that coast, covering it with free and independent Americans."

Unfortunately, now that he was out of office, Jefferson was unwilling to interfere in any way. "From meddling, however, it is my duty as well as my inclination to abstain," he wrote. "They are in hands perfectly qualified to deal with them, and who, knowing better the present state of things, are better able to decide what is right; and whatever they decide on full view of this case, I shall confirm has been rightly decided."

WHILE HE WAS awaiting Jefferson's response, Astor learned of the *Tonquin's* destruction from a returning sea captain. It was horrific news. In their April 14 editions, the New York newspapers treated the incident as a national tragedy: Captain Jonathan Thorn, a naval hero and a member of a prominent New York family, and his crew had been murdered by savages.

There was more bad news to come: the unfavorable response from Jefferson and then President Madison's June 18 declaration of war on Great Britain. Astor had been traveling between Philadelphia and Baltimore on business when he heard the news.

It was one thing to be locked in a trade war with the Nor'Westers—quite another, Astor knew, to take on the British army and navy.

On learning of the declaration of war, Jefferson boasted that conquering Canada would amount to a "mere matter of marching." Maybe so, but in the meantime, Astoria was a prize waiting to be taken by the first British man-of-war to cross the Columbia bar.

CHAPTER 21

UP THE COLUMBIA

AT DAWN ON JUNE 30, THE RIVER WAS PARTIALLY SHROUDED in fog and mist. There was the unseen splash of a Chinook salmon rising upstream. Magpies raised a ruckus nearby. Some of the new men tensed at each sound from the forest, certain that savages lurked in the shadows.

While the engages loaded the canoes and assumed their posts, the Stuarts, the new partner John Clarke, and "Fat" Mackenzie bid farewell to their guests. Sodden and flea-bitten, Captain Sowle and George Ehninger were eager to return to the relative comfort of the ship. "A few minutes only were spent in mutual wishes of health and prosperity between the gentlemen who accompanied us, and those of our party when we embarked and proceeded across Shallow [Grays] Bay," Stuart noted.

It was slow going as the procession of canoes and barges started upriver, the oarsmen exchanging friendly insults as they jockeyed for position. The spring runoff from the winter's snows was receding, but the current remained strong, impeding the Astorians' progress. Between nine and ten that morning the travelers stopped for breakfast. By the time they'd set off again, the sun had burned off the fog and beat down mercilessly on the canoes. Alfred Seton, a newly arrived clerk from New York, complained that he had never experienced such heat, even in the tropics.

For Stuart, the vagaries of river travel had long since become routine. He knew every bend in the broad Columbia, every stretch of rapids, and had traded with most of the tribes who inhabited its banks and its tributaries. One of these, the Wahkiacums, had watched the flotilla pass their village late in the afternoon, and when the traders made camp on a small rise a few miles upriver, they brought salmon and a few beaver skins to trade.

The Wahkiacums were old friends, a small band with sixty-six warriors, by Stuart's count. Lewis and Clark had experienced some minor difficulties with them. Like guests who stay too long at the party, the Wahkiacums had been reluctant to leave the Corps of Discovery's winter quarters when the Americans announced that, at the end of the day, the gates would be closed to visitors. They "are very forward in their deportment," Lewis complained.

Stuart found them peaceful and always willing to trade for wappato, an edible root many Indians thought a delicacy. In his visits to their village, he'd learned how they'd broken off from the Chinooks two generations earlier as the result of a bitter dispute between the then Chinook chief and his brother Wahkiacum, whose name the dissident band had taken as its own. Whatever their remaining differences with the Chinooks, the Wahkiacums posed no threat to the travelers, Stuart told his men.

Despite these assurances, the usually laconic John Day reacted violently when the Wahkiacums appeared at the encampment, reviling them with a barrage of obscenities and insults. Stuart was naturally concerned by this behavior, especially after Crooks confided that Day's wits, as Washington Irving noted, "had been partially unsettled by the sufferings and the horrors through which they had passed, and he doubted whether they had ever been returned to perfect sanity."

Stuart and the others were traveling with an apparent madman. The next morning, July 1, Day seemed stable. Relieved, the Astorians embarked soon after daylight, but during the course of the day, they had difficulty finding dry land on which to stop and kindle a cooking fire. In the wake of the spring runoff, the shores on both sides resembled "an immense swamp," Stuart observed.

When the sixty-two-man flotilla did stop, it was often to mend a canoe that had been damaged by a submerged rock or a sunken tree, torn from its roots by the strong spring currents. The Astorians' canoes were similar to those used by the Nor'Westers on the western side of the Rockies. Composed of cedar boards a quarter of an inch thick and braced by cedar strips to which the boards were sewn by sturgeon twine, these vessels weren't nearly as resilient as the birch-bark canoes used in the East, Stuart claimed, and needed to be kept in constant repair. A collision with a rock or a tree could spell sudden disaster.

Several hours before sunset, the flotilla passed the site some forty-five miles from the mouth of the Columbia where, in 1810, Nathan Winship of Boston, master of the ship *Albatross*, had tried unsuccessfully to establish a trading post. "It is situated on a beautiful high bank on the south side and enchantingly diversified with white oaks, ash and cottonwood," Stuart observed.

Winship had first made the mistake of building the post in the interior rather than on the coast, thereby earning the enmity of the coastal Chinooks, who had heretofore controlled the interior trade and now were threatened. During its construction at the height of spring runoff, part of the post had been partially flooded. Then, during its construction, Winship's men had placed several of the neighboring Echeloot Indians in irons, mistaking them for natives who several years earlier had attacked a Russian schooner from Sitka. The formidable Echeloots, one of nine clans of the Upper Chinookan family, began to make their displeasure known in an intimidating fashion, shooting off muskets in the forest and menacingly aiming their weapons at Captain Winship.

Winship and his small group of would-be entrepreneurs, including several of his brothers, soon began to wish they'd never left Boston. Captain Winship's assistant, William A. Gale, complained that the local chiefs they fed at their table were filling their mouths with one hand while planning to cut their hosts' throats with the other. Following a visit by several chiefs who insisted that the whites leave, Winship and his followers loaded their livestock—pigs and goats—and gear back aboard the ship, released their prisoners, and, as Stuart put it, "left the Columbia without lots of time." The trading post had lasted all of eight days.

The Astorians had far better luck in dealing with the Echeloots than their predecessors. During the previous autumn, Stuart even stationed a clerk and several men in the Echeloot village to capitalize on

the region's excellent duck and geese hunting. The tribe's fishery provided the traders with sturgeon up to nine feet in length and candle-
fish, a delicacy that, when dried, Stuart likened to smoked herring.

An hour before dusk, the travelers beached their canoes three
miles beyond the Echeloot village. As they were settling in for the
night, Day again began showing symptoms of what Stuart described
as "mental derangement," rambling on incoherently in a highly agitated state. Several of the men tried to calm him, but Day went to bed
gloomy and churlish. By the dwindling firelight, Stuart recorded that
the flotilla had progressed twenty-two miles from the previous night's
station and pondered how he should deal with this, his first crisis.

Briefly, at least, Stuart was able put aside his concerns about Day
the following morning as the travelers got off to an early start with a
favorable wind at their backs. Passing the Cowlitz River, which joins
up with the Columbia from the north, Stuart recalled his exploratory
probe the following winter. Heading up a small expedition that
included Russell Farnham, Stuart had canoed up the rapidly flowing
Cowlitz, which rose from Mt. Rainier. He'd been impressed with the
terrain that began about fifty miles to the north: "beautiful high
prairies which make their appearance occasionally interspersed with
a few oaks, walnut and pines and are feeding grounds for a great
many elk, bear and deer."

This was the homeland of the Cowlitz Indians, a powerful Sal-
ishan tribe that was unknown to Lewis and Clark. These Indians,
with whom Stuart spent several days, would later be characterized as
the blue bloods of the region's native peoples. Indeed, Stuart
thought their demeanor somewhat haughty and insolent but conceded they were honest and peaceable, at least toward whites. In
their war canoes, they would descend Cowlitz River to the Columbia
to raid the villages of their enemies—the Chinooks—and take slaves.
The Cowlitz were far too proud to hunt beaver on behalf of the white
traders, although Stuart did manage to barter for 260 skins, a meager
haul in his estimation.

By the following evening, when the travelers camped upriver on
the island named in honor of Patrick Gass of the Lewis and Clark
expedition, the situation with Day had reached a crisis point. Twice,
he tried to get possession of arms with the intention of committing

suicide. Thwarted on both occasions, he eventually seemed to regain his senses, expressing great remorse for his behavior.

A little before daylight, however, the Astorians were awakened abruptly by gunshots. Day had somehow secured a pair of loaded pistols, put both to his head, and in his deranged state, fortunately fired too high. Stuart immediately ordered Day secured and placed under guard in one of the canoes until he could determine what to do with the Virginian who'd become a danger to himself as well as to the entire expedition.

With Day bound like a prisoner and complaining angrily that Stuart and the others were conspiring against him, the Astorians progressed to Cathlapotle Island (now Bachelor Island), home of another band of the Chinookan nation, the Cathlapotles, with whom the Corps of Discovery had stayed on November 5, 1805, and on their return East the following March. There, after conferring with his uncle, Mackenzie, and Clarke, Stuart decided to send Day back to Astoria with a Cathlapotle headman he knew, in exchange for a few trade articles. As a result of his condition, Stuart noted in his journal, Day had "become not only an entirely useless member of the expedition, but likewise kept us continually in alarm, for his own safety and that of some individuals against whom he had evidently some evil design. . . . He [Day] was completely disarmed before embarking with the Chief, who I knew well, and have every confidence in his carrying him down in safety."

Along with Day, Stuart sent a letter back to McDougall detailing the hunter's apparent breakdown and suicide attempt, but when Day arrived back at Astoria on July 9, McDougall found him in "good health without any appearance of having been as crazy as our letter gave us to understand." To McDougall, Day conceded that he might have acted as a madman but only on a couple of occasions. The real problem, he claimed, however, had been McClellan, who treated him in a shameful manner, which he could no longer endure. "He at length gave way to passion, retorted on McClellan, exposed some certain facts and gave his mind freely, on which they endeavored to persuade him he was crazy," McDougall reported.

Unfortunately, the participants in this drama never spoke further of it, leaving us with several intriguing questions. What were the facts with which Day confronted McClellan? Was there some terrible secret, real or imagined, from the previous winter? Why had McClellan been so abusive toward him, if, in fact, that had been the case? Had Day been faking his breakdown? In his letter to McDougall, Stuart expressed doubts about the reality of Day's madness, saying that it may have simply been an excuse for not making the overland journey. These doubts may explain why McClellan was so hard on his onetime friend, and they seem, to some extent, justified. Even in a delirious state, it's unlikely that Day, in trying to shoot himself, would miss not once but twice. Consider, as well, that for the rest of his stay at Astoria, and indeed for the remainder of his days, he seemed as sane as the next man.

Clearly, though, Stuart made the right decision. In verbally assaulting virtually every native the Astorians encountered, Day could very well have triggered the kind of incident that led to the destruction of the *Tonquin*. "He might embroil us with the natives," Stuart said. This was not a risk Stuart could afford to take. Nor could he have Day and McClellan at each other's throats the entire journey. He had no choice but to send Day back, but in doing so, Stuart lost the services of a good man.

WITH DAY GONE, Stuart could take a little time to reflect on the surrounding countryside.

Approaching Cathlapotle Island, he and his companions passed what today is the Multnomah Channel of the Willamette River, flowing into the Columbia from the south. "That large and beautiful stream [is] called by the Indians Wallamat and by Lewis and Clarke Multinamah," Stuart noted, indicating a familiarity with the Corps of Discovery's route, gained probably from McClellan.

The traders had entered what today is the Willamette Valley, which Stuart judged to be perhaps the most appealing region he'd seen in his travels though the Pacific Northwest. Flanked by the Coast Range to the west and the Cascades to the east, the area was home to the Cathlapotles as well as another nation, the Calapooias, whom Stuart described as numbering three hundred men and living in a scattering of villages above Willamette Falls to the south.

On his initial visit, it was the enormous beaver population that had impressed Stuart, but on this occasion, the crofter's son recognized the area's vast potential as farmland. "The country nearly to the falls . . . is delightful beyond expression; the bottoms are composed of an excellent soil with cottonwood, black walnut, birch, hazel, alder and white oaks, ash and pines to give variety to the most beautiful landscapes in nature."

Stuart had a good eye. Thirty years later, emigrants would begin coming here by wagon train along the Oregon Trail. For them, the rich Willamette Valley represented the Promised Land. They arrived in such numbers that, by 1846, the British abandoned their claim to all the land above the Columbia, instead agreeing on the forty-ninth parallel farther north as the Canadian-U.S. border.

THE NEXT FEW days were relatively uneventful as the travelers entered the deep green expanses of the Columbia River Gorge. Beacon Rock marked their way, towering almost nine hundred feet above the passing flotilla. Traveling to the Pacific, Lewis and Clark had encountered the first ocean tides within the long shadow of this giant stone pillar.

Just ahead, the river pinched together and once had been spanned, the Indians believed, by the Bridge of the Gods. Stuart thought the rugged crests of the canyon resembled "the antique towers and fortifications" of Scottish castles, and he noted the succession of waterfalls that cascaded down the lichen-covered cliff face.

Beyond the Gorge, the country changed abruptly, becoming open, rugged, and mountainous. The traders were approaching the Lower and Upper Cascades which rivaled the Short and Long Narrows of The Dalles farther west as the most treacherous rapids on the river. The Cascades, a spumy stretch of rioting, boulder-strewn water, marked the river's passage across the axis of the Cascade Mountains. "In low water by making a portage of two miles, you pass all the bad parts of these Cascades, and may jump the remainder without much risk," Stuart noted. When the river was high, though, as it was in early July, the Lower and Upper Cascades were "one continued rapid" extending nearly six miles.

The Astorians planned to begin portaging the Cascades before the evening of July 6, but rain delayed their progress, and they encamped on Strawberry (Hamilton) Island at the foot of the rapids. As soon as the downpour ceased the following day, the traders put their arms in order and replenished their cartridge boxes, dividing up into two brigades: one to guard the heights as the second group towed the canoes through the rapids by rope from shore or carried cargo.

Stuart was with the group below supervising the tiresome task of hauling the canoes through the strong, treacherous current. The roar of the rapids was so loud that the men had to shout to make themselves heard. They had ascended about three miles when David Stuart's canoe struck a rock, spun sideways, and quickly filled and upset. Immediately some of the men rushed out in smaller canoes to retrieve the errant vessel and its cargo. Meanwhile, Robert Stuart set off with five men in another canoe in pursuit of some of the packages that had been swept downriver.

Returning to Strawberry Island, he recovered several small packages and part of a bale, which had already been opened and partially pilfered by Indians. On his way back, his canoe was crossing a rapid when the water that appeared "as if boiling, gushed at both sides of the canoe at such a rate as to cause real alarm for our safety."

With the few strokes of their paddles, Stuart and his men managed to extricate themselves from danger, but they were badly shaken. "Had the canoe filled, it would have upset in a moment, and no doubt can exist but every soul would have perished in a moment, as we were a great way from the foot of the rapids," he wrote that evening.

The next few days were spent repairing David Stuart's damaged canoe and searching for the remaining merchandise that had been swept away. On Thursday, July 9, the Astorians resumed their portage, but the pace was excruciatingly slow, the work an ordeal even for the fittest of the engagés. At the end of the day, they'd come only a little more than a mile, and they managed only a mile and a quarter on July 10.

On Saturday, two of Clarke's canoes took in considerable water, but fortunately nothing was lost. Even so, the cargo had to be unloaded and carried upriver while the canoes were towed to a spot where the rapids diminished somewhat and they could be reloaded.

Finally, at about 2 P.M., the travelers passed the head of the rapids and, finding it too early to stop, continued on for two more miles, encamping on the Columbia's southern bank near present-day Rock Creek.

Here, Stuart and his companions remained another day to dry the goods from Clarke's canoe and enjoy a respite after the Cascades. William Matthews, one of the clerks, took advantage of the break to invite some of the local chiefs for a counsel. They were given tobacco as a reward for having let the Astorians traverse the Cascades without incident and told that, as long as they remained friendly, they could expect reciprocal friendship from the whites.

Ahead lay The Dalles, where the natives were far less docile. Neither Stuart nor any of the men who'd skirmished with the Wishrams at The Dalles in April were eager to pass that way again.

WHEN THE ASTORIANS arrived at the Long Narrows at midday on July 14, they discovered that the salmon-fishing season was in full swing. From the beginnings of the rapids to Celilo Falls, the banks were crowded with Indians reaping the river's incredible harvest: Wishrams and their Chinookan neighbors from the south side of the Columbia, Wascos; Wahkiacums from downriver; Echeloots; and Indians from the forks of the Columbia and the interior who, like the others, had come to fish, gamble, and trade. "All mix promiscuously at this season," Stuart wrote. "When added to the residents of this quarter, 700 men might be collected in two hours."

Lewis and Clark had come through here too late in the year—and departed too early—to have seen this remarkable spectacle. Along both banks, the fishermen had constructed scaffolds that extended out over the river, usually over narrow channels where the salmon, making their annual spawning run from the sea, would bunch together, often leaping from the water and remaining suspended in midair for a heartbeat before resuming their journey.

From their perches, the natives manipulated long-handled scoop nets to which a large hoop was attached. The fishermen extended the scoop net perpendicularly into the water, allowing it to descend with the current until it encountered a salmon struggling to go upstream. The net was always kept distended and was pulled up with such ease that boys were often employed at the task, succeeding equally with the most robust of their elders, Stuart observed. "The operator hardly ever dips his net without taking one and sometimes two Salmon, so that I call it speaking within bounds when I say that an experienced hand would by assiduity catch at least 500 [Salmon] daily. . . . From this some idea may be formed of the incredible shoals of Salmon which annually ascend the Columbia and its waters."

With any luck, the natives would be too preoccupied with their salmon catch to pay much attention to the passing fur traders. Still, the Astorians weren't taking any chances. Upon their arrival at Long Narrows, they discharged all their weapons, then cleaned and reloaded them. Each man was provided with a musket and forty rounds of ball cartridge. Many were also armed with daggers, short swords, and pistols. Over their clothes, they donned leather armor, a kind of long shirt made of elk skin. It extended from the neck to the knees and was arrow-proof.

That evening, the Astorians camped on the river's south side, which Stuart knew from his previous visit afforded the best and shortest passage. Once the tents were pitched, the partners divided the men into three groups to stand guard through the night in an equal number of shifts. If the Wishrams—"saucy, impudent rascals," Stuart called them—or warriors from the other tribes mounted an attack, they would not take the Astorians by surprise.

The night passed without incident, and in the morning, two-thirds of the party began the portage while the rest remained on guard. Indians were evident everywhere, and when two of the Astorians momentarily abandoned a bale they were carrying to look down from the rocks on the wild rapids below, several of the natives appeared and tried to abscond with it. Realizing they were being robbed, the sightseers sounded the alarm, bringing the guards, one of whom, an excellent shot, deliberately winged a fleeing native in the arm with a musket ball. "The fellow gave a dreadful shout on receiving the ball, but still continued his flight with his comrade until we lost sight of them," Ross Cox reported. "This piece of severity was deemed necessary to prevent repetitions of similar aggressions."

That night, according to a perhaps apocryphal story later told by some of Stuart's family members, David Stuart took the last watch, but when his nephew awoke shortly before dawn, "Old Uncle" had disappeared.

Immediately, the Astorians organized a search party that tracked the elder Stuart to an Indian village upriver. There, they discovered the errant partner convivially sharing a pipe with several dozen natives. Apparently, David had grown restless, taken a walk to the village, and finding the Indians all asleep around the campfire, helped himself to one of their pipes and some tobacco, ensconcing himself by the remains of the fire. When the natives awoke, they were so startled to see the trader in their midst coolly enjoying a smoke and so impressed with his sangfroid that they shook him by the hand and made him a present of the pipe.

Robert Stuart arrived soon after with the search party, the story goes, and the relief he experienced at finding his uncle safe quickly turned to exasperation. When he began to rebuke David for his rashness, the older man reportedly responded, "There is no fear of an Indian if you have no fear for him." In his journals, Stuart made no mention of the incident, except to say that, on the morning of July 16, the Astorians breakfasted in a large Indian village some 500 yards from the previous night's camp.

That evening, the traders stopped on a sandy beach where great numbers of natives, perhaps as a result of David Stuart's diplomacy, visited the camp. "They behaved very much to our satisfaction in consequence of which a present of tobacco was given to the chief," the younger Stuart noted.

By the end of the following day, the whites had half-completed their arduous portage of the narrows and were settling in for the night when two Indians were seen running toward the camp. The cry "To Arms" was immediately sounded, and every man assumed his post, but the visitors posed no threat. Out of breath and clearly terrified, they explained how a war party of Indians from the interior had attacked one of their canoes late that afternoon, killing four men and two women.

The traders didn't entirely believe the report, thinking it might be some kind of ruse; nonetheless, they hastily built a breastwork from their canoes and packages, and Stuart and the other officers examined each man's firearms with all due military solemnity.

According to Cox, several members of the war party appeared soon after. "In language, dress and manners, they appeared to belong to distinct nations," he observed. "The horsemen were clean, wore handsome leathern shirts and leggings, and had a bold daring manner, which we did not observe with any of the tribes from the sea upwards."

From a distance, the mounted warriors sized up these bearded strangers who crouched behind their canoes, arms at the ready. They made no show of friendship and appeared to be a reconnoitering party. With a sense of foreboding, Stuart watched them finally ride off. These were the first Indians from the interior he'd seen, a portent of the dangers that lay beyond the forks of the Columbia.

BY JULY 20, the Astorians had completed their portage. It had taken them fifteen days to traverse the eighty miles from the first rapids at the Cascades to the head of Celilo Falls.

Beyond, the country opened up, and the pines became stunted, giving way to scrub oaks. Snow-capped Mt. Hood loomed to the south, dominating the landscape. In his journal, Stuart sought to measure the mountain's enormous scale within a context that was fathomable to European sensibilities:

> This mountain is entirely detached from any other, and when we consider the great height of the river hills (which in a civilized country would be thought nearly impassable from their magnitude and above which this gigantic mass appears as a steeple overlooking the lowest houses of a city) it will easily be imagined that it is not a hillock of common order. At present the trees are discernible about half way up the acclivity, the tops of others in a higher region begin to emerge from snow, but the summit never knows a change of seasons.

On July 21, after an early start, the flotilla paused for breakfast on the south bank of the river, where natives visited them. Two of the visitors Ramsay Crooks recognized as the culprits who, in April, had robbed him and John Day of their belongings. The pair was seized at once, bound hand and foot and thrust into the canoes. Writing of the incident years later, Alexander Ross, who hadn't been present at the time, claimed some of the traders wanted to hang the thieves or cut off their ears, at the very least. This is unlikely, however, if for no other reason than the resentment it would create among the Astorians' trading partners. Stuart mentioned nothing of this; nor did Irving, who noted that Crooks saw no need for drastic retribution. According to Stuart, he, Crooks, and the others told the Indians they would be freed only after the property that had been taken was returned.

By nightfall, the prisoners' tribesmen returned with the two rifles, but they'd been unable to recover the smaller articles. Even so, the Astorians released their prisoners unharmed. Certain they were going to be killed, the pair fled at once into the night.

With a strong, fair wind at their back, the flotilla traveled forty miles on Wednesday, July 22, and an additional thirty miles the following day. They had now entered the Columbia plains, a sandy desert that is bounded to the southeast by the Blue Mountains, where Crooks, Day, and the voyageur Dubreuil had gotten lost in the snow the previous winter. Except for infrequent clusters of willow, cottonwood, and stunted red cedar, the desert region was almost totally bereft of firewood, and it was infested with rattlesnakes.

Landing on the river's rocky south shore in the heat of midday, the traders discovered hundreds of the deadly reptiles basking in the sun or nestling under the rocks. In a killing frenzy, they claimed the landing site as their own. Firing together with muskets loaded with goose shot at a batch of snakes under one of the boulders, half a dozen men dispatched thirty-seven snakes, by Cox's count. Dozens of others were similarly killed or driven away.

Rattlers, the traders knew, were repelled by the smell of tobacco, so they spread loose tobacco leaves around their camp at night for protection. During the day, however, they weren't always as vigilant. At one point during a rest stop, an engagé named Pierre LeCourse dozed off in the afternoon heat with his head resting on a small package of trade goods. To their horror, his comrades watched as a three-and-a-half-foot-long rattler slithered across his chest and then coiled itself in the snug of LeCourse's left shoulder.

The men wanted to wake him, but another voyageur, an old Canadian, said, no, the snake would probably move on. Meanwhile, one of the group came up behind the napping LeCourse, hoping to disengage the snake with a seven-foot long-pole. As he gingerly eased the pole under the snake, the rattler raised its head, flicking out its tongue and angrily shaking its rattles. Finally, the man with the pole was able to pitch the snake a good ten feet from LeCourse, who was awakened not an instant too soon by his comrades' shouts of joy—the disoriented voyageur's first indication he'd been in danger.

ON MONDAY, JULY 27, the traders arrived at the juncture of the Columbia and the Walla Walla, a bold, rapid stream about fifty yards wide that flowed in from the east. Here the Columbia began its broad arch north to its headwaters in the Canadian Rockies. To the immediate north, it was joined by the Snake and Yakima Rivers at the so-called forks of the Columbia.

Most of the expedition would continue on to the Columbia's forks, but for Stuart and John Clarke, who was bound for the Spokane River, the mouth of the Walla Walla marked the end of the river journey. The flotilla would remain here for several days, while both partners and their men made preparations for their respective overland journeys.

For the Walla Walla Indians, the arrival of the traders was a cause for celebration. These were the people who had succored Day and Crooks when the gaunt, forlorn pair had finally found their way down from the Blue Mountains. Lewis and Clark described them as "the most hospitable, honest and sincere people that we have met with on our voyage."

Stuart was similarly impressed, although as a fur trader, he was disappointed the Walla Wallas had neither the aptitude nor the inclination to trap beaver. "They are good Indians, about 200 in number, but as yet entirely ignorant of the modes and destitute of the means to ensnare the furred inhabitants of their lands," he wrote.

The Walla Wallas greeted the Astorians with the same unbridled enthusiasm they'd shown when the Corps of Discovery had stopped at their village six years earlier. The women were particularly solicitous of the whites' well-being, but their hospitality did not encompass bedding down with their guests, the Astorians quickly discovered. Observed Cox, "The females . . . were distinguished by a degree of attentive kindness, totally removed from the disgusting familiarity of the kilted ladies below the rapids, and equally free from affections of prudery; prostitution is unknown among them; and I believe no inducement would tempt them to commit a breach of chastity."

Late into the night, the Walla Wallas—men and women—danced for their guests around a great bonfire that had been built at the far end of the fur traders' camp. To the beat of hide drums and rattles, the whites were no doubt encouraged to participate in the hop-and-chant dance and perform Scottish reels and exuberant French Canadian folk dances to the delight of the onlookers.

The following day, Tuesday, July 28, Stuart began trading for the horses he needed for the overland trip. He'd already acquired eight horses from the Walla Wallas' neighbors a few miles downriver but still needed a dozen more, some to serve as pack animals, the rest as mounts for him and his men. One powerful, handsome stallion Stuart purchased for himself, intending, according to Irving, to present the animal as a gift to Astor when he arrived in New York.

Stuart doesn't mention the stallion in his journals, but he indicated he'd overpaid for the remaining twelve horses and the high deerskin saddles and bridles fashioned from braided horsehair he obtained from the Walla Walla. "I gave merchandise to the amount of $179.82, but had I been in possession of proper articles, they should not have cost more than half that amount," he complained.

The next afternoon when the trading had been completed, the Astorians crossed the Columbia and camped at the mouth of a small creek. On July 30, Clarke and his men left for the Spokane, but Stuart hadn't completed outfitting his packhorses and waited until the last day of July to depart. By 7 A.M., he and his men had breakfasted, bid "perhaps a last adieu" to their companions, and crossed the Walla Walla River. With Stuart in the lead, seated uncomfortably on his crude Indian saddle, the tiny caravan ascended into the hills and steered a southwesterly course, bound for the Blue Mountains on the distant horizon.

CHAPTER 22

THE SNAKE

ON THEIR NINETY-MILE journey between the Walla Walla
River and the Blue Mountains, the riders passed through a region of
gentle hills and deep ravines that was in the grip of a severe drought.
The country, Stuart observed, was "without the least appearance of
having experienced any share of the dews of heaven since the time of
Noah's flood." The blowing sand and dust were suffocating, and the
excessive heat added to the travelers' discomfort. By midday, Stuart
and his men were so parched that LeClair drank his own urine.
Along the way, the group's mascot, "a fine, young dog," collapsed
from lack of water and had to be left behind.

By dusk, the horsemen had progressed nearly forty-five miles—a
long, hard ride even in temperate weather—without finding a trace
of water, but in the fading light, they spotted a distant line of cottonwoods to the south. Ben Jones, who functioned as the expedition's
scout as well as its hunter, was confident the trees bordered the
banks of the Umatilla River, whose then rain-swollen waters he had
crossed in January.

In darkness, Stuart and his men pressed on, prodding their
exhausted mounts until the horses scented water and bolted for the
river, drinking so greedily when they finally reached the Umatilla's
banks that Stuart feared they would be sick. Their own thirst sati-
ated, the men led the animals across the river's shallow rapids to the
first suitable campsite, a gravel beach on the opposite bank, and fell
asleep under a horned moon listening to the horses cropping grass.

After a late start the following morning, Stuart's party followed

an ancient Indian trail east through the swampy terrain outside present-day Pendleton, Oregon, passing a succession of beaver ponds and
marshes that reverberated with the high, slurred "tee-err" of red-
winged blackbirds. It was near here in early January, Stuart noted in
his journal, that one of Hunt's men, the Canadian Michael Carriere,
had ridden off to hunt with a friendly Shoshone Indian and vanished,
never to be seen or heard of again.

The Blue Mountains were close now, another day's ride over a
gradually ascending plain known today as Tutuilla Flats. On Sunday,
August 2, the riders stopped for the night on the banks of a nearly
dry streambed. Departing before sunrise the following morning, they
continued east six miles, then began their ascent of the Blue Mountains, following a well-worn Indian path, the Canadians cajoling and
badgering the pack animals up the steep, rocky slopes and the tired
horses sucking in the thin mountain air.

Two days later, on July 4, after crossing the dividing ridge, the
travelers stopped midmorning at a deep hole in the Grande Ronde
River to spear seven salmon, then proceeded on through what Stuart
described as "a most enchanting tract where the gloomy heavy-
timbered mountains subside into beautiful hills, checkered with
delightful pasture ground."

They followed the Grande Ronde River east, descending by way
of a narrow valley flanked on both sides by steep, high slopes. The
banks on both sides were narrow and rugged with extended widen-
ings at only three or four stretches. To get from one to the other, the
Astorians had to keep crossing and recrossing the river, much to the
displeasure of their horses, until after twelve torturous miles they
came out onto the western rim of the Grande Ronde.

This lush, level, circular plane, by Stuart's estimate, was at least
sixty miles in circumference. It was set, like some enormous natural
amphitheater, in the middle of the mountains. Stuart called it the
"Big Flat," which the French traders later named "Grande Ronde."
Hunt had been the first American to come through here.

Encamping on the Grande Ronde River on July 5, where La
Grande, Oregon, is now situated, Stuart lingered long enough to
mend the saddles that had been damaged crossing the mountains
and to take inventory of the wildlife that was indigenous to the val-

ley. There were deer, raccoon, beaver, otter, and elk, which, Stuart deduced, flocked each year to a hot springs and sulfur lake along the valley's western periphery. The hot springs, Stuart noted, were "greatly agitated as if boiling and for 500 paces around, the olfactory nerves were sensibly affected. . . . It is much frequented by elk, which animal is tolerably plenty in the adjacent mountains and it would appear from their numerous horns, strewed everywhere around the margin of the pond, that they visit it mostly in the spring of the year [antler shedding season]." Marshy in places and crisscrossed by multiple streams, the area, with its rich soil and great growths of willows and dwarf cottonwood, was home to "incredible multitudes of the furred race," Stuart noted.

On August 8, the traders were on the move again, adhering to a southeasterly trace through the broad expanse of the present-day Baker Valley, which is bounded to the west by the Blue Mountains and the east by the Wallowa Mountains. After the two-day respite at Grande Ronde, Stuart was eager to make up time and connect with the Snake.

Traveling along the left bank of the Powder River, then south-southeast across a high prairie and low sandy hills, the returning Astorians reached what Stuart called Wood Pile Creek (today the Burnt River) on August 10. As they followed that stream east by southeast, believing it to be a tributary of the Snake River, the party, Stuart reported, "saw no less than 19 antelope, a sight so uncommon in this country that . . . we doubted the evidence of our senses. We tried all possible means to get a shot at some of them, but they were so exceedingly shy as to avoid our every endeavor at approach."

After traversing a "very stony and bad" road on both sides of Wood Pile Creek, passing a deserted Indian fishing camp, and descending a long, steep slope, Stuart, on August 12, got his first glance of the river that had so bedeviled Hunt. "It is about 400 yards in breath, has high sandy banks, little or no willow and a rapid current," he noted after the Astorians had made camp on a grassy flat projecting from the left bank of the river. "It is the main branch of the right-hand fork of Lewis's river, called by Lewis & Clark, Kimooenem; by some Indians Ki-eye-nim, by the Snakes [Snake or Shoshone Indians] Biopaw and by the generality of whites, the Snake River."

He planned to follow the long, serpentine arch of this mighty river though the bleak sage deserts and high lava plains of what today is southern Idaho and then on to the Tetons, adhering to the Snake's southern bank. Ahead, perhaps after an eight-day march, McClellan and Crooks estimated, were the caches Hunt's overlanders had left behind. From these, Stuart planned to draw the provisions, ammunition, traps, and armament he and his men needed to complete their journey.

WITH ITS HEADWATERS in today's Yellowstone Park, the Snake is the principal tributary of the Columbia, draining much of the northwestern Rocky Mountain area. On their first day, the returning Astorians covered eighteen miles, stopping for the night at a sight where the river began a sharp turn toward the south. Soon after they had settled in, a lone Indian, whom Stuart identified as a Shoshone, rode boldly into their camp with what Stuart described as "grateful tidings." Using sign language, the Shoshone claimed that two whites were staying with his people at an encampment upriver about a day's march away.

The Astorians were delighted by this news, but mystified as to the whites' identities. The pair, Stuart reckoned, had to be members of one of the two groups from Hunt's party who'd stayed behind: the engages who had briefly reunited with Crooks and Day the previous winter, or the hunters and the disgruntled Joseph Miller, who, at Fort Henry the previous October, had decided to winter in the Rocky Mountains trapping beaver rather than continuing on. Nothing had been seen of either group since.

Traveling across bottomland dense with willows and salt wood and over low, sandy, sagebrush-covered hills, Stuart's party did not arrive at the Shoshone village his visitor had described until the afternoon of August 15. It was a small encampment, ten lodges set at the confluence of the Owyhee River and the Snake. After its inhabitants confirmed that indeed there were whites nearby—they were on the other side of the Owyhee, the Indians claimed—the traders decided to make camp there. Stuart dispatched one of the Indians to retrieve these mysterious white men.

THE SHOSHONE, or Snakes, as Stuart and other whites sometimes called them, had their roots in the Great Basin of Nevada and Utah. They were a diverse nation of nomadic digger-hunters whose common bond was the Shoshonean language. For thousands of years, they'd subsisted on whatever scant resources their barren homeland yielded—roots, berries, seeds, salmon, mountain sheep, antelope— but in the early 1700s, two of the Shoshone tribes, the Utes and Comanches, who lived on the borders of Spanish New Mexico, first acquired horses; soon the rest of the Shoshones had them as well.

Astride these fearsome beasts, the Shoshone intimidated their enemies. In about 1730, according to ethnologist John C. Evers, the Shoshone surprised the Piegan Blackfoot with big, four-footed animals "on which they rode swift as a deer," one aging Piegan told the NWC's David Thompson decades later. The mounted Shoshone roamed far out onto the Great Plains to hunt buffalo, there acquiring many of the traits of the plains tribes.

But while the Shoshone had horses, their enemies—the Blackfoot and the Atsinas of Canada—began acquiring firearms from French and British traders. With guns, these Indians quickly obtained horses themselves, many of them taken from the Shoshone, who were ultimately driven back into the Rockies of Wyoming and Idaho.

The Shoshone Sacagawea and several of her tribesmen had guided Lewis and Clark on much of their journey to the Pacific and had extended the whites their hospitality in the mountain-sheltered valley of the Lemhi. Of these Indians, Lewis wrote, "They live in a wretched state of poverty. Yet . . . they are not only cheerful but even gay, fond of gaudy dress and amusements; like most other Indians they are great egotists and frequently boast of heroic acts which they never performed. They are also fond of games of risk. They are frank, communicative, fair in dealing, generous with what they possess, extremely honest, and by no means beggarly."

Stuart was well aware of the Shoshone's reputation for "rectitude and integrity of conduct," but he had reason to question their credibility after the Indian who'd been sent to look for the mysterious whites found nothing. Perhaps the rumors of whites being in the area were unfounded.

Disappointed and cranky—the relentless mosquitoes had kept

them awake much of the night—the Astorians pressed on, crossing the Owyhee early Sunday morning. They had progressed only a few more miles when a lone rider, an Indian, came galloping toward them as if on a mission of some urgency.

THE RIDER WHO overtook Stuart's Astorians was one of the two young Shoshone guides who had led Hunt's brigade over the Teton Pass—what Stuart referred to as Mad River Mountain—and had stayed behind to watch over Hunt's horses. McClellan and Crooks and the other veterans of Hunt's expedition recognized him at once.

From his tribesmen he had learned that the whites were in the vicinity and looking for several of their countrymen, he explained in rudimentary English. Had he seen them?, the Astorians asked. Yes. Ten nights ago, he'd parted from three white hunters. These men had trapped a great many beaver, but the Absarokas (Crows) had discovered where the hunt was concealed and carried off everything. The Absaroka had also taken most of their belongings so that they'd been left with "only a horse each and but one gun among them."

Their names, he said, were Michel, Alexis, and Makan.

There was a Louis St. Michel and an Alexander Carson among the Canadians who'd wintered with the Shoshone, but the name Makan bore no resemblance to the names of any of those who'd stayed behind. The Astorians were baffled.

As Stuart and the others puzzled over this information, the Shoshone mentioned, offhandedly, that there was a shorter, more direct route through the mountains than that by which Hunt had traveled last autumn. The information galvanized Stuart. Traversing the rugged Rockies was the most arduous and time-consuming part of his trip. A more direct route to the south could save the Astorians weeks of travel and ensure they'd clear the mountains before the dreaded advent of the first snow. Stuart's journal entry that night is an indication of the excitement he experienced at this revelation. "Hearing that there is a shorter trace to the South than that by which Mr. Hunt had traversed the Rocky Mountains and learning that this Indian was perfectly acquainted with the route, I without loss offered him a pistol, a blanket of blue cloth, an ax, a knife, an awl . . . a fathom of blue beads, a looking glass and a little powder and ball if he would guide us to the other side."

The Shoshone accepted. He was eager to return to the far side of the mountains and again hunt "La Vache" (buffalo). The salmon, which sustained his people on this side of the mountains, were not as good as "La Vache," he said. First, though, he had to return to his camp on the Wooded River (the Boise River) for his arms and possessions, but he assured his new employers, he'd rejoin them the following morning.

True to his word, the guide returned the next day, meeting up with the Astorians about four miles from the previous night's camp. Stuart had gotten off to a late start. The mosquitoes were again out in force during the night and so aggravated the horses that they had wandered far from camp. The Canadians and Ben Jones spent hours rounding them up and packing the short-tempered animals.

As a result, it was already midmorning and the travelers had gone only a few miles when the guide reappeared. Stuart and the others greeted him enthusiastically and readily acquiesced when the Shoshone suggested they make camp after traveling only five more miles. There was a shortcut across the hills, he explained, but as it would take a full day to reach the river again, they might as well stop now and get off to an early start the next morning.

That night, Stuart determined that his "Express" had progressed no more than nine miles on August 17, but with their guide now leading the way to this southerly trace across the mountains, they would no doubt make up for lost time.

ON THE MORNING of August 18, Stuart and his companions experienced a rude awakening. The Shoshone had slipped away during the night. At first, the traders thought he might have wandered off somewhere, but in rounding up the horses, they discovered that both the Indian's mount and Stuart's prized stallion were gone. The whites followed the tracks for some time. They led north a few miles, and then crossed over to the far side of the Snake. Apparently, the guide was headed west, perhaps to hunt "La Vache" without the encumbrance of white companions and pack animals. With him, he had taken Stuart's mount, a bounty in trade goods, and his knowledge of the shortcut.

Stuart registered his disappointment and anger in his journal, "From his former conduct we had not the least suspicion that he should attempt committing an act of this nature," he lamented. "Concluding from our lesson of yesterday morning that no dependence would be placed on Indians, notwithstanding their uniform good behavior, we determined to keep a constant guard during the remainder of this voyage—the night to be divided into three watches and one person to stand at a time."

IT WAS ONE OF those chance encounters that defy probability. For several days, the horsemen had been skirting the steep banks of the Snake, but near midday on August 20, they struck a southerly bend in the river and rode down to the bank to get a drink and to water their mounts. There to the Astorians' amazement, they discovered a solitary white man fishing from the riverbank. Badly emaciated, bearded, and nearly naked, he proved to be John Hoback, one of the hunters who'd left Hunt's party at Henry's Fort.

The raucous, emotional greeting between Hoback and Stuart's men brought the hunter's companions, Edward Robinson, Jacob Reznor, and Joseph Miller, from the willows where they, too, had been fishing. All three resembled Old Testament prophets who'd been wandering too long in the wilderness.

Had Stuart stopped earlier or decided to go on to the next bend, he surely would have bypassed the foursome, who were famished but otherwise fit, given their remarkable ordeal of the past ten months. Stuart at once fed them "with the best our small pittances of luxuries could afford" and made camp a few miles downriver at a site with excellent grazing and fishing.

Robinson, Reznor, and Hoback were among the original mountain men, the spiritual forefathers of more fabled fur trappers like Jedediah Smith and Jim Bridger, who wouldn't come west for at least another decade. All three were Kentuckians who, by any conventional measure, were far too long in the tooth to endure the rigors of the fur trade. Robinson, the oldest, was nearly sixty-eight, and wore a kerchief tied over his head to conceal the fact that he'd lost his scalp as a young man on the Kentucky frontier. "He was one of the first settlers in Kentucky," said the Englishman John Bradbury, who had met Robinson and the others when they joined Hunt's party on the Missouri. "He had been in several engagements with the Indians there, who really made it to the first settlers, what its name imports, 'The Bloody Ground.' In one of these engagements he was scalped, and has since been obliged to wear a handkerchief on his head to protect the part."

Robinson had been one of the original employees of Manuel Lisa in Lisa's initial fur-trading venture up the Missouri River. In 1809, he and his fellow Kentuckians, Reznor and Hoback, had signed on as hunters in a large MFC expedition organized by Lisa to penetrate to the Three Forks of the Missouri. Its field captain was Andrew Henry, a tall, slender Pennsylvanian with a commanding presence and a talent for fiddle playing.

At the Three Forks, the traders had been relentlessly harassed by the Blackfoot, and eventually had fled across the Continental Divide with Henry to the Snake, where they'd built Henry's Fort and trapped until the spring of 1811. Returning east, the trio had encountered Hunt's Astorians near the juncture of the Niobrara and Missouri Rivers on May 26, 1811, and had agreed to guide the Astorians as far as Henry's Fort on the north fork of the Snake. There they remained behind to trap, joined by another hunter, Martin Cass, and Joseph Miller.

The scion of a good Maryland family, Miller was a former U.S. Infantry officer, who'd resigned from the army in a pique when denied a furlough. Hunt had recruited him for Astor's venture, providing him with two and a half shares in the PFC, a stake that Miller quickly decided was inadequate. His dissatisfaction was aggravated by an unspecified physical ailment, which made horseback riding extremely uncomfortable, and his apparent unhappiness with Hunt's leadership. With his affliction, Miller had been one of those lobbying for Hunt to switch to canoes, but by the time Hunt decided to take the water route at Henry's Fort, Miller was so thoroughly fed up that he went off with Robinson's crew.

Reunited now with the Astorians, the trappers recounted their experiences of the past ten months. A crude map of the Rockies was drawn in the sand. In the course of ten months, the foursome had explored much of the western wilderness. On leaving Hunt, they had gone two hundred miles south to a sizable river (probably the Bear), which they reported flowed south and west into the Pacific. From there they traveled another two hundred miles east to the lower valley of the present-day Green River in Wyoming's Sierra Madre, encountering a large camp of rogue Arapahos who'd broken off from the main tribe.

After the Indians—the trappers referred to this dissident band as "Arapahays"—robbed them of several horses and most of their belongings, the whites continued on another fifty miles to the western slopes of the Medicine Bow Mountains, where they wintered. With the spring thaw, the beleaguered trappers were again overtaken by the Arapahays, who on this occasion robbed them of all but two of their remaining horses and most of the scant possessions remaining to them. One of these mounts, the trappers claimed, was later taken by Martin Cass, who had villainously deserted them (there was later some speculation that the starving trappers may have eaten Cass over the winter).

With their remaining horse, which eventually was stolen as well, they'd started west again, subsisting largely by fishing, and, according to Stuart, "traveling about 950 miles in which they suffered greatly in hunger, thirst and fatigue."

Eager to elicit information that could prove helpful in charting his own path eastward, Stuart questioned the trappers about their return route. Unfortunately, Robinson and the others had no first-hand knowledge of the shortcut through the mountains described by the Shoshone guide. Perhaps it didn't exist.

He took careful note in his journal of the extensive knowledge that they had gained about the fur trade in the Far West—intelligence Stuart knew would be invaluable to Mr. Astor in New York:

All the unknown Indians they became acquainted with during their perambulation in that quarter (the southern water courses, particularly in the vicinity of the mountains) are a southern band of Snakes, the Arapahays, who may probably muster 350 warriors;

the Arapahos, 2,700; and the Black Arms (Utes), about 3,000 strong; The latter two nations are generally at enmity with each other, but are very friendly to the whites and possess the best beaver country on this side of the mountains, particularly the latter, whose territories extend to the neighborhood of the Spaniards.

Perhaps one day, they'd return to the southern Rocky Mountains, but for now the trappers claimed they'd had their fill of their wilderness, as had Miller. All four wanted to return with the Astorians to St. Louis and to civilization.

WITH FOUR NEW passengers aboard "the Express" and his own mount long gone, Stuart needed to trade for additional horses and reach Hunt's caches upriver, which the Astorians hoped would yield supplies and weapons. Robinson and the others had been stripped of almost everything except a small amount of ammunition.

But horses were difficult to come by. On August 21, the Astorians discovered some thirty lodges of Shoshones encamped on the left bank of Rocky Bluff Creek (the Bruneau River). The Indians had ponies, and although they readily exchanged their salmon for awls, they refused to surrender any of their herd, saying they hadn't enough for their own needs. Eventually, Stuart and his companions had to settle for swapping two of their exhausted animals for a pair of fresh mounts.

The wear and tear on the animals was brutal. Lava rocks along the riverbank cut through the horses' unshod hooves while sage and greasewood ("these abominable and detested shrubs") slashed the animals' legs and flanks. Stuart reported that feed for the mounts and pack animals was extremely scarce. What little the Astorians could procure "was generally the rankest grass and coarse weeds."

Of all the wilderness Stuart passed through, none was more desolate and unyielding than this desert region along the southern banks of the Snake. Only the river provided sustenance and that was often marginal. Continuing east, the Astorians passed a few huts "of wretched Indians. . . . So poor are they that we seldom or never get even a single salmon of them." These were so-called Digger

Shoshone, who pried roots from the ground and trapped small game with snares.

After encamping on a small stand of grass, the travelers saw more Digger Shoshone, who were reduced to swimming after dead and wounded salmon that were floating on the surface of the water. But at Salmon Falls, another day's travel upriver, Stuart's party met up with a large band of Shoshones who seemed far more advanced than the Digger Indians and proved highly adept fishermen. Unlike the Chinook, who relied on scoop nets, these Indians used ingeniously constructed spears tipped with hollowed-out elk horns. Stuart studied the devices carefully:

Their spears are a small straight piece of elk horn, out of which the pith is dug, deep enough to receive the end of a very long willow pole & on The point an artificial beard is made fast by a preparation of twine and gum. The point of the spear is about seven inches long and from a little below where the pole enters a strong string of the same length is attached, which is fastened in a like manner to the handle so that when the spearman makes a sure blow, the wicker catches, pulls off the point and leaves the salmon struggling with the spear through his body while the spear is on one side & the handle on the other.

The travelers spent the night at the falls and watched as shortly after sunrise the salmon began their ascent of the falls, some of them trying to surmount the nearly twenty-foot-high perpendicular pitch on the north side, the less ambitious jumping up the series of cascades on the south side. Meanwhile, the Indians situated themselves on rocks and in the water and began spearing the fish that, exhausted with their struggle, became easy prey. Miller claimed that coming downriver he had seen one salmon clear the entire cataract with a single, spectacular leap of upwards of thirty feet.

Believing the Shoshone to be one homogeneous tribe, rather than the highly diversified people they were, Stuart couldn't fathom why some of the Indians lived in wretched conditions while the Shoshones at the falls were obviously flourishing. "With the greatest facility prodigious quantities are slaughtered daily, and it must have been from this place that the dead and wounded came which we saw picked up by the starving wretches below," he observed. "Am completely at a loss to conceive why these poor creatures do not prefer mingling with their own nation at this immense fishing place (where a few hours of exertion would produce more than a month's labor in their own way); rather than depend on the uncertainty of a fish ascending close along the shore or catching part of what make their escape wounded from these falls."

The Astorians remained long enough at Salmon Falls to replenish their supplies with dried salmon, and then continued along the Indian trail that paralleled the Snake's southerly bank. Along the way they were joined by a small band of Shoshone—two men, their two wives, and a child—who asked to travel with them and tarried with the whites through the night.

It was an amicable interlude, which concluded the following morning with Stuart trading for one of the Indians' horses. Yet when the Shoshone set out again, the cautious Scot decided to remain behind for another night. With the caches nearby, Stuart feared that the natives would see him and his men digging up the belongings Hunt had buried. As a result, he'd let the Indians go on ahead. "By this day's march the savages will be too far off for us to fear being seen by them while taking out of the caches what articles belong to the gentlemen and Canadians along with me," he reasoned.

SATURDAY, AUGUST 29. The Indian path Stuart had been following looped too far to the south to suit the Scotsman. He took a shortcut, steering across twenty miles of dense sage and greasewood and reconnecting with the Snake at the stretch of wild water where Hunt's Astorians had lost a canoe and one of their Canadians.

The sight that awaited him unnerved the frail Crooks. It had been his pirogue that had struck the boulder. At the entrance to the canyon below, he'd run into a stretch of rapids, no worse than the tumultuous runs Hunt's party had encountered earlier. The lead canoe had shot through unscathed, but Crooks's craft, the second in the flotilla, had smacked into a rock that rended the soft cottonwood hull like paper. Clappine, the steersman, had been swept away while

Crooks and the four other Canadians onboard had floundered through icy water to the bank.

Ten months after the accident, the shattered canoe was still lodged among the rocks. Momentarily, Stuart considered going down into the canyon to see what condition the craft was in, but the lava-rock bluffs on his side of the Snake were four hundred feet high and so steep that such a descent would be foolhardy, he decided.

Studying the Snake at this juncture, Stuart could readily understand why Hunt had been forced to abandon his canoes here. Just below the site of Crooks's accident was a terrifying stretch of water at the foot of a waterfall, which the explorers called Cauldron Linn. Flanking the river here on both banks were cliffs composed of immense piles of rocks. "Nothing that walks the earth could possibly pass between [these cliffs] and the water, which in some places is never more than 40 yards wide, rushing with irresistible force over a bed of rocks as makes the spray fly equal to the ocean," Stuart noted. "Hecate's caldron was never half so agitated when vomiting even the most diabolical spells as this Linn."

With the caches nearby, the Astorians settled on a campsite that was surrounded with good grass. While the rest of the men unloaded the pack animals and set up quarters, Stuart, Crooks, and McClellan, all eager to determine what state the property was in, proceeded to the cache site.

Trappers, initially the French, typically used caches as wilderness storage bins for their belongings and furs. In preparing a cache, the trapper usually dug a deep vertical pit—ideally in dry, easily excavated soil—and insulated it with leaves and sticks before storing the goods therein. The key in securing a cache from wild animals, Indians, and unscrupulous rival trappers was to make the earth look exactly as it had before the excavation. The sod was carefully replaced and, on occasion, the cache maker would build a campfire over the site to obliterate all evidence of digging and to divert attention as well.

Whatever camouflage techniques Hunt had employed hadn't worked. Hunt's men had dug nine pits, and Stuart, Crooks, and McClellan were shocked to discover that six of them had been ransacked. Except for some books that had been discarded, the pages scattered by the wind in every direction, the contents had been removed entirely.

Stuart noted that the grass in the immediate area was criss-crossed with footpaths that appeared to have been created recently by the vandals. He speculated that wolves had initially discovered the hiding places, drawn to the caches by the scent of the pelts they contained, and theorized that Indians had later looted the site. Subsequently, he would learn that the Canadians who had withdrawn from Hunt's advancing column in eastern Oregon to winter with the Shoshone had overtaxed their welcome with the Indians. To compensate, they had led their hosts to the caches as a means of reinstating themselves in the Shoshone's good graces.

Vastly disappointed, Stuart and his two companions cursed their luck and started back, only to be caught in a thunderstorm, the first the Astorians had encountered since leaving the Walla Walla. Soaked through, the three men discovered at the camp that there was next to nothing to eat. The addition of Miller and the three hunters to the party had exhausted the travelers' meager provisions.

The following morning, Stuart dispatched Jones and Reznor upriver to bring back whatever game their guns and traps could produce. Meanwhile, Miller and McClellan fished the greater part of the day, while Stuart returned to the caches with the rest of the men to dig up the remaining three pits. The contents included a few dry goods, traps, and ammunition. At least the Indians hadn't taken everything.

That evening, over a supper of thirteen cutthroat caught by Miller and McClellan ("an excellent species of trout," Stuart adjudged) and a little rice, the trappers announced they'd had a change of heart about returning to St. Louis. With the traps and weapons that had been removed from the remaining caches, they could stay in the area and continue collecting beaver pelts. Frankly, Robinson confided, they far preferred "their present ragged condition to civilized society."

Stuart knew better than to argue or try to reason with the tough old Kentuckian. He agreed to outfit the hunters "as far as lay in my power" and reminded them that Reed, the Irishman, and his men were due to come through here in the fall. It was hoped that Reed would bring the additional supplies the hunters needed to get through the winter.

The following day, August 31, the eastbound Astorians, now seven in number with the addition of Miller, made final preparations to move on. Throughout the day, they mended saddles and, in the lingering late summer twilight, closed the caches, taking several small items for the expedition and leaving behind merchandise they wouldn't need for the remainder of the trip.

On a nearby pole, Stuart left a letter for Reed, informing him of the condition in which he had found the caches and of his party's safe journey thus far. It was the last word the white world would have of Stuart and his men for another eight months.

CHAPTER 23

SHORTCUT

LEAVING THE REMAINING CACHES, STUART AND HIS companions followed the broad arch of the Snake as it extended across today's southern Idaho. The party continued to retrace Hunt's route in reverse, although they traveled the opposite side—the rugged southern banks—of the river.

The disagreeably cool night of September 2 served as a reminder of the impending winter and the need to get across the mountains before the cold weather set in and snow blocked the passes. Already some of the cottonwoods and aspens were partially burnished with the first yellows and golds of autumn.

Stuart's immediate challenge was to traverse a big portion of the Snake River plain, a desolate, kidney-shaped stretch of arid flatlands, modest calderas, and craters that had once been the mouths of two-thousand-year-old volcanoes. Covered by snow when Hunt's overlanders had passed this way the previous winter, the surface here was a bed of lava rock covered, Stuart noted, with a parched soil of sand, dust, and gravel and an abundance of sage and greasewood. Stuart, whose legs, like those of his companions and their sore-footed horses, had repeatedly been scratched and torn passing through dense clusters of high sage, detested what he termed "these abominable . . . shrubs."

Their provisions gone, the returning Astorians were now living literally from hand to mouth, supping on whatever food they could trade for, kill, trap, or catch during the day. Like Lewis and Clark and Hunt before them, they relied increasingly on the kindness of the natives, notably the Shoshone. On the morning of September 2, the riders came upon an Indian lodge trace, a trail created by natives dragging tepee poles from the backs of their horses. Such trails were usually an indication that the Indians ahead were disposed to be friendly. "Ordinarily a lodge trace denoted peaceable Indians because war parties rarely encumbered themselves with tentage," Philip Rollins notes.

Following the trace along the base of cedar- and pine-covered hills, they rode into a small Shoshone encampment on present-day Marsh Creek. Here, Stuart was able to make good on the boast he and his fellow partners had made to Captain Thorn: They'd eat dog if necessary. Stuart traded for one of the camp animals as well as some dried salmon and what he characterized as an excellent sort of cake made of pulverized roots and berries. "Last night we made a hearty supper on the dog carcass and between the evening and this morning's pastime caught a sufficiency of trout for breakfast which we found delicious, they being fried with the dog's fat and a little flour we still preserved," he reported.

He had less luck trying to secure a horse from the Indians, paying what he complained was an extravagant price, only to have the animal's owner return the trade goods and ask for his horse back. Given the sorry shape of the expedition's own mounts, Stuart reluctantly agreed. "This I would not have assented to but considering the great distance we had to travel through this country, and the facility of stealing these creatures, I thought it best to save at least the articles I had given him rather than run the risk."

After a fourteen-mile ride along the Indian trail the following day, Stuart and the others unpacked their horses and plied their rods for several hours, hoping to catch cutthroat trout, so named because of the vivid red-orange slash under their bottom jaw. As he neared the Missouri's Great Falls, William Clark had discovered these fish, which were indigenous to the Rocky Mountain West. The eastbound Astorians much favored them over the chubs and whitefish that also frequented these rivers.

They were fishing what Stuart dubbed Trout Run—a stream that later would be known by travelers of the Oregon and California Trails as the Raft River, a jumping-off point for emigrants bound for the

California gold fields. The catch was insufficient to feed seven ravenous men. Fortunately, one of the party, probably LeClair or Valle, managed to trap a small beaver to supplement the evening's modest fare.

The course of the Snake had by now begun its northeasterly arch. By September 5, the traders had reached the thirty-five-foot-high Portage Falls (now American Falls), just below what today is Pocatello, Idaho. During the next few days, Stuart, Crooks, McClellan, and the newcomer Miller began to reassess their course. Stuart had originally intended to follow Hunt's route to the Spanish or Green River valley—that is, follow the Snake one hundred miles or so north to Henry's Fort, cross the Teton Pass into today's Jackson Hole, then go down the Hoback River to the Green River valley. At least that had been the plan upon leaving Astoria.

Since then, however, Stuart had become privy to some new information, notably the claim of the Shoshone guide that there was a far shorter trace across the Rocky Mountains than that taken by Hunt. If such a track did exist, Stuart believed, it lay at the southeast end of the Green River valley. Finding the pass would mean Stuart's party wouldn't have to negotiate either the Wind River or Bighorn Mountains. Even though the Shoshone had made off with Stuart's prized stallion—and Robinson, Hoback, and Reznor had never heard of such a pass—Stuart wasn't ready to discard his claim.

Miller, too, had added a new element to the geographic puzzle Stuart was struggling to resolve. Stuart's party was now almost directly west of the Green River valley, separated by a range of the seemingly impassable Caribou Mountains. Miller claimed that there was a river ahead they could follow more or less directly east into the valley. Robinson and the others had traveled this route on returning from their hunt the previous autumn.

On Monday, September 7 after encamping with several families of friendly Shoshone, the riders came to what Miller recognized as the shortcut. Miller was insistent—and he rallied support from others in the party as well—that Stuart take this path rather than continue up the Snake. It would not only save at least ten days' travel but would enable the travelers to keep a wide berth from Blackfoot territory to the north.

Stuart was easily persuaded. After all, as leader of the Express, his charter was to get to John Jacob Astor with all possible expediency. "This being the water course which guided Mr. Miller . . . and having determined by very urgent persuasion on taking his tract as less circuitous and more out of the walks of the Blackfoot Indians . . . than that by Henry's Fort, we . . . followed up the left bank for 25 miles SE and encamped a mile above the discharge of a small branch [today's Mink Creek] coming in from the West."

The fate of the expedition now hinged on the former army officer's ability to retrace the path he and the Kentuckians followed nine months or so earlier. It soon became apparent, however, that as a frontiersman, the Marylander was no Hoback, Reznor, or Robinson.

LEAVING THE SNAKE, Miller led the riders east by southeast in hopes of finding the trail he recalled traveling the previous autumn. We were "hoping by this route to fall in once more with the Lodge Trace which Mr. Miller supposes we had left to our right six miles below Portage Falls," Stuart wrote on September 8. The traders followed today's Portneuf River into the Marsh Valley, a thirty-mile stretch sheltered by the Portend Mountains to the north and east and the Bannack and Malad ranges to the south and west.

As they continued up the valley, Miller grew more and more disoriented. He'd spot what seemed a familiar landmark only to second-guess himself a few minutes later. There was no sign of the travois trail he remembered. Growing anxious, Stuart sent Ben Jones ahead to search out the Indian road. "After walking a considerable distance, [Jones] returned without discovering any thing of it, and he says further that the tract we had followed all day bent still more to the west," wrote Stuart.

Miller now conceded that he must have taken a different route, one farther to the north. Perhaps he meant he had traveled today's Blackfoot River, which enters the Snake thirty or so miles above the Portneuf. At any rate, he had no knowledge of the valley through which they were presently riding.

The traders had the choice of turning back in an attempt to find this northern river or continuing through this valley along the stream they'd been following since leaving the Snake, the Portnuef. "We thought it advisable to continue up the creek more particularly as it lay directly in our course," Stuart said.

Around midday on September 9, Stuart's party passed through a gap in the mountains and began descending to a broad plain. This was today's Bear River valley. Continuing due east, the traders saw considerable sign of a buffalo herd, which they hoped to overtake in a few days.

After the earlier missteps, there was a sense now, unspoken, that they were back on course. Even the tired horses seemed suddenly exuberant, pricking up their ears, their nostrils flaring at the smell of water ahead. After a ride of eighteen miles across the parched valley, the party at last reached the present-day Bear River. "Mr. Miller at once pronounced [this] the stream where he had made his last fall's hunt," a relieved Stuart noted in his journal that night. He had sufficient confidence in Miller to assert his explorer's prerogative and give the river Miller's name. By his calculations the Express had covered forty-one miles between sunup and dusk.

CHAPTER 24

CROWS

THE VISITORS CAUGHT THE ASTORIANS ENTIRELY OFF guard. Stuart and the others had been fishing for their dinner in the north branch of Miller's River (the Bear River). When they returned to their camp at dusk, they found a dozen or so Indians waiting for them.

They were Absarokas, members of the Crow Nation. Where they had come from, Stuart couldn't imagine. The Astorians had spent most of the day, September 12, crossing "a beautiful, low plain," without seeing any sign of Indians. Now, here were the Crow, strutting boldly about the fur traders' camp as if it was their own. "Their chief came forward with a confident air," Irving wrote. "He was a dark Herculean fellow, full six feet four inches in height, with a mingled air of the ruffian and the rogue."

Though alarmed, Stuart couldn't help but be impressed by the Crows' striking physical appearance. Taller than the coastal tribes, they dressed in soft, supple, exquisitely decorated deer, elk, and buffalo skins garnished with porcupine quills and ornamented in a variety of ways. As the frontier painter George Catlin would later note, the Crow males were "fine looking, with an ease and grace added to their dignity of manners . . . most of them six feet tall or more . . . and many have cultivated their hair to such an almost incredible length that it sweeps the ground as they walk."

Closely related to the Hidatsa Indians on the upper Missouri, the Crows roamed from southern Montana down to the Bighorns and the Wind River and Green River valleys. While the Shoshone were the first Indians in the Northwest to acquire horses, the Crows and the Black-

191

Ba-Da-Ah-Chon-Du (He Who Outjumps All), a Crow chief on horseback by George Catlin.

foot readily obtained weapons from Canadian traders. Armed with the white man's gun, the Crows terrorized the Shoshone, seizing their territory as well as many of their horses and women.

By the early 1800s, the Crows owned more horses than any western tribe, by one estimate as many as ten thousand. As Stuart and his companions were well aware, the Crows continually added to their herds through thievery. William Clark had discovered the Crows' talent for stealing horses on his return journey from the Pacific. On his way to reunite with Meriwether Lewis, Clark and his men camped on the Yellowstone River. When they awoke on the morning of July 21, 1806, twenty-four of their fifty horses had vanished. The raiders had managed not only to elude Clark's apparently dozing sentinels but also to obfuscate the horses' tracks leaving the camp so they couldn't be followed.

Along with making contact with an enemy in battle and wresting

away a foe's weapon in hand-to-hand combat, the theft of horses pick-
eted in a hostile camp was one of the greatest deeds of valor a Crow
warrior could perform. It was an endeavor these nomadic buffalo
hunters and raiders pursued with passion, artistry, and saucy humor.

The traders' uninvited visitors appeared peaceful and even
returned to their nearby camp to bring the whites some buffalo meat;
nonetheless, Stuart remained cautious. "Knowing the adroitness of
these fellows in stealing horses, we doubled our watches."

By midnight the Indians, now numbering twenty-one, became
loud and abrasive, taunting the whites so aggressively that Stuart's
entire party kept guard for the remainder of the night. At daybreak,
after Stuart traded for additional meat, the Crows insisted on selling
the Astorians horses and demanded gunpowder in return. "Their
behavior was insolent in the extreme and indicated an evident intention to steal if not to rob," Stuart reported. "We kept close possession of our arms, but not withstanding our vigilance, they stole a bag
containing the greater part of our kitchen furniture."

According to Washington Irving, the traders were mounted and
ready to depart, having declined to provide the Crow with gunpowder, when the hulking Crow chief approached Crooks in a threatening manner. Thumping his chest, he made it clear he was a great
chief and as such was entitled to a present commensurate with his
importance. What he wanted was the horse upon which the white
men's chief, Stuart, was already mounted.

After Stuart denied the request with a firm shake of the head, the
imposing Crow leader walked over to Stuart, seized him by the waist
and "moved him backwards and forwards in his saddle, as if to make
him feel that he was a mere child in his grasp," Irving wrote. When
Stuart, outwardly at least, remained calm and again shook his head,
the Crow seized his horse's bridle with such a forceful jerk that Stuart's startled mount reared, almost throwing its rider. Recovering,
Stuart swiftly produced a pistol that was now level with the Crow
chief's head. His own mount only a few feet away, the Crow immediately ducked behind the animal just as Stuart ordered Crooks, McClellan, and the others to produce their own weapons but not to fire.

Immediately, the twenty or so warriors who had witnessed this
confrontation disappeared into the bushes, leaving their leader

behind. After a moment of uncertainty, the Crow chieftain burst into laughter as if the entire confrontation had been an elaborate ruse. "The chief now said it was all play. He did not want the horse," Stuart later said.

The crisis passed as abruptly as it had begun, as Stuart and the other traders put away their weapons and haltingly joined in the laughter—Stuart even going so far as to give the Crows the gunpowder they had initially demanded as compensation for his refusal of the horse. As Stuart noted in his journal entry of September 13, this helped "to prevent an open rupture and left them happy at getting off on no worse terms,"

AT THE TIME of the Crows' visit, Stuart was only 160 miles or so due west of his intended destination, the road through the Rockies that later would be known as South Pass. Another few days down the Bear River would have brought the traders into the southeastern corner of the Green River valley. From there, it was an easy march northwest across the valley to the pass through the mountains the Shoshone guide had described.

But not long after the incident with the Crows, Stuart opted to abandon this route entirely and regain in reverse the path that Hunt had followed. This meant going back to the Snake, riding north all the way to Henry's Fort, then crossing the Teton Pass and following the Hoback River back down into the Green River valley, thereby adding another four-hundred-plus miles and more than four weeks' travel to the journey.

Some early Western historians such as Hiram Chittenden, who didn't have access to Stuart's journals, harshly criticized Stuart for this seemingly incomprehensible decision. "It is difficult to conceive the state of mind which could lead men to such a path of absurdity as indicated by their route for the next month," Chittenden wrote. "Had not these bewildered overlanders forgotten that the sun rises in the east?"

Clearly, though, the Crows had badly unnerved the eastbound traders and made them aware of how truly vulnerable they were. Continuing east after the Crow encounter, Stuart and his companions spotted "smokes" on several of the surrounding mountains. They concluded these were "signals for the purpose of collecting a reinforcement of these rascals to pursue and attack us," Stuart explained.

Likely because of the locations from which the smoke signals arose, the overlanders also believed that the Crows were on the Bear River to the south. Stuart explained, "We thought it best to vary our former course . . . the better to keep out of their way."

The presence of the Crows, however, wasn't the only determining factor in causing Stuart to abandon Miller's shortcut. Miller distinctly remembered following the Bear River south into the Green River valley. But the Bear follows an extremely serpentine course, as Miller was apparently aware. With its headwaters in Utah's Uinta Mountains, the swift-falling five-hundred-mile-long watercourse flows north into Wyoming, then west into Idaho and finally turns south back into Utah, where it empties into the Great Salt Lake fewer than one hundred miles from its origin. On September 13, after seeing the Crow smoke signals, the traders made their way east, where they came upon the north-flowing Thomas Fork of the Bear River. Fearing the Crow were to the south, Stuart's party, at Miller's urging, headed up the Thomas Fork, believing it would soon turn south.

But Miller was badly mistaken. Thomas Fork did not reverse its direction. Consequently, on September 16, the traders, all the time looking over their shoulders to see if the Crows were in pursuit, began following a well-worn Indian trail east that led to another river. Stuart and the others briefly thought they might have regained the Bear, but this was today's Greys River. Stuart was crestfallen to discover that it, too, flowed north. Clearly, the Astorians had overshot the elusive southerly flowing portion of the Bear. "On striking this watercourse, we easily discovered how far we had failed in attaining the object in view," Stuart wrote. "For, from all we had learned concerning Miller's River, we ought to have struck it hereabouts, whereas the one we are on runs quite a contrary course and must be a branch of the Snake River."

There was no turning back with the Crows possibly behind them. And there was no continuing east in hopes of reaching the Spanish

River valley. Stuart sent Ben Jones out to see if passage was possible in that direction. The Virginian returned with word that the mountains to the east were far too rugged to traverse.

That left but one choice: follow this fast-flowing mountain stream north in the hope of regaining the Snake. Stuart summarized the decision in his journals:

> Having thus lost the intended track by which we proposed crossing the Rocky Mountains, knowing it must be to the south and the great possibility of falling in again with the Crows, the large band of whom we did meet, our horses would undoubtedly be sacrificed, [the] property forcibly taken from us, and our lives perhaps endangered, we at once concluded that our best, safest and most certain way was to follow this river [the Greys] down and pass the first spur of the mountains by the route of the party who came across the continent last year.

For three more days the traders continued their hellacious march up the Greys. Since the river ran so close to its steep banks, there wasn't room for the horsemen to pass. The current of the Greys was far too swift and dangerous to wade. Consequently, for much of the trip the Astorians had to travel through the densely forested slopes of the Caribou Mountains. When the river valley finally opened up on the last day of the march, the traders' pace was slowed by a succession of beaver dams and surrounding swamps.

At least Stuart had been correct in assuming the Greys was a tributary of the Snake. On September 18, the returning Astorians regained the south fork of the larger river, camping near present-day Alpine Junction, Wyoming. From the time they had started up the Greys, there had been no sign of the Crows, and Stuart was confident he'd left the Indians far behind. For the first night in a week, the Astorians slept without grabbing for their weapons at every sound from the woods.

With the first light the following morning, Stuart and the others were up and making preparations to move on after their breakfast. Stuart, Ben Jones, and several others had started down to the river to freshen up when they heard an Indian yell raised near the camp and the ensuing cry "To Arms! There's Indians!" They just had time to grab their weapons when two Indians rode by at full gallop three hundred yards from the camp, emitting war whoops that Stuart described as "the most horribly discordant howling imaginable."

Another Crow was stationed conspicuously on a nearby hill, waving what appeared to be a brightly colored flag elevated on a pole. When the war whoops sounded, the Astorians' startled horses looked up to see what was causing all the commotion. At that moment, the flag-brandishing Crow on the hill spurred his own mount. Seeing it bolt away in apparent panic, the Astorians' horses, which were tethered and hobbled, broke away and started after it, Stuart said, "as if a legion of infernals were in pursuit of them."

Stuart and the others had started after the horses when they heard repeated yells in the direction of the camp. "[These] made us desist from the pursuit in order to defend ourselves and baggage; for there being only two Indians after the horses, we very readily imagined that the main body were in reserve to attack our rear did we follow the foremost, or to plunder our camp if opportunity offered," he noted. If the Astorians went after their horses, they would probably lose all their belongings. If they stayed behind to protect their luggage, the Crows would take their horses.

In an instant, Stuart opted to return to the baggage, reasoning that the chances of catching their mounts before the Indians drove them off were at best remote. No sooner had he and the others regrouped at the camp when, he said, "the savages whose yells made us return to the baggage passed soon after at full speed in the others tracks, and we [discovered] that the whole party amounted to [no] more than 20, which had we known only three minutes sooner, a few horses might have been saved and a scalp or two fallen into our hands.

"From the few words we heard they were no doubt of the Absaroka nation, and I believe [the same] band we met on Miller's river," he continued. "On the whole, it was one of the most daring and intrepid actions I ever heard of among Indians, and convinced me how determined they were on having our horses, for which they would unquestionably have followed us any distance."

The Crows galloped off, shouting and laughing derisively at their victims. One of them even turned his backside to the whites in what Stuart later described as "an insulting manner." An enraged Ben Jones drew up his rifle and begged Stuart to allow him "one crack at the Indian," even offering a good part of the wages due him in exchange for the satisfaction of shooting at the Crow. Stuart insisted he hold his fire, reasoning that if Jones managed to wound or kill the Indian, his tribesmen would return to kill them all.

CHAPTER 25

TO THE TETONS

THE CROW RAID LEFT THE RETURNING ASTORIANS
stunned, angry, and badly demoralized. "Destitute of horses, the
party hardly knew what to do," Stuart later admitted. "Some even
proposed to give up all [hope] and die where they were, as it seemed
hardly possible to cross the immense prairies on foot, weak as they
had become and destitute of provisions."

Stuart was at his best at a time of crisis. In April, he had prevented the badly frightened men in his party from panicking during
the fight with the Wishrams. Now, calling up all the persuasiveness
and resolve he could muster, he put the best possible face on the
expedition's grim prospects, urging the men to continue upriver to
the plains below Henry's Fort, where, he asserted, "we have hopes of
meeting with some of the Snakes [Shoshone] from whom . . . we can
procure a couple of horses."

With horses, they might be able to reach the Cheyenne River, a
tributary of the Missouri, before the cold weather set in. With any
luck, they could winter on the Cheyenne on the far side of the Rockies, he assured McClellan, Crooks, and the others. "Should we fail in
this, our winter quarters will probably be somewhere on the Spanish
[Green] River." One way or another, Stuart fully intended to continue. By spring he would be in St. Louis drinking whiskey and
savoring a first-class meal. The others could either come with him or
remain here in the wilderness to fend for themselves.

He cajoled, bullied, and pleaded. By midafternoon, the others
were making at least desultory preparations to continue up the Snake

Eagle Ribs, Blackfoot *by George Catlin*.

COURTESY SMITHSONIAN AMERICAN ART MUSEUM,
GIFT OF MRS. JOSEPH HARRISON, JR.

by foot. Stuart had rallied them, but privately he conceded a near miracle was needed if they were to survive. "We have just enough food for one meal, and rely with confidence on the inscrutable ways of Providence to send in our road wherewith to subsist from day to day," he wrote in his journal. His chances of ever returning to the civilized world or seeing Betsy Sullivan again were all but nonexistent.

That night, Jones had set the party's only remaining trap at a nearby beaver dam. Early the following morning, Sunday, September 20, on his way to check the trap, he spotted two members of the Crow raiding party skulking in the aspens. Stuart became infuriated when Jones told him what he'd seen. He was certain the Crows had remained in the area to see where their victims cached the belongings they were unable to take with them, now that their horses had been stolen. "To prevent the villains benefiting more from us," Stuart ordered everything he and the others couldn't carry "committed to flames . . . and the remainder we threw into the river."

Burdened down with their heavy bundles, Stuart and his six companions got underway by midmorning of September 21. They traveled downstream on the left bank of the Snake's south fork through what would later be known as Swan Valley. The already snowcapped peaks of the Snake River Range rose to the northeast, the Caribou Range to the southwest.

After an exhausting ten-mile march, the sore-limbed travelers stopped while there was still enough light left in the high western sky to fish for supper. "Forty-five trout were the produce of Mr. Millers and my fishing rods," Stuart reported, but the cutthroat that had been caught at the close of the spawning season made for an unsatisfactory meal. "Were it not for the little meat we occasionally fall in with, I really think they would not even support life," Stuart noted that evening.

After covering only a few miles the following morning, the Astorians decided to cross to the far bank of the river where there was more timber for firewood. The Snake at this juncture was too fast and deep to ford, however, so Stuart and the others fashioned two log rafts. Even in some rough water, these crude vessels proved so sturdy that, instead of simply crossing the river, the weary travelers—four on one raft and three on the other—continued on for another twenty miles where they encamped "on a beautiful low point." There, after pulling the rafts on the shore to dry, Jones killed a fallow deer and a wolverine while Andre Valle caught a large beaver in the Astorians' remaining trap and shot another. The creature was so fat it sank before Valle could recover it.

Their rafts were now laden down with dried beaver and venison. Even so, the travelers made good time. Game was everywhere, but Stuart and his men soon discovered they weren't the only hunters in the region. After passing through the lower canyon of the Snake's south fork, the party discovered a small herd of elk grazing on a little island. One of the animals bolted for the water after being shot and tried to swim away. The hunters frantically pursued it on their rafts for more than a mile before overtaking the wounded animal, killing it, and hauling it ashore.

With a storm gathering in the mountains, they decided to stop for the night at the spot where they'd beached the elk. The following day, Friday, September 25, in rain that later turned to hail and finally snow, they discovered a ball and a broken arrow embedded in the elk's carcass as they dressed their kill. Both were fresh wounds, no more than a week old. "This leads us to believe that the Blackfeet were here not long since and were the persons who wounded it [the elk]," Stuart wrote that evening with the wet snow still falling and elk meat roasting over the fire.

FROM THE PERSPECTIVE of the American fur traders, the Blackfoot made the Crows seem benign. They were to the northern plains what the Apaches and Comanches were to the Southwest— fierce warriors who prided themselves on killing as many of their enemies as possible. "Many older men among the Blackfoot tribes bragged of killing fifteen or twenty of the enemy," ethnologist John C. Ewers notes. "He was but a modest warrior who could claim less than ten scalps."

The Blackfoot Nation consists of three tribes: the Bloods, the Pie-gans, and the Blackfoot proper. Given their name by the neighboring Cree Indians, perhaps because at one time they may have dyed their moccasins black, the Blackfoot are an Algonquian-speaking people who, by 1800, had emerged as the dominate military power on the northwestern plains.

They had long-standing trade relations with both the HBC and the NWC, providing fresh and dried buffalo meat from their fall hunts and pemmican in exchange for trade muskets, ammunition, and rum. They called the Canadian traders "The Northern White Men." One of their best friends among the Northern White Men was David Thompson, who spent the winter of 1787–88 on the Bow River at a Piegan village and helped secure the Blackfoot trade for his then-employer, the HBC, and more recently for the Astorians' rival, the Nor'Westers.

In contrast, the Blackfoot intensely disliked the "Big Knives," as they called the American traders. This hostility was exacerbated by an incident that occurred while Meriwether Lewis and several members of the Corps of Discovery were searching for the source of the Marias River in northern Montana on their way back from the Pacific

Coast. Lewis's party was to join up with Clark at the end of July 1806.

On July 26, Lewis encountered eight seemingly friendly young Piegans a few miles below the junction of Badger Creek and Two Medicine River and ended up camping with them that night. Near dawn, one of the Indians tried to make off with a gun that Joseph Fields, one of the four men in Lewis's group, had briefly left unattended. While Joseph was struggling to retain the weapon, his brother, Ruben, ran up and stabbed the Piegan in the chest, killing him.

At this point, the Piegans started to make off with the white men's horses when Lewis shot and wounded another of the Indians who was taking aim at him with his rifle, causing his companions to flee the scene. Before hastily moving on, Lewis inexplicably left one of the presidential medals Jefferson had given him and Clark to present to friendly chiefs on the dead Piegan's chest so "that they might be informed who we were." For generations, the Blackfoot angrily recalled this encounter with the Big Knives.

From that day forward, the Blackfoot harassed and killed almost every American trader with whom they came in contact. Blackfoot drove both Manuel Lisa and Andrew Henry out of the upper Missouri, killing twenty traders in the spring of 1810 alone. Staying at the Nor'Wester post on the Saskatchewan that same winter, Henry saw all kinds of booty the Blackfoot had taken from their victims, including beaver traps, dirks, and even banknotes. He also learned that the Indians "had murdered and probably butchered and eaten an American officer or trader to avenge the death of several red men at his hands," says Evers.

Stuart had likely heard Hunt relate how on his way from St. Louis to the Nodaway camp, he and some of his overlanders, including the English naturalist John Bradbury, who was briefly with the expedition, had run into the Virginian John Colter, the able, one-time Corps of Discovery hunter. Now retired from the fur trade and married, Colter had spent several years trapping the northern Rockies after serving with Lewis and Clark. Hunt, Bradbury, and the others had heard from Colter how a large Blackfoot war party captured Colter and another Corps of Discovery veteran, John Potts. After killing

Potts, the Blackfoot stripped Colter naked and made him run for his life, after giving him a head start of several hundred yards.

It would have been better to be pursued by the hounds of hell. Colter miraculously escaped, outracing his tormentors and hiding under several dead logs on the Jefferson Fork of the Missouri with the Indians on the riverbank above him screeching and yelling, as he put it, "like so many devils."

The ball and arrow that Stuart's party extracted from the elk were a chilling reminder that the eastbound Astorians would now have to make their own run through Blackfoot country.

WITH THE RIVER now turning west, Stuart had come as far as he could by raft. On September 27, the traders camped on the Snake's west bank near today's Heise, Idaho. There they intended to cross the river in the morning and proceed northeast by foot, but their departure was delayed a day so that the men could rest and prepare themselves for the long march ahead. "We remained in the same camp all this day, making moccasins and other preparations for our journey," Stuart wrote on September 28. He had Ben Jones divide the dried meat and distribute it. Each member of the party was to carry twenty pounds of elk and beaver meat in his parcel.

Stuart and the others were haggard and filthy. The layover presented a rare opportunity for them to bathe and do their laundry. In their largest remaining kettle, the men soaked their frayed flannel shirts—Stuart was the only member of the party whose wardrobe included an extra shirt—in boiling water and a strong liquid soap they made from wood ashes, called lye. "The prime object was to make a very strong lye . . . into which the flannel was plunged and concocted for a couple of hours, under the ardent wish of putting an end to certain vagrants of a particular genera [fleas] with which most Indian voyagers are well acquainted," Stuart later explained.

"It would have been truly ludicrous to have witnessed one of our washing parties . . . During the boiling, the votaries of cleanliness cloaked in a blanket or buffalo robe, almost in a state of nature, watched the ebullitions of the kettle . . . each washed his own [shirt] and walked around until it dried, almost in a state of nature."

These infrequent washing parties were usually jocular, but the mood of the camp on this occasion was solemn. Since the Crow raid, each member of the group had seemingly retreated into himself. Jones was still sulking about not having gotten off a shot at the Crows. The fragile Crooks was listless; nothing seemed to bolster his usually buoyant Celtic spirits. And McClellen had been in a foul humor for days. When he spoke at all, it was to grumble about his sore, badly blistered feet or reiterate his displeasure at Stuart for following Miller's route and getting them lost. Had the Astorians continued along Hunt's route as originally planned, they'd have been across the Rockies by now. Instead, with winter fast approaching, they had yet to cross the Teton Pass. Already, there was considerable snow in the high country, and the bitter winds had begun to strip the yellow leaves from the aspens. McClellan and the other members of Hunt's party had spent one horrendous winter in the wilderness. It was not an experience they wished to repeat.

Stuart did his best to ignore the carping. During this brief respite, he occupied himself by recording his observations of the region's fauna, its geological makeup, and its potential as a future trading site:

> The body of the mountains and hills is black rock, the former produce great numbers of pine species and some red cedars, but the latter are little else than barrens with a growth of short, stinted grass. Immense quantities of beaver inhabit Mad River and its tributary streams and whenever the soil is the least propitious, a great abundance of small cottonwoods and willow are everywhere to be found.

With so many pelts here for the taking, it was easy for him to understand why Hoback, Robinson, and Reznor had been so eager to stay behind and trap in the region the previous winter. In another twenty years this area would become one of the hubs of the American fur trade.

Leaving on the morning of September 29, before the sun had cleared the mountains to the east, Stuart's party crossed to the east bank of the Snake, where they abandoned their rafts. They traveled north along the foothills of the Snake River Range, then veered southwest to cross the broad valley that the mountain men would later call Pierre's Hole.

At the head of the valley loomed the Tetons, a series of jagged granite peaks, now snowcapped, that rose straight up almost a mile and a half. On clear days, they were visible for one hundred miles and served as a beacon for wayward travelers. Hunt had called them Pilot Knobs, as did Stuart, while the more romantically inclined French trappers were reminded of upturned women's breasts and gave them the name that stuck, Tetons.

Their passage across Pierre's Hole took the Astorians through largely open country. Stuart could only pray that the little caravan would escape the sharp-eyed scrutiny of the Indians. When Ben Jones spotted three antelope within rifle range, Stuart thought it imprudent to shoot "fearing the Blackfeet may be in the vicinity and well aware that if discovered by them inevitable destruction must be our lot."

On September 30, the expedition came upon a large trace made by Indian horsemen, probably Crows, Ben Jones believed. The trail was seemingly one month old and mysteriously separated in every direction after a few miles. That night after traveling nineteen miles, the party billeted in a deep gully where the light of their fire wouldn't be seen in the distance. Nearby, while looking for water, one of the Canadians discovered a series of hot springs, an extension of the thermal waters within present-day Yellowstone National Park. John Colter had traversed the Yellowstone area in 1807, returning east with fantastic stories of burning lakes, towering geysers, and boiling springs, but Stuart was the first to record these wonders for posterity:

> A little to the side of our camp [were] several very astonishing springs of various qualities and temperatures, some of them are cold, others hot; one of the cold we found to be acidulated and impregnated in a small degree with iron; but the principal one in the group is very hot and sulfuric, the water is oily to the touch, and foams like soap suds; its margin is covered with a yellow efflorescence of sulfur, which affects the sense of smelling at some dis-

tance, and the volume of the smoke that issues immediately from this spring may be distinguished at least two miles off.

At the camp that night, Crooks developed a considerable fever and was, Stuart noted worriedly, "a good deal indisposed." Then, the next morning, the short-tempered McClellan and Stuart got into a bitter, senseless argument. First, the aging frontiersman petulantly refused to take his turn carrying the Astorians' remaining beaver trap. Nor would he carry his allocated portion of dried meat, claiming he could kill enough for his subsistence on a day-by-day basis.

The dispute didn't end there. Ahead was a small pine-covered mountain, a toe of the Snake River Range. Stuart wanted to go over it, reasoning that the timber would provide cover and decrease the likelihood of their being spotted by the Blackfoot. McClellan angrily dismissed this notion as balderdash. Why waste valuable time trudging up and down through the timber when the mountain was easily circumvented through the open country to the south? Stuart was being overly cautious, much as he had been in trying to elude the Crow. And that effort, of course, had been disastrous.

As the exchange grew more heated, McClellan abruptly stalked off on his own. He would make it back to St. Louis on his own. The rest of them could go straight to hell with the Scot leading the way. Stuart refused to go after him, instead stubbornly striking out on his intended route, only to get bogged down in deep snow as he and his now further-diminished party crossed the mountain. "We reached the other side by the middle of the afternoon and found the passage of the mountain somewhat difficult on account of the snow which in many places was of considerable depth," he later conceded. By the time he and the others finally encamped on the south fork of the Teton River, McClellan was well ahead of them.

The day's rugged march, sixteen miles through knee-high drifts, had drained Crooks of whatever strength he had in reserve. Stuart fed him castor oil, which revived him briefly, but Crooks was soon delirious with a high fever and was in no condition to travel farther. Stuart determined to stay put until his fellow Scot had recovered sufficiently to go on.

The decision was not well received by Miller, Jones, or the Canadians, who pressed Stuart to reconsider. They simply couldn't expose themselves, they argued, "by any delay in this unknown and barren tract, among most inveterate enemies of whites, and in the midst of impervious mountains of snow." Remaining here, with only a day's provisions, they couldn't even hunt for fear of attracting Indians with the report of a gun shot.

Miller, Jones, and the others were right, of course. If they abandoned Crooks, Stuart and the others would be across the pass and out of Blackfoot country in a matter of a few days. "Such a prospect I must confess made an impression on my mind that cannot be easily described," Stuart conceded, "but the thoughts of leaving a fellow creature in such a forlorn state were too repugnant to my feelings to require long deliberation, particularly as he might be well in a few days; this hope I suggested and at length prevailed upon them, though very reluctantly to abide the event." Unlike Hunt, Stuart refused to leave the incapacitated Crooks behind.

That night in the piercing cold, Stuart recalled with bitter irony the supreme self-assurance he'd felt in New York and Montreal when contemplating his trip to the wilderness. How confident he'd been then of his abilities to overcome the worst the frontier had to offer. Now, writing by the light of a small fire, hundreds of miles from the nearest white outpost, he felt utterly lost and hopeless. "The phantoms which haunt a desert are want, misery and danger, the evils of dereliction rush upon the mind," he reflected. "Man is unwillingly acquainted with his own weakness, and mediation shows him only how little he can sustain, and how little he can perform."

STUART'S EDICT AGAINST using firearms until the expedition cleared Blackfoot country went by the boards early the next morning, when Jones set out looking for a promising site to set the beaver trap. Not far from camp he encountered an angry grizzly—a "white bear" as the hunters called the king of American beasts, because of its silver-tipped coat—that hadn't yet gone into hibernation.

These creatures often weigh as much as fifteen hundred pounds and loom seven feet high when rearing upright on their back legs. When the animal charged, Jones had to shoot in his own defense, wounding the animal and driving it off. When he returned to camp, Stuart sent him out again in quest of game, reckoning that if the Blackfoot hadn't heard Jones's initial shots, they must be long gone. If they had, Stuart and his companions were probably doomed anyway. Promptly, the Virginian downed five elk from a big herd that had come down from the Tetons.

At least the traders were no longer in danger of imminent starvation. "We immediately moved forward supporting Mr. Crooks for six miles to where the dead animals lay and encamped in the vicinity," Stuart reported.

Crooks, meanwhile, failed to show any improvement. He could barely move his limbs, let alone travel. Acting as the expedition's physician, Stuart exhausted the supply of castor oil and then decided to try a remedy he'd learned from the Chinooks. Working with the Canadians, he built an "Indian sweat," a dome-shaped erection of branches covered with pelts and blankets. Inside, he placed red-hot stones, then poured cold water over them, producing a dense cloud of steam that filled the small structure. The patient, stripped naked, was left to swelter among the stones. Stuart was encouraged by the results. "[The sweat] had a good effect, and we are in great hopes of moving on again tomorrow." The traders, especially Crooks, owed a debt of gratitude to old Comcomly and his people.

Though still extremely weak, Crooks improved to the extent that by October 5, he could continue as long as Stuart and the others helped him carry his things. After eight miles, they stopped for the night on the Teton River near Teton Creek, after coming upon another grizzly. "On our way here we killed a white bear which had three and a half inches of fat on the rump, and proves an agreeable addition to our stock of elk meat."

The six traders set out early the next morning to begin the long ascent to the top of the Teton Pass. Happily, Crooks was continuing to improve. "Mr. C. mends slowly and was able to carry part of his things," Stuart noted. Even with Crooks lagging the others, the party ascended seventeen miles that day and thirteen the next. Following a steep, narrow, rock-strewn Indian trail, the traders finally reached the apex of the pass by midafternoon, October 7. Fortunately, there was little snow on the western slope of the mountain, and the weather, though "piercingly cold" for the past few days, remained clear.

From the summit, Stuart paused long enough to recoup from the arduous climb and get his bearings. The vast landscape to the east was dominated by a seemingly endless succession of mountain peaks: the Gros Ventre to the east, and to the south the Winds, their snowcapped summits glittering brilliantly in the autumn sunlight. As far as Stuart could see, the cordilleras to the east presented a seemingly insurmountable barrier between the returning Astorians and their destination.

CHAPTER 26

HUNGER

THAT AFTERNOON, OCTOBER 7, THEY DESCENDED INTO the Snake River valley, today's Jackson Hole. Hunt had passed through here, but John Colter was probably the first white man to view this spectacular setting, having come through on his 1807–1808 winter odyssey that took him up the Wind River valley, into Jackson Hole and across the Tetons.

Before dark, Stuart's small party reached the valley's thickly forested river bottom and crossed the Snake, wading across a succession of thirty-to-sixty-foot-wide channels one and a half to three feet deep. The water was frigid, and the current so rapid it could knock a man off his feet.

Heading south, the travelers ascended the foothills of the Gros Ventre range, settling for the night just above the mouth of today's Horse Creek. The campsite was no more than thirty miles east of the mouth of Greys River, where the traders had been three weeks earlier.

By now, shortage of food was becoming critical. Since they'd left the Walla Walla, Stuart and his companions often had to subsist on the most meager fare, but Jones, the Canadians, or Stuart and Miller—the fishermen of the party—had always managed to come up with something at the end of the day. Recently, however, game had become so scarce or elusive that the travelers went entire days without food.

On October 8, Stuart and the others, passing the site where the Snake River turns southwest into the mountains, saw several herds

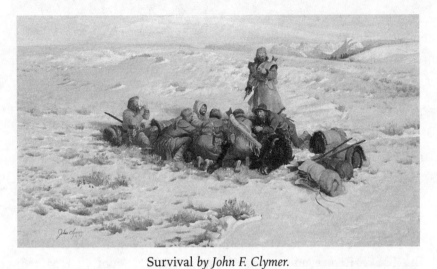

Survival *by John F. Clymer.*

of pronghorn antelope. Easily spooked and able to run up to forty miles per hour, these animals bolted whenever Jones tried to get within range. That night, the travelers retired without a mouthful to eat. Fortunately, they were now approaching the Spanish (Green) River valley, where Stuart expected to find buffalo in abundance.

Crooks, McClellan, and the others who had traveled this way with Hunt the previous summer remembered Hoback Canyon all too well. Now headed south—they'd been traveling up the canyon to the Teton Pass on their previous visit—the traders trod cautiously along the steep right bank of the river Hunt had named after his guide. "The track is often so perpendicular that missing a single step you would go several hundred feet into the rocky bed of the stream below," Stuart wrote.

Despite this "abominable road," Stuart and the others trekked nineteen miles on October 10, before stopping at the juncture of present-day Jack Creek and the Hoback River. One of the party had shot a small, sinewy buck antelope the previous day, and in the darkness (which now came earlier every night), Stuart and the others finished off most of the buck, leaving just enough meat to provide an unsatisfactory breakfast.

Continuing their descent of Hoback Canyon, they arrived at McClellan's day-old campsite. At one point, due to Crooks's illness,

McClellan had been several days ahead of them, but he was clearly slowing down. Next to the ashes of his still-smoldering fire, Stuart and the others discovered "the carcass of a poor wolf" upon which McClellan had supped. At least he had eaten. Deciding to camp on the same spot, the traders again went to bed without supper, everyone in a foul humor.

A hard scramble the next morning brought the party to the top of the ridge enclosing the Green River basin to the south. From the rimrock, Stuart looked out on what historian David Lavender describes as "sagebrush plains immense beyond seeing." When Hunt's overlanders had traveled this way, Hunt described the region as a near-paradise. "We were surrounded by mountains in which were disclosed beautiful green valleys where numerous herds of bison graze," he wrote.

Entering the valley, Stuart, Crooks, and the others grew apprehensive. Where were the buffalo, the great herds that had been here the previous autumn? By the time they finally reached the Green—"a stream about 60 yards wide with no great depth of water, no timber and but few willows," Stuart said—around noon on October 12, it had become became evident that the bison had entirely vacated the region. "A few old Bull tracks were all we had for hope," a bitterly dejected Stuart wrote.

There was at least one encouraging sign on the horizon—significant smoke rising to the southwest. After making camp on the left bank of the Green, Stuart sent LeClair to see what had caused it. "We had great hopes of its being Indians and consequently sat up late waiting his return in expectation of getting something to eat, but at last despairing of his coming we went to bed about 11 o'clock, again supper less."

That night, Ben Jones set the beaver trap. At dawn, the traders visited their trap "in anxious expectation" of finding their breakfast. Instead, they found the forepaw of a large beaver that had chewed off its own leg during the night in order to escape the trap. This "has greatly dampened our spirits," Stuart reported.

The traders could scarcely muster the will or the strength to continue much farther, but there was still the prospect—remote, given the run of their luck—that LeClair might have secured food. Stuart and the others encountered him soon after starting out. His news could scarcely have been worse. The smoke hadn't come from a Shoshone encampment. Rather, McClellan had accidentally set fire to his camp while he was some distance away fishing. He had lived on little or nothing since going off on his own. Near starvation, McClellan, LeClair reported, was eager to rejoin Stuart and the others. He was counting on them to bring him food.

"When we arrived, we found him lying on a parcel of straw, emaciated and worn to a perfect skeleton and hardly able to raise his head or speak from extreme debility," Stuart reported. "He was happy of our being near as well he might."

The arrival of his companions revived McClellan, but he was unwilling to go any farther. "He said it was just as well for him to die there as anywhere else, there being no prospect of our getting any speedy relief," Stuart said.

Somehow Stuart, Crooks, and the others got him upright, helped him collect his things, and prevailed on him to continue. Carrying McClellan's bundle, the party proceeded another seventeen miles—a remarkable jaunt for a man who only a few hours before had apparently been near death—before stopping for the night, after seeing several antelope in the region.

Leaving McClellan by the fire, Stuart and the others went off in hopes of killing at least one of these creatures. Again, the pronghorns eluded the hunters. Perhaps these animals were mirages, similar to the water a man dying of thirst sees in the distance. In this instance, a delusional wretch, about to succumb to hunger, is tantalized as bucks and does skitter on the vaporous horizon just out of rifle range and then disappear entirely just as the hunter cocks his musket. A blink of the eye and they're gone. Regardless, Stuart had no luck, nor had the others. "After dark [we] returned to camp with heavy hearts but I must confess we could not in justice enter the same complaint against our stomachs," Stuart wrote, somehow managing a weak joke.

In the past week, the traders had subsisted on a beaver, a few trout, and a small duck. They had had nothing at all to eat in the past three days, and on the night of October 13 were again preparing to bed down without supper, when one of the Canadians—Irving maintains it was LeClair, but Stuart doesn't say—advanced toward Stuart with rifle in hand. After an awkward moment of silence, the Canadian gathered his nerve to make a little speech. The game had entirely abandoned this region, he began. And it would take three or four hard days, perhaps longer, to cross to the other side of the basin. Surely, they would die of starvation first. Unless . . .

Unless what?, Stuart demanded.

If they cast lots, the Canadian offered, only one of the party need die to preserve the others.

It took Stuart a moment or two to grasp what the engage was proposing: the sacrifice of one of the party to ensure survival of the rest. They would cannibalize one of their own. As an added inducement to gain Stuart's support, the Canadian explained that as the expedition's leader, the Scot would be exempt from the draw.

Stuart initially tried to reason with the man; he tried to shame him into disclaiming such a gruesome proposal, assuring him that on the morrow they would surely fall in with some game. But he soon realized the futility of trying to reason with a wild-eyed French Canadian engage who was starving to death, clutching a loaded weapon, and—to Stuart's horror—apparently on the verge of converting others in the party to his cause.

Before that could happen, Stuart snatched up his own weapon, cocked it, and leveled it at the Canadian "with the firm resolution to fire if he persisted."

To Stuart's immense relief, the Canadian, terrified now, instantly fell to his knees, begged the whole party's forgiveness, and solemnly swore that he would never again suggest such a thing.

The crisis had passed, but Stuart was badly unnerved by the incident, later writing: "My thoughts began to ruminate on our hapless and forlorn situation with the prospects before us until I at length became so agitated and weak that it was with difficulty I crawled to bed and after being there for the first time in my life I could not enjoy the repose my exhausted frame so much wanted."

HAVING NO BREAKFAST to prepare, the traders were off before daylight. Weakened by hunger, it took them the better part of a day to proceed nine miles southeast, where they came to the base of some low, dun-covered hills, which they ascended heading directly east toward the Wind River. Here to their unbounded joy, they encountered three buffalo bulls that had remained behind while the rest of the herd went off to winter in less frigid climes.

Two of the bulls, both young, eluded the hunters, who were semi-delirious with hunger and so weak they were barely able to stand. Even the usually sure-eyed, steady-handed Ben Jones missed his targets. Fortunately, the remaining bison, a tough old bull, was too feeble to elude them. As they closed around him, he snorted defiantly at his attackers and seemed prepared to charge when a shot finally felled him.

In a lupine frenzy, the Astorians descended on the animal, hacking and slashing through his thick winter coat with their knives. "So ravenous were our appetites that we ate part of the animal raw," Stuart recalled later.

They cut up what they hadn't eaten, steam rising from the bull's belly as they removed the entrails, then retired to a small brook nearby, where they stayed up most of the night roasting the remaining meat and devouring it, though not before Stuart took precautions to ensure they didn't get sick. "I was very much alarmed at the ravenous manner in which all ate, but happily none felt any serious effects there from, probably in consequence of my not allowing them to eat freely before they sipped a quantity of broth."

CHAPTER 27

SOUTH PASS

SATED FROM DEVOURING THE BETTER PART OF A BULL buffalo, the Astorians spent a day and a half resting and cutting up to dry what remained of the buffalo meat. It was midafternoon on October 15 before they collected themselves and set out again. Stuart was fully determined now to find the pass to the far side of the Rockies. "This was not a time for indecision and delay. . . . We at a late hour left camp with the intention of going down this river [the present-day New Fork] so long as it lies in our course or at least to the point of the mountain we see to the east near which we expect to find the Missouri waters," he wrote.

Shortly before they stopped for the night at a bend in the river, the traders discovered why so few buffalo remained in the area. Not far from their campsite they had come upon a large Indian trail that seemingly had been made by the Crows. It was perhaps two weeks old. The surrounding area in every direction was littered with numerous buffalo skeletons. Clearly, the Indians had hunted in this country for most of the summer, killing hundreds of bison during their stay.

On October 16, the rising sun silhouetted the rugged peaks of the Wind River Range as they broke camp. From Stuart's vantage point, these mountains presented a formidable barrier, extending as far as the eye could see to the south. Other than the word of the errant Shoshone guide, he had no assurances that these towering granite peaks, many of them over thirteen thousand feet, didn't continue indefinitely without a breach. Yet he and his companions jour-

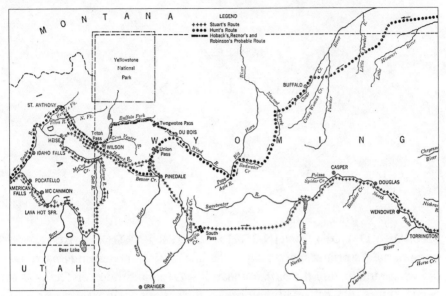

Routes of Stuart and Hunt in eastern Idaho and Wyoming.

PHILIP ASHTON ROLLINS, *THE DISCOVERY OF THE OREGON TRAIL*
(NEW YORK: EDWARD EBERSTADT, 1935).

neyed on. With each mile, they distanced themselves farther from the known routes across the Rockies—Union and Togwotee passes to the north—and descended deeper into wilderness never before explored. Without game to sustain their passage, there could be no turning back.

Leaving the New Fork and traveling southeast across flat, sage-cluttered terrain, they headed toward a sizable stand of trees to the southeast. Near present-day Pinedale, Wyoming, they waded across the swift, cold waters of a large stream (Pine Creek). On the far banks, they discovered a large, recently abandoned Indian encampment. By the looks of the place, several hundred natives, probably Crows, had summered in this piney enclave. Dried and blackened carcasses of buffalo were strewn everywhere.

In the center of the camp stood a lodge 150 feet in circumference supported by twenty trees, each about twelve inches in diameter and forty feet high. The structure was covered by branches of pine and willow to provide shade.

The traders hung back, perhaps sensing this was a sacred place where the Crow shamans, or *batse' maxpe'*, practiced their medicine. As trespassers, they risked earning the wrath of the Absarokan spirits.

This apparently was a burial lodge. At its west end, immediately opposite the door, three corpses lay with their feet pointing to the east. Stuart recorded the scene in his journal:

> At their head were two branches of red cedar firmly inserted in the ground and large buffalo skulls painted black [and] placed close by the root of each. This building is circular; on many parts of it were suspended numerous ornaments . . . quantities of children's' moccasins, and from the quantity and size of the materials [the lodge] must have required great labor and time in erection, from which we infer that the personages on whose account it was constructed were not of the common order.

Later, recalling his visit to this abandoned encampment, Stuart would say it had been an act of providence that their horses had been stolen. Otherwise, they would have arrived at the camp when the Crow were still there and would likely have been murdered.

There was still no sign of a breach in the mountains as they continued southeast, crossing today's Boulder Creek and the East Fork River, both of which Stuart correctly surmised were tributaries of the Green. Both streams "take their rise in the ridge of mountains to the east, which is the main range of the Rocky Mountains," he noted. "[These mountains are] stupendously high and rugged, being composed of huge masses of blackish colored rock, [and] almost totally destitute of timber and covered in many places with snow."

By October 17, the traders had exhausted all their food except for several dried strips of buck antelope and bull buffalo meat—both "too bad to be eaten except in cases of starvation." Fortunately, they met up with half a dozen friendly Shoshone who led them back to their modest winter encampment, a village of some forty huts made largely of pine branches.

"Poor but hospitable in the extreme," the Indians invited them to camp nearby. In exchange for a pistol, a breechcloth, an axe, a knife, a tin cup, two awls, and a few beads, they gave Stuart their only horse, a mare well past her prime. For men who had been lugging heavy packs for weeks across what Stuart described as "the most rugged and barren country I ever beheld," the aging animal was a godsend.

The Shoshone also imparted perhaps the most welcome information Stuart had received since leaving Astoria. The Crows, they explained, had recently stolen a number of Shoshone women and the rest of their horses, taking them to the other side of the mountains. Stuart was almost afraid to ask the obvious question for fear the answer might not be what he hoped. How had the Crows gotten to the far side of the mountain?

Through a pass several days to the southeast, the Indians responded. The white men simply had to follow the Crow trail to arrive at this opening in the mountains. But once their visitors reached the other side, the Shoshone cautioned, they must be careful to stay well clear of the Crow village.

Despite his own self-doubts—and second-guessing on the part of McClellan and perhaps others in the party—Stuart had stubbornly sought out this elusive gateway through the Rockies. In confirming its existence, the Shoshone had vindicated Stuart and given fresh hope to the expedition.

That night the Shoshone provided their guests with badly needed leather for moccasins and dried buffalo meat for their coming journey. They fed the whites from clay jars and dishes they'd crafted. Now that he'd recovered from what he termed his "hungry spell," Stuart took a moment to admire the natives' handicraft. "There is a species of clay which is very fine, and light, of an agreeable smell . . . [from which] the natives manufactured jars, pots and dishes of different descriptions," he commented. "These vessels communicate a very pleasant smell, and flavor to the water that is put in them, which undoubtedly proceeds from the solution of some bituminous substance contained in the clay."

He also remarked favorably on the Shoshone's use of metallic earths, or chalks of various colors: green, blue, yellow, black, white, and two kinds of ocher—one pale, the other a bright red. "These are held in high estimation by the natives and neighboring tribes, who use them to paint their bodies and faces, which they do in a very fanciful manner."

During this powwow, the Indians informed the whites of a number of deprivations their fellow traders had suffered at the hands of rival tribes, most of whom were far less amicable to whites than the Shoshone. The previous summer, they claimed—accurately as it developed—a trader named Champlain (Jean Baptiste Champlain) had been murdered in his sleep by Arapahays, a renegade band of Arapahos, while he was on a beaver hunt some distance down the Spanish (Green) River. They also told the visitors that two of the Canadians left behind by Hunt the previous winter had accompanied one of their bands to hunt buffalo on the headwaters of the Missouri. There, the Canadians and many of the Shoshone with whom they were hunting were killed by Blackfoot. "It undoubtedly was those two unfortunate wretches who conducted the Indians to our caches on the Snake River," Stuart later concluded.

Finally, the villainous Crows had attacked two additional hunters from Hunt's party who were also making their way to the upper Missouri the previous spring, their packhorses weighed down with the pelts they'd collected. The whites had fought back, killing seven of their attackers, but the Crows had finally overpowered and massacred them.

Listening to these tales, Stuart must have felt further justified in not allowing Jones to fire upon the fleeing Crow horse thieves. For the benefit of their hosts, however, Stuart, Crooks, and the others adopted a militant tone. "When we told them the day was not far distant when we should take signal vengeance on the perpetuators of these deeds, they appeared quite elated, and offered their services which were of course accepted."

The evening ended with the traditional smoking of the calumet pipe of peace. Packed with a small-leaf, wild tobacco the traders found superior to their own Virginia blend, the long pipe was passed around among the newly bonded allies in ritualistic silence.

IN THE THIN, canted glow of sunrise, the eastbound Astorians christened their new packhorse "Rosinante" after Don Quixote's famous steed, and they loaded the animal with six days of buffalo meat and all their belongings except their bedding. This made for "easy loads compared to what we have carried for . . . some time past," Stuart reported.

By the time the sun had cleared the mountains, they had traveled three miles over exceedingly rough terrain, joining up with the Crow trace leading southeast. Based on the lines in the soil left by the horse-drawn lodge poles, the Canadians estimated the caravan consisted of at least sixty lodges, perhaps more.

Their destination was in view now, the long sought-after passage to the other side of the mountains. "We . . . made the best of our way for a gap discernible in the mountains in a southeast direction," Stuart said. He was hopeful that they could reach the pass by nightfall, but after a storm moved in without warning from the northeast that afternoon, the traders decided to encamp early on present-day Big Sandy Creek. Despite the snow and a frigid wind, Valle and LeClair managed to kill a young buffalo bull that evening. Their bellies full for the second consecutive night, Stuart and the others retreated into their blankets early to escape the cold. Stuart was determined that the following night they would sleep on the far side of the Rockies.

The traders awakened the following morning, October 20, to find their bedding covered by a thin layer of snow that had fallen during the night. By breakfast, however, the weather had cleared, allowing Stuart to admire what he described as beautifully undulating country as he and the others completed a "hard tramp of 18 miles" to the gap. "The ridge of the mountains which divides the Wind River from the Columbia and Spanish waters ends here abruptly," he reported. Directly to the east was the pass the Shoshone had described: a broad plateau of sage flats bounded by the Wind River and Rattlesnake Mountains to the north and the less imposing Sweetwater Mountains to the south. Nothing obstructed the horizon save two buttes rising in the distance.

The travois trail of the Crow bore to the northeast side of the gap. "Being somewhat apprehensive of falling in with some of their spies," the traders veered to the southeast, leading an overburdened Rosinante across a barren sage-covered plain and camping on a little drain (Dry Sandy Creek). Whatever exaltation the returning Astorians might have experienced at finding their way through the mountains was quickly forgotten as the weather turned for the worse. Hunkered down in their buffalo robes around a modest sage-fueled fire, the traders ate supper and tried without much success to warm themselves. The wind, a nor'easter, was so brutally cold and unrelenting they "were again obliged to take refuge in [their] nests at an early hour."

The following morning, they lingered in camp waiting for the now fully revived McClellan to return with part of a buffalo he had shot the previous night. When they finally got started, the wind and snow hampered their progress. After fifteen miles, less than two-thirds the distance they often covered on a good day, Stuart decided to billet on the eastern slope of a hill immediately northeast of present-day Pacific Springs and well within the western entrance of the pass. Stuart sent LeClair and Valle out to fetch water while he and the others gathered dry aspen for firewood. Not far from camp they discovered another fresh Crow trail—this one, Stuart believed, made by a hunting party returning from the lower Green.

Despite the cold and the unsettling proximity of the Crows, Stuart took careful note of the landmark he and his companions had discovered—this "handsome, low gap." In the Rockies, mountain passes are typically narrow gorges flanked by steep escarpments; traversing them is best left to mountain goats.

With the exception of this pass—South Pass, as it would later be called—virtually all the passes through the Rockies are high in the mountains, accessible by a difficult ascent, often along steep switchback trails and through nearly impenetrable forest. Both Togwotee and Union Passes, which Hunt's party traveled, are more than twenty-five hundred feet above their trailheads in the upper Wind River valley. Togwotee traverses the Continental Divide, North America's backbone, at an elevation of ninety-six hundred feet. Those who had crossed the Rockies prior to Stuart—Hunt, Alexander Mackenzie, David Thompson, and particularly Lewis and Clark—had a terrible time making their way over the mountain passes, none of which proved remotely suitable for transcontinental wagon travel.

In contrast, South Pass forms a corridor that at some points is twenty miles wide. It also presents an easy grade across the Continental Divide, rising to an elevation of seventy-four hundred feet. As a result, the four hundred thousand or so emigrants who later passed through here along the Oregon and Mormon Trails found the slope so gradual—a bump on the road—and easy that they often had difficulty believing they were actually astride the great Rocky Mountains.

Though they were preoccupied at the time of the crossing with immediate life-and-death concerns—finding firewood, food, and water and retaining their scalps—the returning Astorians clearly understood the significance of what they'd discovered. For seasoned fur traders, such as Crooks and McClellan, this newly found pass would provide direct access to the rich fur country of North America. St. Louis–based traders would no longer have to ascend the Missouri to collect pelts.

As he later told the Missouri *Gazette,* Stuart fully grasped that this gateway through the Rockies opened up settlement of the Far West to anyone with a wagon and the oxen or horses to pull it. All his perseverance and stubborn courage had been rewarded. "Let him [to whom] difficulties and distresses were only things imaginary . . . but visit these regions of want and misery," he wrote, reflecting on what he and his little party of adventurers had endured. "His riches will prove an eye sore, and he will be taught the advantages of prayer."

SETTING OUT AS USUAL at daylight on October 22, the traders ascended the gentle slopes of the pass, stopping after a few miles to breakfast at a spring of excellent water. Before noon, they scrambled to the top of a large butte that was south of the pass's main corridor—Stuart referred to it as a mountain, which he and his companions named Bighorn. Here they found the head drains of a watercourse, Sand Creek, which ran eastward, winding its way down through low somber hills crowned with blue-gray sage.

The traders were straddling the continent. On Bighorn's summit, Stuart sensed correctly that he was "in the midst of the principal chain"—astride the Continental Divide. As he was well aware, the water flowing west from the divide ultimately finds its way to the Pacific, the water flowing east to the Atlantic—largely by way of the Missouri and the Mississippi.

Now well within the western entrance to South Pass, Stuart and the others were astride a world no white man had ever visited. The soil had a strange tint, which caused Stuart to surmise it had a high copper content. At one time, this terrain had been an ocean bottom. Seashells, which "doubtless had been deposited by waters of the deluge," were scattered all across the volcanic summit of the Bighorn. At its center was a lake filling what Stuart believed had once been the volcano's crater. Following Sand Creek east, the traders discovered whitish water oozing from the earth. Crooks and McClellan said it tasted much like the muddy waters of the Missouri.

They camped farther down Sand Creek, where Jones shot two bighorn sheep, the first they had killed since departing Astoria. The sheep made for excellent eating, a welcome change from their largely bison diet.

They weren't having much luck with the weather. In a snowstorm the next morning, they continued east, heads bowed against the wind. When the snow finally stopped by midafternoon, Stuart could see that they were now "on the east side of all the Rocky Mountains, which on either side of us were stupendously tall."

Surely, the worst was behind them now. With their vastly foreshortened sense of western geography, the traders believed the stream they had been following, Sand Creek, was a tributary of the Missouri. By continuing east along its banks, they would find their way to St. Louis in no time.

CHAPTER 28

THE CHATEAU OF INDOLENCE

EMERGING FROM SOUTH PASS, STUART'S PARTY CAME
out onto the northern fringes of today's Red Desert and Great Divide
Basin, four and a half million acres of rainbow-colored badlands,
towering buttes, high desert, and shifting, 150-foot-high sand dunes.
No white man had yet visited this vast region, much of which
remains pristine wilderness today.

This desert terrain was not what the returning Astorians had
expected—not the rolling, high plains country Hunt's party had
encountered as it approached the Rockies in the summer of 1811.
Nothing about this strange, seemingly endless landscape was familiar. Stuart and his companions might have been in the Sahara Desert.

Still, they hoped one of the streams flowing eastward out of
South Pass would debouch into a western tributary of the Missouri,
likely the Cheyenne or the Rapid Water River (today's Niobrara).
Crooks and McClellan had crossed the Cheyenne on their way to the
Columbia and had traded with the Ponca Indians at the juncture of
the Missouri and the Rapid Water. On reaching either of those rivers,
they would continue on to the Missouri, from there proceeding to St.
Louis.

But Stuart and the others had badly miscalculated where they
were in relation to the few landmarks they knew. The Cheyenne
River drained out of the Black Hills far to the northeast and the
Rapid Water in northwestern Nebraska. They were nowhere near
either river. The Missouri itself was much farther east than they realized. As they soon discovered, getting back to St. Louis was going to

be a significantly more difficult, prolonged, and dangerous endeavor than they had anticipated.

Through no fault of their own, Stuart and the others became disoriented almost as soon as they cleared the pass. Unbeknownst to them, the Continental Divide splits to surround the Great Basin Divide. As a consequence, almost all the streams within the Basin drain to neither the Atlantic nor the Pacific but are contained within the region.

On a piercingly cold October 23, Stuart's party set out along Sand Creek, the little stream they had first begun to follow on the Bighorn. To their consternation it abruptly turned south, and then was swallowed up by the arid land, disappearing entirely. Disappointed, Stuart fixed on a landmark on the eastern horizon. "We at once concluded to give up all idea of taking the creek for our guide, and to make the best of our way for a range of mountains [the present-day Seminoe Mountains] in the east about 60 miles off, near which we are in great hopes of finding another stream," he wrote. On reaching the Seminoes, the traders were determined to establish a winter camp.

They were heading east now along the southern edge of today's Antelope Hills. Ironically, just on the other side of those hills was the east-flowing, present-day Sweetwater River and what would become the main corridor of the emigrant trail. For the traders, this would have been the far more preferable route, one where good water was continually available from the aptly named Sweetwater, but in skirting the Crow, Stuart had chosen the presumably safer trace.

But at a price. Water was in short supply here. During their eastward trek of October 23, the traders found a few puddles from which they extracted drinking water but not a single stick of firewood. Instead, they had to burn buffalo dung, which generates relatively little heat. Remarkably, they hiked twenty-two miles the following day in the face of a bitterly cold northeast wind and heavy snows. Stuart characterized the day's effort as "a march truly disagreeable." Without water that night, the traders made do with melted snow. Fortunately, they had saved enough buffalo dung from the previous night to build a fire.

———————

BY OCTOBER 26, it was evident that Stuart's party could no longer steer toward the Seminoes along a route that was all but bereft of water, firewood, grass, and game. There were signs of numerous buffalo but only a few were actually visible—and those at a great distance. As soon as these animals got wind of the hunters, they "scampered before we could approach close enough to do execution," Stuart said.

Poor Rosinante was seemingly on her last legs, having gone several days without grass or water. On October 26, Stuart and the others had begun following another stream (Lost Soldier Creek). Like Sand Creek, it turned due south and vanished into the earth. Not a drop of water ran over its sandy bed, Stuart noted.

By now, the situation had become desperate. Stuart's party couldn't turn back, and couldn't risk continuing east. Ten miles to the northeast was a wooded ravine. Where there are trees, logically, there is water. So far, though, the Basin had defied logic but, happily, not in this instance. The party reached the ravine before nightfall. "We discovered to our great joy a creek [Muddy Creek] with muddy banks and a great abundance of willow . . . running with considerable body of water N.N.W. where we stopped for the night," Stuart reported.

ENCAMPING AT THIS little oasis, the traders obtained fresh meat—a beaver that Jones trapped and two buffalo bulls—and "feeling ourselves, as well as our horse pretty much fatigued." They remained in camp for an entire day.

At last, Stuart and the others had discovered a stream that didn't disappear into the soil. Continuing along Muddy Creek ten miles northwest on October 28, the party passed through today's Muddy Gap, coming out onto what Stuart described as "a handsome plain." Still, the Basin continued to mystify. After camping the following night again on Muddy Creek, Stuart noted that this eight-foot-wide stream had inexplicably grown into a twenty-yard-wide river.

In truth, Muddy Creek had merged into the Sweetwater. The eastbound Astorians had now regained the future Oregon Trail. They were heading east along a road that was widely traveled by the Indians but entirely unknown to whites, the one watered course that extended from South Pass all the way to the Missouri. Stuart and his companions had no inkling of this—nor would they grasp what they had discovered for another few months.

Ninety miles from South Pass, they encountered one of the important landmarks of the Oregon Trail, Devil's Gate. Here, the Sweetwater River has cleaved a spectacular V-shaped gap through a nearly four-hundred-foot-high granite cliff. About seven miles east is Independence Rock, a 136-foot-high granite dome, which the Jesuit Pierre DeSmet would later call the "register of the desert," because of the thousands of pioneers who would pause here to inscribe their names on the dome's surface.

Farther east, they descended into low country that afforded excellent pasture for the numerous herds of buffalo that blanketed the landscape. Crooks and the other members of Hunt's party had seen such herds before, but for Stuart, this was a first. The entire plain was black with bison.

Jones shot three buffalo cows, the first cows they'd killed. Encamped on the Sweetwater among several large white willows, the traders roasted their hump steaks, which Stuart enthused were "by far the most delicious I have ever tasted." That night it snowed again. Fortunately, it was warm enough during the day so that the snow melted. Otherwise, the accumulation would have been several feet deep by then.

In near darkness on the morning of October 30, they renewed their march along the Sweetwater, quitting the river that afternoon after it, too, turned to the south. Crossing it, the party came to another river after a short hike. This was the North Platte, though Stuart and the others mistook it for either the Cheyenne or the Rapid Water. Its waters coursed northeast through a canyon that grew increasingly deep. Stuart's party was traveling along the left rim. Far below a "foamingly tumultuous" current dashed over the huge masses of rocks that crowded the riverbed. Stuart had viewed the wildest stretches of the Columbia and Snake, but this river all but exploded. "To form somewhat of an adequate idea," Stuart explained, "let one imagine numerous streams pouring from the mountains into one channel, struggling for expansion in a narrow passage, exasperated by rocks rising in their way, and at last discharging all their violence of waters by a sudden fall through the horrid chasm."

Making camp on the rim, the traders needed water, since neither man nor horse had tasted a drop since leaving the Sweetwater hours earlier. Since there was no water at hand on the canyon rim, the party decided to descend a steep ravine heavily timbered with scrubby cedars in an effort to reach the river. But Stuart and the others misjudged the difficulty of hiking to the bottom. Carrying a heavy load, Rosinante lost her footing several times and almost went plunging down the slope, a reddish colored-precipice of stone that in some places Stuart estimated was five hundred feet high.

It was too dangerous to proceed. As the darkness set in on another frigid night, the traders took refuge among the cedars. Stuart feared that, without water or grass, Rosinante might well not make it through the night. LeClair volunteered to make another attempt to reach the river below, a foray that was doubly dangerous because of the gusting wind and the fading light. Miraculously, he made it, returning with enough water to provide a drink for each member of the party, including Rosinante.

STUART'S PARTY REGAINED the canyon rim at daylight the following morning. It was the last day of October 1812. Game was everywhere—big herds of buffalo on the high plains and bighorn sheep and black-tailed deer in the ravines below. Travel was slow, since the canyon bluffs along which this little caravan marched often extended well into the interior. Late in the morning, the traders reached a bluff overlooking the river. Below, a channel had torn through great piles of red rocks, descending in a series of steep cataracts. "The spray extends at least a quarter of a mile; the noise may be plainly heard at the distance of 30 miles," Stuart marveled.

By the end of the day, they reached the canyon's lower portal and came down to the riverbank, where the traders butchered a buffalo cow Jones had killed earlier. Stuart doesn't say so, but the morale of the party had clearly lifted. They had found their east-flowing river, though which river they were still not certain. Game abounded, and there was no sign of Indians. Certainly the odds of getting back to St. Louis were considerably better than they had been a few weeks earlier.

THEY CROSSED to the right bank of the river the following morning at a site below the sandstone precipices, which Stuart dubbed the Fiery Narrows. It had rained and sleeted before dawn. Low, threatening clouds harbingered another storm, but the traders continued on, following the river through a gap between today's Bessemer and Coal Mountains. On the far side of the gap, the North Platte made a large bend to the north and the country opened up to reveal what seemed an ideal campsite—a beautiful bottom of cottonwoods enveloped by a thick growth of willows. Here, probably at the confluence of Goose Egg Creek and the North Platte, about ten miles outside today's Casper, Wyoming, they bedded down for the night. In the darkness, Stuart fell asleep listening to the gentle murmur of the river whose name he didn't know.

It had become evident the previous afternoon that this stream was most likely not the Rapid Water nor the Niobrara River. As McClellan and Crooks were aware from their stint in the Missouri fur trade, the Niobrara conjoined with the Missouri at what today is the northeast corner of Nebraska. Given its projected northeasterly route, the traders estimated that this river they had been following would debouch into the Missouri farther north. They decided, then, that it was most likely the Cheyenne, which emptied into the Missouri above today's Pierre, South Dakota, several hundred miles northwest of the confluence of the Niobrara and the Missouri.

Just to make sure, on November 2, they continued along the river's right bank for six more miles. "Seeing that the river still bent its course to the north of east, doubts were no longer entertained of our being on the Cheyenne, in consequence of which I held a general consultation," Stuart noted.

If they continued down the Cheyenne, Crooks and McClellan argued, they could be assured of encountering the Indians from whom the river took its name. The Cheyenne were harmless enough, but their closest allies were the Sioux—the same Sioux who'd driven

Crooks and McClellan from their post on the Missouri and had intimidated almost every white who traveled the Upper Missouri, including Hunt's large, well-armed party. Seven bone-weary fur traders wouldn't have a prayer against the mighty Sioux.

From the Cheyenne, "their worthy relations on the Missouri," the Sioux would "of course soon be advertised of our approach and lay in ambush for us along the banks of the river in spring," Stuart noted, likely summarizing an argument proffered by Crooks and McClellan, one with which he had come to agree.

To continue on, then, was foolish, especially since the traders, even by their own overly optimistic estimates, still had to cross hundreds of miles of open prairie before reaching even the westernmost American settlements. At that time of year, finding fuel on the prairies was extremely dicey. Why not winter at the previous night's campsite, Stuart urged, where there was wood for building a shelter and fires, there was water and there was more game than they'd seen anywhere in the course of their journey?

When he put the matter to a vote, the decision was unanimous. Stuart wrote in his journal: "Returning to camp according to agreement, we have determined on passing the winter here and will leave it in the opening of the navigation in perhaps two buffalo-hide canoes, till which time we entertain strong hopes of living in peace and quiet without being honored with the intrusive visits of our savage neighbors."

By November 10, Stuart and the others had settled in, building the first cabin in present-day Wyoming. It was a crude but comfortable structure, six feet by eighteen feet, with the fire in the middle, Indian style, and the whole covered with buffalo skins. After sleeping out in the open for almost five months, the traders were now living in comparative comfort. Perhaps in a wry reference to the great houses of the Montreal fur barons, Stuart dubbed their new home the "Chateau of Indolence."

CHAPTER 29

REVERSALS

IN THE FOUR MONTHS THAT STUART HAD BEEN TRAVELING east, the war had gone badly for the United States. The British easily thwarted an uncoordinated summer offensive against Canada, and then went on the attack themselves, capturing Fort Mackinac, Fort Dearborn, and Fort Detroit, all in a two-week span in August 1812. Detroit fell without the Americans firing a single shot.

In mid-October, the British, outnumbered three to one, routed an American invasionary force at the Battle of Queenstown Heights after many of the American militiamen refused to cross the Niagara River into Canada, leaving their comrades to the mercy of the British and their Iroquois allies. Fourteen British soldiers were killed while the Americans lost 250 men; another seven hundred were captured.

In Manhattan, John Jacob Astor monitored the war's progress with mounting concern and frustration. The loss of the Western frontier and Mackinac, the hub of the region's Indian trade, was potentially a mortal blow to his AFC. Fearing that Astoria might soon come under attack as well, he wrote to Captain Sowle at Canton, almost as soon as war was declared, with orders to return at once to the Columbia with supplies for the traders and there put himself under Hunt's orders.

From halfway around the world, Astor had no way of knowing that the former Nor'Wester Duncan McDougall, not Hunt, was in charge at Astoria and that Hunt had sailed with Sowle aboard the Beaver. In his letters to Astor, Captain Thorn had made it clear he didn't trust McDougall or, for that matter, any of the Canadian traders. With war underway, the last thing Astor wanted was a former Nor'Wester determining the fate of the PFC.

According to Washington Irving, who clearly had gotten his information from an embittered Astor, Sowle, after finally arriving in Canton to find Astor's letter waiting for him, flatly refused to comply with his employer's command. Instead, he chose to sit out the war in Canton. Worse, from Astor's viewpoint, Sowle, thinking he could do better, turned down a $150,000 offer for the furs he brought with him to Canton, a sum that could have made the difference between success and failure for the PFC. Instead, he ended up not selling a single pelt and having to borrow money on Astor's account at an exorbitant interest rate. Astor never forgave him.

As for Hunt, after departing Astoria, he had endured round-the-clock bargain sessions with the constantly besotted, bullying Alexander Baranov, who headed up the Russian-American Company at New Archangel on the Alaskan coast. Subsequently, in October 1812, the *Beaver* continued on to St. Paul's, one of the Bering Islands, to pick up sealskins and was damaged there in a severe Arctic storm. Hunt wanted to return to Astoria, but Sowle was unwilling to risk taking his damaged ship across the Columbia bar at a time of year when dangerous Pacific storms were prevalent. Instead, he was determined to continue on to Canton by way of the Sandwich Islands, where he would stop for the necessary repairs.

By some accounts, Sowle and Hunt quarreled bitterly over this matter, but Sowle had a letter of instruction from Astor telling him to go to Canton. Moreover, neither man knew yet about the war or the grave danger confronting Astoria. Rather than continue on to China, Hunt opted to remain on the Sandwich Islands late in 1812 and await Astor's next supply ship from New York. He had a much longer wait than expected. With the British navy blockading the entire East Coast, Hunt wouldn't see another of Astor's ships until the following summer.

Had Astor counted on Hunt or Sowle for Astoria's salvation, he would have been sorely disappointed. On a matter of such magnitude, however, Astor was far too cautious not to hedge his bets several times over. Within weeks of President Madison's declaration of war, Astor had a ship ready to sail for the Columbia in hopes that he could find a way of somehow getting it past the iron-tight British blockade of New York harbor. Concurrently, he concocted what James Ronda describes as the PFC's most daring exploit, a scheme worthy of any of history's great spy masters. A month after the war started, Astor met with two of his veteran sea captains, Richard Ebbets and William J. Pigot. He wanted them, he explained, to travel undercover to London with drafts for twelve thousand pounds. They were to use these to discreetly buy arms, ammunition, and trade goods and to charter a ship that they ostensibly planned to sail to Canton under a neutral flag. Their real destination, however, would be the mouth of the Columbia River.

Arriving in England in September, Ebbets and Pigot went one better. At the suggestion of Astor's commercial agent in London, Thomas Watson, they chartered an English brig, the seventeen-gun *Forester*, and recruited a crew and master at a final cost to Astor of nearly sixty thousand dollars. Remarkably, Ebbets and Pigot somehow managed all this without arousing suspicion. Ostensibly bound for China, the *Forester* departed from Portsmouth in March 1813 with Pigot as her supercargo and Captain Ebbets posing as a lowly clerk. Surely, Astor must have relished a belly laugh or two when he learned this spy ship of his sailed under a British flag as part of a large British convoy.

Ironically, this likely was the same convoy in which there was another ship sailing for the Columbia, the twenty-gun raider *Isaac Todd*. All the while Astor's agents had been working in the shadows to outfit the *Forester*, the NWC was busy securing permission from the British government to send the *Isaac Todd* to Astoria accompanied by two British warships, the *Phoebe* and the *Raccoon*.

Late in 1812, Astor learned of what the Nor'Westers were up to from one of his agents in England. "I have just now a letter from London dated 19, November which states that they are fitting out the ship *Isaac Todd* of about 450 tons for the northwest coast, and she will, I have no doubt, go to the River Columbia," he wrote Secretary of State James Monroe in February 1813.

After being politely rebuffed by the Madison White House and Thomas Jefferson, Astor was still hoping that the government would recognize the strategic importance of his Columbia River outpost and come to his aid in keeping it from falling into British hands. At an earlier meeting in Washington, Secretary of State Monroe had seemed sympathetic to Astor's plight. Perhaps, now that he'd been informed the *Isaac Todd* and two naval ships were soon to leave for the Northwest, Monroe could get the President to act.

"I pray you, sir, to have the goodness and bring this subject under the President's consideration and if permitted I would request the favor of being informed of the result," Astor wrote to the secretary of state. "I am sure the government will readily see the importance of having possession and command of a river so extensive as the Columbia, the fountain of which can not be far distance from the waters of the Missouri, as well as the impression which such an enterprise would make in favor of the American nation."

All Astor needed, he informed Monroe, were forty or fifty soldiers, a reasonable request given that the British were sending the *Raccoon* and *Phoebe* in support of the Nor'Wester ship. "If such were there, they could with the aid of the men already there repel any force which the British might at this time send," he concluded.

As Astor anxiously awaited a response from Washington, the *Forester* and the *Isaac Todd* embarked from Portsmouth, each bound for the same destination—one intending to destroy Mr. Astor's factory, the other to save it.

CHAPTER 30

UPROOTED

BY THE TIME THE EASTBOUND ASTORIANS REACHED their winter campsite, Stuart estimated they had covered 2,174 miles including the fruitless four-hundred mile detour in search of Miller's River. After months of harrowing travel, Stuart's party welcomed their prolonged respite. For men who had endured so much danger and hardship, the "Chateau of Indolence" was a safe haven. Snug in their isolated retreat, they supposed themselves sufficiently concealed to elude what Stuart termed "even the prying investigation of Indian spies."

For once, Stuart and the others didn't have to worry where their next meal was coming from. The traders had lain in eighteen buffalo—"black cattle," Stuart called them. That was enough meat to last out the entire winter. They dressed and butchered the buffalo meat, saving only the choicest parts—the hump steaks, tongue, marrowbones, and liver—and using their thick, woolly hides as robes.

After a week or so of bitter cold—the river froze over—and heavy snows that kept the traders mostly in their hut close to the fire, the weather abruptly turned mild. LeClair and Valle took advantage of the change to hunt for animals whose skins they could use for leather for moccasins and clothing. They returned that evening with eight mountain sheep and deer hides.

Stuart and the others joined them over the next few days, collecting twenty more skins and felling a grizzly. The grizzly hadn't gone into hibernation yet and had surprised them. It took the entire hunting party to bring the animal down.

This little ragtag crew of adventurers had become gentlemen of leisure. Instead of rising each morning before dawn to begin their endless eastward march, Stuart and the others often slept in, lazed most of the day by the fire, or tended to menial chores—dressing leather to make moccasins, gathering firewood, or cleaning their weapons.

Even Stuart loafed during this well-earned hiatus, neglecting to make his daily journal entry for almost a month. When he ventured any distance from the cabin, it was to hunt and explore the mountains to the southeast (the Casper Range). "The mountains to the southeast are at a distance of two miles," he wrote on November 12, his last journal entry for almost a month. "The declivities are thickly wooded with Firs and Red Cedars shooting promiscuously out of the crevices of the rocks, but in the upper region the extensive tracts of Pitch Pine are occasionally checkered with small patches of quaking aspen."

Defining nimbleness, bighorn sheep by the score scrambled over the rocky summits of these mountains, while bear and black-tailed deer frequented the slopes below. Game was everywhere, and there was nary a sign of Indians. It seemed the traders could not have chosen a more ideal site to wait out the long winter.

THIS PEACEFUL SOJOURN ended abruptly on the morning of December 10 when the Astorians were awakened abruptly by a "savage yelp" near their cabin. Someone shouted "Indians," and they immediately seized their weapons and stumbled outside where they found an Indian war party gathered at their front door. The Indians—twenty-three by Stuart's quick count—seemed nearly as astonished by the encounter as the Astorians. Miller recognized them as Arapahays, a renegade band of Arapahos. These, he suspected, were the same Indians that had twice robbed him and the Kentuckians.

The traders had been so confident they were secure that hadn't bothered to draw up a plan to defend themselves in case of attack. Fortunately, these unwelcome intruders seemed amicable. "After the first surprise was over, they advanced in a friendly manner telling us they were on a war excursion against the Absarokas who had some time ago stolen a great many of their horses, taken some of their

women and were then on a river six days march to the northward
were they were going in hopes of obtaining revenge," Stuart noted.

It had been sixteen days since they'd left their village, the Arapahays continued. It was on a large stream (the South Platte) that joined
the river on which the white men were encamped far to the south.

This was one tribe Lewis and Clark had missed during their journey of exploration. Though distantly related to the Algonquians in the
East, the Arapaho had long been residents of the Northern Plains. A
handsome people, notable for their Roman noses and complexion
that was lighter than that of their arch enemies, the Shoshone, the
Arapaho by disposition belied the stereotype of the stoic Plains
Indian. "They have a keen sense of humor and are great practical jok-
ers," tribal historian Virginia Cole Trenholm observes. "Even in time
of frustration or adversity they can manage to laugh."

How had they discovered this camp?, the Astorians wanted to
know.

The answer was simple enough. Two days earlier, the Arapahay
chief explained, he and his men had been passing through the mountains when they'd heard the reports of firearms; on searching they'd
found where two of the whites (LeClair and Valle) had killed several
deer and had simply followed their trail to the cabin.

Badly outnumbered and caught by surprise, the Astorians had little choice but to extend these visitors their hospitality. With their
weapons always within reach, they barbecued buffalo steaks, which
the Arapahays devoured throughout the day in gargantuan quantities.
By nightfall, the Indians were sated and threw up two breastworks of
logs where the party, obviously weary, bedded down for the night. The
Astorians invited the chief and his deputy to sleep in their hut.

Stuart hadn't forgotten the Shoshone account of Arapahos mur-
dering Champlain in his sleep nor Miller's claim that he had been
victimized by these natives. He made sure one of his party was awake
at all times to keep an eye on the guests, but their behavior, he conceded, "was far more regular and decent than we had any reason to
expect from a war party."

In the morning with their hosts' acquiescence, they took a good
portion of the Astorians' remaining meat, selecting only the choice
cuts, and begged and cajoled their hosts for ammunition with no suc-

cess. "We are poor now," Irving has their chief saying, "and are obliged to go on foot, but we will soon come back laden with booty, and all mounted on horseback, with scalps hanging at our bodies. We will then give each of you a horse to keep you from being tired on your journey."

"Well, when you bring the horses, you shall have the ammunition, not before," Stuart responded.

Having been refused, they good-naturedly relinquished their demands and, as a gift, left the whites a crude map of the region presumably drawn on an animal skin. By midmorning, to the Astorians' great relief, they left peaceably on their mission of retribution.

No sooner had they departed than Stuart and the others sat down to reassess their situation. With the Crows, whom they'd followed through South Pass, several days' ride to the west and the Arapahays—"the villains who robbed Mr. Miller and the hunters," Stuart wrote—to the north, their winter camp suddenly seemed vulnerable. The traders agreed that the good conduct of their visitors was merely a ploy to lull their suspicions. Stuart and the others were convinced that the Arapahays would later return with reinforcements and, Stuart noted, "surprise us when least on guard."

Perhaps they were overreacting, but the traders now believed they had no choice but to move on. "We determined to abandon our Chateau of Indolence as soon as we can finish the dressing of a sufficiency of leather for moccasins (and leggings) . . . that we may be better able to withstand the severity of the weather," Stuart wrote that evening. "Our present intention is to extricate ourselves out of the paws of our rascally neighbors by going a very considerable distance down this river."

As he had in the past when the party's prospects appeared bleakest, Stuart seized upon a positive note. In studying the Arapahay map with Crooks and McClellan, Stuart now believed they were on the Rapid River (Niobrara), not the Cheyenne. If that was the case, the traders could proceed by canoe downstream to the Missouri without having to worry about the Sioux. First, of course, they had to settle on a new winter camp. Stuart was hopeful it would be situated on the banks of the Missouri.

CHAPTER 31

WINTER MARCH

BY AN EXTRAORDINARY ACT OF WILL, STUART AND THE others set out again, leaving behind their comfortable retreat to troop across the high plains of today's eastern Wyoming in early winter, following the southeasterly course of what the traders once again believed was the Rapid River.

They hastily completed dressing their leather, and by December 13, two days after the Arapahays' departure, were again on the move. At least they still had Rosinante to carry their remaining buffalo meat and gear. The Indians either thought the animal too feeble to bother with, Stuart surmised, or planned to return for her.

The barren, windswept country they traversed was covered with as much as a foot of snow. Even so, they averaged twenty miles the first few days of their march. The snow made passage almost unbearably uncomfortable as the crust was not hard enough to support their weight, and their moccasins afforded little protection from the cold and wet. "As a result our feet are excessively sore, which make us begin to think of taking up our quarters in the first eligible situation and rather than die on the march, fall valiantly on the field of Mars," Stuart noted.

Still, they soldiered on, welcoming a thaw that began on December 16 and continued for several days, melting some of the snow. When the temperature dropped again, they frequently walked on the now-frozen river rather than cut out a path along the snow-covered banks.

To the southwest, the traders could see present-day Laramie Peak and the Laramie Range. These mountains marked the transition along the Oregon Trail from the Great Plains to the Rockies. The California- and Oregon-bound emigrants called them the Black Hills because of the darkly hued pines that covered their slopes. They were the last mountains the eastbound Astorians would see on their journey.

At night, the traders dried their moccasins over the fire and warmed their near-frozen feet and hands. It was a wonder that no one on the expedition became a victim of frostbite. For all their discomfort, though, they were fortunate to have this watercourse to follow eastward. Without the river's life-sustaining resources, they never would have gotten across what explorers Zebulon Pike and Stephen Long would later call the Great American Desert, and certainly not in winter.

Trees covered much of the river bottom. The timber provided shelter and firewood—and food, at least for the horse. Since the grass was largely buried under snow, the traders had nothing to feed Rosinante but cottonwood bark and willow tops.

Though Stuart and the others sometimes had to break through the ice to retrieve it, there was a continuing source of water, and ample game. In the winter, buffalo, antelope, deer, and what Stuart called ibex—mountain sheep—were all drawn to the river bottoms. Nearly every day Jones, Valle, and LeClair managed to bring fresh meat back to the camp.

Frustrated with its meandering, the traders made the mistake of leaving the river on December 18 in hopes of shortening their route but soon found the going so rough they returned to their original course. For the remainder of their journey, they wouldn't depart again from what Merrill J. Mattes called the Great Platte River Road, this natural corridor Stuart's party had discovered linking the Missouri and the gateway through the Shining Mountains, South Pass.

BY DECEMBER 20, they had made it through today's Lower Canyon of the Platte, a stretch that was not dissimilar from The Dalles on the Columbia. "These narrows are composed of high rocky hills and bluffs and precipices on each side of the river, on the declivities of which are numerous cedar interspersed with Pitch Pines affording an asylum to great numbers of ibex and deer," Stuart wrote. The country was level now. The snow that tormented them had miraculously disappeared. "The weather has every appearance of a mild autumn," he noted.

On the morning of December 22, Stuart noted the natural attractions of a tongue of land created by the convergence of today's Laramie River and the North Platte. "Soon after leaving camp the country opened greatly to the eastward and a well-wooded stream apparently of considerable magnitude came in from the southwest," he wrote. This was the first recorded description of the juncture of a well-traveled north-south Indian trail: the Laramie River and the Platte River corridor. It would become one of the most important crossroads on the American frontier.

To seasoned traders such as Stuart, Crooks, and McClellan this was an ideal site for a trading emporium. It would be another twenty-one years, however, before the fur traders William Sublette and Robert Campbell built the first post here—Fort William. In 1841, the AFC followed with the adobe-walled trading post called Fort John. Eight years later at the height of the California gold rush, the U.S. military established Fort Laramie at this juncture to protect the thousands of emigrants bound for the gold fields.

In their wildest reveries, the Astorians could not have imagined the waves of humanity that would pass through here within their lifetimes. "Up to this morning 476 wagons have gone past this point, and this is but an advance guard. At Fort Laramie we switched to a pack train, passing '10,000 wagons' before reaching South Pass," a witness to the surge of migration in 1849 wrote. "Every state, and I presume almost every town and county in the United States is now represented in this part of the world. Wagons of all patterns, sizes and description, drawn by bulls, cows, oxen, jackasses, mules and horses are daily seen rolling along towards the Pacific guarded by walking arsenals. . . . Such a migration as is now passing over the plains has not had its parallel in any age."

BY CHRISTMAS EVE, Stuart and the others were becoming anxious. During the day's twenty-seven-mile march they noticed that the timber was gradually disappearing. Stopping for the night among a few cottonwoods near today's Mitchell, Nebraska, they didn't see a single tree to the east. Fortunately, there were still plenty of buffalo. Stuart noted several big herds grazing on the river bottom. Scattered among the buffalo were a number of wild horses feeding with them.

Christmas passed unnoticed and uncelebrated. That day, the traders hiked twenty-one miles over sand hills and barren prairie, managing to retrieve just enough driftwood from the riverbed to build a fire when they finally stopped for the night. To the south Stuart took note of "remarkably rugged and bluffy hills." These were Scotts Bluffs, a familiar landmark on the emigrant trail. To the Astorians, who had seen peaks that extended several miles into the sky, they weren't especially noteworthy, but after traveling for days over monotonous, level prairies, the emigrants were often roused by the spectacle. "How can I describe the scene that now bursts upon us," a California-bound traveler named Thomas Eastin wrote in 1849. "Scotts Bluffs lay to the north . . . tower, bastion, dome and battlement vie in their majesty before us."

Conditions worsened the following day with a sharp drop in temperature. Though no snow had fallen since they left the Chateau, the traders again found themselves trekking through knee-deep drifts. Finding driftwood was near impossible. "Not a twig to be seen eastward," Stuart wrote on December 26. Save for a few "old scabby bulls" that probably had been run off by younger, stronger rivals, the buffalo had seemingly vanished as well. The traders couldn't continue much farther under these conditions.

That evening, before they lost the light, Stuart and the others climbed a hill northeast of their campsite. In the clear, pale light of a cold winter afternoon they could see at least fifty miles eastward. Not a tree or a buffalo was visible.

The following morning, Stuart called the members of the expedition together to assess their next move, given what he termed "the wretchedness of our situation." Ahead was "such an inhospitable waste as even to be deserted by every kind of quadruped." In attempting to cross this desolate stretch of open, snow-covered prairie, there was a good chance they'd be overtaken by a blizzard. They, in fact, had been expecting a snowstorm daily for the past week. Without shelter, firewood, or food they wouldn't have a chance of surviving such a storm. The alternative was to return upriver where there were buffalo and firewood for their support.

There was another compelling reason to turn back, Stuart wrote. In the past few days, the river had divided into multiple channels, the riverbed widening to nearly a mile. "This being so different from the character we ever heard of the Rapid River; our having southed so much of late and its appearance coinciding exactly with that of the Great River Platte, we have strong inducements to believe that we are on the main branch of the last mentioned stream," he wrote. If that was the case, the traders needed timber to build canoes—timber they could readily obtain by turning back.

Stuart put the matter to a vote: continue on or turn back. By a margin of five to two, the traders decided to return up the river.

ON THE LAST day of 1812, Stuart's party took up residence at their second winter camp close to the north bank of the Platte a few miles east of today's Torrington, Wyoming. By midday, they had built a shelter, butchered the four buffalo they'd killed the previous day, and scaffolded the meat. The next morning, Stuart declared a New Year's Day holiday, describing the modest celebration in his journal:

> Friday 1st, January 1813—Was solely devoted to the gratification of our appetite, all work was suspended. We destroyed an immoderate quantity of buffalo tongues [puddings] and the choicest of the meat, making it a rule to eat the best meat first so that we would always have the best.

Their stock of Virginia tobacco had long since disappeared, but in commemoration of the New Year, they cut up Miller's tobacco pouch and smoked it.

CHAPTER 32

SURRENDER

ON THE COLUMBIA, THE REMAINING ASTORIANS HELD their own New Year's celebration, a characteristically boisterous, drunken reverie that extended well past the holiday. "Labor of every kind was laid aside and a treat given to all hands, that they might make merry on the New Year," Duncan McDougall wrote in the post's journal on Friday, January 1, 1813. Three days later, several of the men, including William Cannan, one of the blacksmiths, were so hung over they were unable to work.

In the six months since Robert Stuart's departure, the situation had become increasingly grim at Astoria. Food was in such short supply that, by January, the men were subsisting entirely on strict rations of flour, occasional salmon, and whatever game the post's hunters managed to kill. On January 9, McDougall reported purchasing four fresh salmon from some Indians. It was probably the last fish "that may be seen this season," he lamented. "It requires now the greatest economy in giving out our little provisions in order that it shall last until the season of fish may arrive."

McDougall would soon have many more mouths to feed. On January 16, "Fat" Mackenzie arrived unexpectedly with most of his party. Mackenzie had been wintering at his newly built post on the Clearwater River, a few miles from its convergence with the Snake near present-day Lewiston, Idaho. It's difficult to understand why a trader with Mackenzie's experience should have chosen the Clearwater site. According to Mackenzie's clerk, Alfred Seton, not a tree was to be seen in the area. Consequently, Mackenzie's men had to build the post—a store and two cabins—out of driftwood. Worse, this was poor beaver country. The local Indians, the Nez Perce, with whom Lewis and Clark had established a strong friendship, flatly refused to trap for the traders or to allow whites to trap in their territory. Game was so scarce that the traders were reduced to eating horses they secured from the Indians. By November, the Nez Perce had begun asking so much in return for their animals that Mackenzie feared their trade goods would be depleted before spring.

In late November, Mackenzie made the hard, four-day ride to John Clarke's post on the Spokane River, Fort Spokane, to confer with Clarke about conditions at the Clearwater post. His arrival coincided with that of John George McTavish, who was now running the NWC's rival Spokane House.

The PFC partners built Fort Spokane in close proximity to the NWC's Spokane House as an indication they weren't prepared to cede an inch of trading territory to the Canadians. Fort Spokane was also meant to serve as the regional trading headquarters for today's eastern Washington and Oregon; western Montana, where Russell Farnham and Ross Cox were trading with the Flathead Indians; and northern Idaho.

The Canadians had stood by as the Americans aggressively expanded their trading network. Now, it was the Nor'Westers' turn to respond. McTavish had come to Fort Spokane bearing news he knew would unsettle his rivals. The United States and Great Britain were at war, he informed Clarke and Mackenzie, producing a copy of James Madison's proclamation that had been sent to him from the NWC's interior headquarters, Fort William. McTavish also informed the PFC partners that a British ship, the *Isaac Todd*, would be arriving at the mouth of the Columbia in the spring on behalf of the NWC. McTavish would be joining her there.

This was the first that Clarke and Mackenzie had heard about the war, but the news was not unexpected. There had been talk of war well before either man departed for Astoria. A British ship, however, bound for the Columbia was cause for the utmost alarm. Though McTavish hadn't said so—according to Seton at least—the British clearly intended to seize Astoria as enemy property. And McTavish was coming to take the post over on behalf of the Nor'Westers.

No sooner had McTavish departed than Clarke and Mackenzie decided that Mackenzie and most of his party should return to Astoria immediately to alert McDougall of the *Isaac Todd*'s imminent arrival. Alfred Seton and a few men would stay behind to close down the Clearwater post and cache the trade goods and supplies.

WITHIN A FEW days of Mackenzie's January 16 arrival at Astoria, the fate of the PFC and Columbia River headquarters was sealed by the only two partners then present at the post. Fearing that Astor would be unable to send help, McDougall and Mackenzie called a war council, to which the clerks of the factory were invited pro forma, as they had no vote in the deliberations. Careful to cover his own tracks, McDougall made no mention of the council in his official headquarters log. One of the attending clerks, however, Gabriel Franchere, summarized the meeting in his own journal: "Having maturely weighed our situation . . . we concluded to abandon the establishment in the ensuing spring, or, at the latest in the beginning of summer."

The first British cannon had yet to be fired on the Columbia, yet McDougall and Mackenzie, without waiting to confer with any of their partners, had decided to surrender the fort and, in effect, the entire Pacific Northwest trade to their former employers. Of course, there was the off chance that one of Astor's ships would slip through the British barricades—neither Mackenzie nor McDougall knew about the *Forester*—and arrive in time. "The only hope to be cherished that a ship shall be here in season is that Mr. Astor may have anticipated the event and arranged accordingly," McDougall wrote on January 26. McDougall thought the prospect so unlikely that he had already begun implementing plans to cease all trade and shut down the PFC's operations.

CHAPTER 33

DOWN THE PLATTE

STUART'S PARTY PASSED THE REMAINING WINTER months without another visit from the Indians. "We . . . found ourselves once more in a snug hut, where we remained in peace and plenty," Stuart reported. The traders had made the right decision in turning back rather than continuing on. At this second winter camp on the right bank of the North Platte, there was all the game, water, and timber they needed.

In hopes that the Platte would transport them to the Missouri, the eastbound Astorians spent much of January and February hollowing out two cottonwood logs to serve as canoes. Stuart and his companions knew little about this broad, muddy river. The largest tributary of the Missouri, its name comes from the French word for flat or shallow, while its headwaters were rumored to be in the high mountains of Spanish New Mexico (in fact, they are in northern Colorado). From there it extends one thousand miles across today's southeastern and central Wyoming and Nebraska, entering the Missouri at a juncture that marks the beginning of the Upper Missouri country.

On their way up the Missouri, Lewis and Clark had attempted to enter the Platte's main channel in a bright red pirogue paddled by expert canoe men, but it had been so buffeted by the strong, thick current that they had turned back after little more than a mile. Following the same Missouri River route, Hunt's party had breakfasted on one of the islands which lay at the mouth of this mysterious river that drained much of the land obtained in the Louisiana Purchase.

By March 8, the ice was gone from the Platte. The traders proudly

Approaching Chimney Rock *by William H. Jackson.*

launched their canoes. The smaller and lighter of the craft floated easily downstream, as buoyant as a cork, but the larger canoe, which carried Stuart and McClellan among its four passengers, grounded on
one of the river's numerous sandbars after only a few hundred yards.

Still hopeful, Stuart and the slightly built McClellan climbed out,
certain that without their weight the canoe would clear the impedi-
ment. It did—and promptly got caught on a second sandbar.

Frustrated—if this scheme didn't work they would have to
resume their march to the Missouri—the traders spent the better
part of the day towing the craft downstream through cold water—
recently melted snow that rarely came above their knees—all the
while being careful to circumvent frequent patches of quicksand. By
midafternoon when the weather turned frigid and Stuart and the
others decided to camp in an abandoned Indian shelter, they'd come
only eight miles. "Finding an Indian pen sufficient to screen us from
the severity of weather we stopped in it, determined to wait out the
rise of the water," Stuart wrote.

After five days of waiting, the Platte had risen only three inches,
but Stuart had devised a new scheme. On March 14, he sent one of

the Canadians back to the second winter quarters to fetch "our good old Rosinante." After having been put briefly out to pasture, the poor animal was again pressed into service as a beast of burden.

On this second attempt to launch the vessels, only Stuart, Crooks, McClellan, Miller, and a small part of the baggage would be transported in the canoes, two men to a canoe. Meanwhile, Valle, LeClair, and Jones were to proceed on foot with Rosinante carrying the bulk of the baggage.

They set out again resolutely on the morning of March 15. A storm the previous night caused the river to rise another four inches, and at first, the canoes proceeded smartly downstream. Once the travelers reached the juncture of the Platte and present-day Horse Creek, however, the river widened and became so shallow that Stuart and the others only managed to reach an abandoned Indian shelter on the north bank after great exertion. There, "seven miles past our last station . . . we found our people who had gone by land," Stuart wrote that evening. "Here we took up our lodgings pretty much tired of this new mode of inland navigation."

So much for the canoes. Stuart later summarized the failure: "We made two canoes expecting to get down by water in the spring freshes, but to our great mortification the river did not rise more than three inches." Thus ended the first recorded attempt to navigate the Platte. It would be another twenty years, Merrill Mattes notes, before "the fur captains again attempted to put the Platte to work when it was swollen with melting snow from the Rockies."

THE TRADERS HAD begun their journey revitalized from the two-month layover and confident they would soon be in St. Louis. But Stuart and the others still underestimated the distance from their second winter camp to the Missouri. The country seemed to go on forever, and they hadn't counted on having to proceed by foot.

The abrupt changes in weather didn't help. Spring on the Great Plains is a season of extremes. The weather in mid-March was the worst the party had experienced throughout the winter. A blizzard hit on March 16 and continued through the next day. Several days later, a north wind "blew with violence and was withal so cold that our bedclothes appeared as if converted into a sieve for we were on the bare prairie," said Stuart. After several days of numbing cold and unrelenting wind, Miller's feet were so badly blistered he was completely unfit for travel. Fortunately, Jones and the Canadians killed three buffalo bulls that had wandered near their camp, and the Astorians made a comfortable shelter from their hides, where they could hold up until conditions improved.

By the March 20, they had crossed over into present-day Nebraska and were well within the western perimeters of the Great Plains and the Platte River valley, which would later become the central corridor of America's westward expansion. As such, it took several names: the Oregon Trail, which led from Independence, Missouri, to Oregon's Willamette Valley; the California Trail, as this road was known during the Gold Rush; the Mormon Trail, by which the followers of Brigham Young made their way to the Great Salt Lake; and the Holy Road, as the Sioux called it.

Stuart's narrative was the first written record of the trail and the surrounding region. Even though he predated the westbound immigrants by thirty years or more, the pristine country he witnessed during this 1813 crossing closely resembled the terrain the pioneers would encounter coming in the opposite direction. "Nothing but a boundless prairie plentifully stocked with animals appears before us," he wrote on March 22, "and the river running east south east so shallow as makes us happy at having abandoned our canoes for its bed for the most part is upwards of a mile wide and the sandbars so numerous and flat that it would require more water than we have any right to expect to have made it fit for our purposes."

This prairie ocean, as Stuart described the landscape unfolding before him, rose and fell in broad swells that extended to the distant horizons. In passing through the region in spring, he was seeing the Platte River valley when the dynamics of its complex ecosystem come into full play. As the remaining snow melted, the dark, rich prairie loam along the river bottom bloomed with wildflowers, buffalo grass, and straw and grass that would be waist high by the time the Astorians reached the Missouri. Soon the sand hills to the north would become carpeted with sand bluestem, switchgrass, blue grama, sunflowers, and wild rose.

Stuart proved a diligent and astute observer of the unfolding countryside and its vegetation and wildlife, taking time on most days to record in his journals important observations about the landscape. At the time, there were few trees along this stretch of river bottom, and those were mostly cottonwoods which in spring produce blizzards of cottonlike tufts. Oddly, though, the islands that choked the river were often densely forested with a variety of trees, all faintly verdant now with new leafage. Observing the riparian forest, Stuart catalogued elm, box elder, cedar, pine, white ash, white willow, and an almost impenetrable undergrowth of what he called arrow wood, which was probably dogwood.

From the soil, the traders extracted roots the Oto Indians called toe and the Canadians pommes de terre. "They are but seldom larger then hens' eggs with a rough warty brown skin, are never more than six inches deep in the earth and when boiled resemble very much in taste the sweet potato," Stuart wrote.

As the Astorians preceded downriver, great cacophonous clouds of wildfowl—geese, brants, swans, cranes, and "an endless variety of ducks" returning from their winter habitat—alighted in the many swamps and marshes along the Platte. Traversing the bottoms, the Astorians raised pheasants, "or as they are called in this country prairie hens," Stuart noted. He spotted oldfield larks, long-billed curlews, and scores of wild turkey and sharp-tailed grouse.

Not one ordinarily to boast about his prowess as a marksman, Stuart claimed that in hunting for supper on what he called Cedar Island, he killed three swans and a goose with a single shot from a distance of 170 yards.

Game was as profuse as the bird life. There were still elk on the plains as well as deer, and more buffalo than the Astorians had seen anywhere on their journey. "For the past 3 days march, the country is . . . literally covered with buffalo," Stuart observed in his journal entry for March 26.

That afternoon, Stuart's party crossed today's Blue Creek, which entered the Platte from the north. Here in 1855, General William Selby Harney would attack a Brule Sioux village, killing more than one hundred men, women, and children after refusing the Brule chief's surrender offer, thereby earning the nickname "Squaw Killer Harney."

Three miles west of Blue Creek, Stuart took notice of a sizable stream that entered the river from the south. "It is thickly wooded a short distance from its mouth, but with what we could not distinguish . . . For a considerable distance above but more particularly below its juncture the river bluffs are very near and sometimes constitute its banks. They are composed principally of blue limestone and possess many cedars on which account we call the last mentioned branch, Cedar Creek—saw sixty wild horses."

Merrill Mattes maintains that this was the first mention in literature of what would become known as Ash Hollow, a wooded canyon that converges on the Platte and was one of the most important way stations on the emigrant trail. "Here at long last was an abundant supply of firewood and the most copious supply of pure water this side of the Missouri," Mattes wrote. "Here were often found peaceful encampments of Sioux Indians, noble-looking and colorful savages who did not belie the romantic notions of easterners. Here also was a wealth of sinister campfire legend, inspired by many actual incidents of ambush and violence within these canyon walls."

As for the wild horses, Stuart claimed, in a postscript to his journals, that he and his companions captured and tamed one of the animals, but he makes no mention of this in his daily notations.

THE TRADERS HADN'T seen any sign of another human being since their visit from the Arapahay war party in December, but on March 29, while collecting driftwood for fuel in the sand hills some seven miles northwest of the present-day city of North Platte, Nebraska, they discovered a number of logs that had been cut by an axe or hatchet. The cutter, or cutters, could have been Indians or whites; there was no way of telling. "We . . . are at a loss to say at what season or who the people were who left these vestiges," Stuart wrote.

The following morning they passed several deserted Indian villages, one of them of considerable magnitude. Stuart paused long enough to describe the settlements in some detail:

> From all appearance [these camps] were occupied last fall by people who seem to have valued the animals they killed, for we found numerous marks of their having stretched skins; all the buffalo skulls had the brains taken out; the dung lying in heaps contrary to the custom of wolves convinced us that even the paunches had been preserved and at the last camp we found a number of cobs of

Indian corn—from all of which we suppose these signs were made by Pawnees or Otos.

This was likely a Pawnee village, since the Otos lived along the more easterly reaches of the Platte. Among the largest of the Plains tribes—in the early 1800s they numbered between ten thousand and fourteen thousand—the Pawnees "seem to be a sober, good kind of people," a writer for the Louisiana *Gazette* noted in 1812. "The men are not so stout as the Osage and Kansas, nor so active and enterprising, though they are handsome and well formed; the women are ugly and filthy but very ingenious and industrious."

The Pawnees were distinct from other Indians in that they spoke a language from the Hokan-Siouan linguistic stock that was little used by other tribes. Though they dressed much like other Plains tribes, the Pawnee wore their hair in an unusual way: the scalp lock dressed by buffalo fat so that it stood erect. Until the practice was stopped by the great Pawnee chief Pitalesharo in the early 1800s, these Indians occasionally sacrificed a virgin to the god of vegetation, one of the few examples of human sacrifice among North American natives outside Mexico.

Known as the "Wolf People" because of their close identification with this animal, the Pawnee had much the same relationship, that of a quasi ally, with the Spanish as the Blackfoot maintained with the British. In fact, in 1806 when the explorer Zebulon Pike visited a large Pawnee village on the banks of the Republican River, he learned that a large force of Spanish cavalry from Santa Fe had been there only weeks earlier. The Spanish commander had presented the Pawnee with numerous gifts and a Spanish flag that flew over the village, one Pike ultimately convinced the Indians to replace with Old Glory.

Like the Blackfoot, the Pawnee were fierce fighters. They often clashed with their traditional enemies, the Sioux and Cheyenne, and in later years terrorized fur traders after more and more whites encroached on their hunting grounds to the south. Josiah Gregg, author of *Commerce of the Prairies*, characterizes them as "among the most formidable enemies of the Santa Fe traders." Early on, though, the Pawnee were generally friendly toward Americans. Stuart and company had nothing to fear from these Indians.

FOLLOWING AN INDIAN trace along the Platte's left bank, Stuart noted that the countryside was changing markedly. To the south, there were hills and large forests, which seemed to indicate the travelers were nearing the end of the plains. Antelope and the scattering herds of wild horses had disappeared altogether, "but our beloved friend the buffalo still remain to comfort our solitary wanderings," Stuart noted.

Thunder, lightning, and heavy rain impeded their progress for the next few days, but on April 3 they traveled twenty-five miles, encamping due south of present-day Lexington, Nebraska. There the Indian trace disappeared. Suspecting that the road resumed on the southern, or right, bank of the Platte, the Astorians the next morning crossed the river at a spot where it braided into ten channels. As usual the water was shallow, the quicksand so treacherous they almost lost Rosinante.

After regaining the trail, which soon split into numerous parallel paths, they came upon another village that was deserted except for three old Pawnee squaws living in a straw hut. Even though one of the Astorians, probably Valle or Crooks, spoke to them reassuringly in the language of their neighbors and friends the Otos, and Stuart offered them some dried meat in a demonstration of friendship, the women were terrified of their visitors. Throughout the Astorians' brief stay, they remained highly agitated, telling their visitors little they could comprehend except that there were white people at no great distance to the east. Stuart surmised that the old women had become sick and had been "abandoned to their fate by their savage relatives."

Encouraged by the news that whites were in the area, the travelers accelerated their pace, reaching the largest of the Platte's many islands on April 7. Stuart estimated that this landmark, which he named Grand Island—the name that remains today—was seventy-two miles long and perhaps twenty-four miles wide and described it as possessing "great bodies of timber, affording shelter and subsistence to a great many deer, some elk and a few beaver."

They had now, Stuart recognized, exceeded the eastern limits of the buffalo range. The herds had disappeared entirely. There was no sign even of their dung. Fortunately, the party still had a small stock of dried meat, and Jones and the Canadians were able to shoot deer as needed.

It appeared the region had experienced a severe winter. Snow still

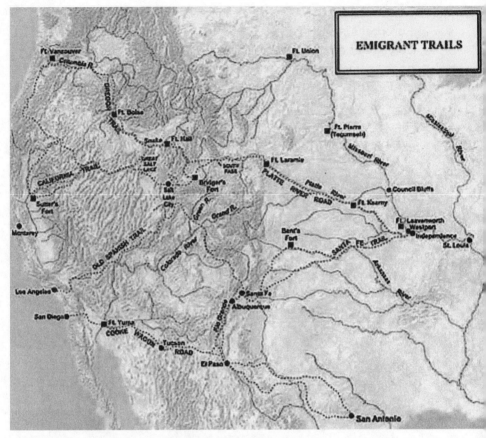

Map of emigrant trails.

clung to the hills to the north. The Pawnee villages along the Platte were all deserted. As was their custom every spring, the Indians had departed to follow the buffalo herds, which had migrated south to escape the cold.

But not all the Indians were off hunting buffalo. On April 10, Stuart's party was overtaken by a member of the Oto Nation. The tribe—whose name, for reasons which can only be imagined, means "lovers of sexual pleasure," according to Rollins—lived in permanent villages of oven-shaped, earth-covered lodges at the eastern end of the Platte. There they farmed and hunted the Salt Creek and Little Nemaha River valleys and the neighboring plains. They were also enthusiastic traders who had been dealing on a regular basis with Europeans since at least 1795, when Spanish traders based in St. Louis built a post in their territory. Both Crooks and McClellan had done business with the Otos before joining the PFC.

On April 11, Stuart sent Valle and Crooks back with the Oto to his village to gather news and determine their location. Soon after, the expedition arrived at the Loup Fork of the Platte, a clear, rapid stream some two hundred yards wide that came in from the north and would later prove difficult for the emigrants to ford because of its soft banks and quicksand. Along this river, Stuart was aware, the Pawnees had many of their major villages. The nearest, the Grand Pawnee village under the leadership of Long Hair, or Ku-taw-row, was the home of "about nine hundred warriors."

As Stuart noted in his journals, these Indians ranged as far west as the frontier villages of New Mexico hunting buffalo, but unlike the nomadic Plains Indians, the Pawnee maintained permanent villages, where they supplemented their hunting efforts with farming. Noted Stuart:

> These Indians come to their towns early in April, plant their corn, pumpkins and beans towards the end of May, stay till it is a certain height, when hoeing it, they then abandon it to the benign care of the All seeing Providence and return to the plains to pursue the humpbacked race. In August they again revisit their village and after gathering in the harvest [and] depositing [it] safely and secretly in excavations made for the purpose in the earth, they once more leave their homes for their favorite pursuit of the buffalo at which they employ themselves till the following April.

In the heart of Pawnee territory, the Astorians made camp at a large point of woods and waited for Valle and Crooks to return. In high spirits, Stuart reported that the party had traveled some twenty-eight miles, capping their day by killing a wild turkey for supper.

CROOKS AND VALLE caught up with the expedition shortly after sunrise on April 12. Anxious to overtake Stuart and the others, they had walked until well after sunset. Unable to find the camp in the darkness, they had slept nearby. By the first light, they appeared with news. The Otos, two families they had visited, told them that for the past year the United States and Great Britain had been at war. The Shawnee Prophet had sent a messenger offering them wampum to fight on the side of the British, but they declined, arguing pragmatically that they could make more by trapping beaver than by making war against the Americans.

Naturally, Stuart and the others found this information unsettling, but the Otos seemed confused and uncertain of their facts, Crooks explained. Perhaps they were wrong. Of more immediate interest to Stuart was something else Crooks and Valle had learned. The Otos also claimed that a white man, a trader named Francois Derouin, was living in their main village. "As to the distance of the town, they said we would not sleep more than two nights," Stuart wrote.

The traders set out immediately, traveling twenty miles downriver until a heavy downpour forced them to make camp at a point of woods on the Platte. On a cold April 13 after a dismal twenty-four-mile march though intermittent sleet and hail, Stuart's party reached the Oto settlement. The village, which was made up of some thirty lodges each housing from two to four families, was set on a hill several hundred yards from the right bank of the river. The residents immediately took the visitors to meet Derouin and Jean Baptiste Antoine Roy, another trader from St. Louis. Both had recently arrived at the Oto camp after a six-week journey up the Missouri from St. Louis.

The St. Louis traders confirmed what Stuart termed "the disagreeable intelligence of a war between America and Great Britain . . . but in such a confused manner was it related that we could comprehend but little."

Roy and Derouin seemed more concerned with the weather in the region and its impact on the fur trade than the war. The snow, Derouin complained, had been four and a half feet deep, two feet deeper than normal, and no outdoor work could be accomplished without snowshoes.

In exchange for Rosinante, who had served them so well, the Astorians bartered for enough provisions from the traders to get to Fort Osage, a government trading post on the Missouri, which had been built in 1808. As part of the bargain, Derouin threw in a canoe as well, or at least the makings of a canoe, since no extra vessel was available.

The Otos on the traders' payroll soon began building the craft, which consisted of five elk and buffalo hides stretched together with strong sinews and drawn over and made fast to a twenty-foot-long frame. Normally, the work wouldn't have taken more than a day or two, but on April 14, it had snowed and had been so cold during the day that not much could be done beyond putting the hides in the Platte to soak.

STUART TOOK ADVANTAGE of the delay to explore the village. The Otos, he learned, lived here with members of the Missouri Nation, a tribe that had been nearly wiped out after an attack by the Sac and Fox Indians; the surviving Missouris had later joined up with the Otos, who had lost many of their own people in a smallpox epidemic in 1800. They had later begun sharing the same village, and by 1813, Stuart noted, the two tribes were all but indistinguishable. "They have resided together for a number of years and by marriage have become so intermixed that we may at this day justly call them the same people; more particularly as their habits, manners, customs and pursuits are exactly the same."

By his estimate, the Otos and the Missouris were of equal force and could together muster about two hundred warriors. More important, from a trader's vantage point, they annually produced about 250 packs of high-quality pelts.

The Oto lodges in particular interested him in that they were unlike the Indian dwellings he had seen elsewhere on his journey. With the number of new lodges being built to accommodate an influx of expected summer residents, Stuart had a firsthand opportunity to witness the various phases of the complex construction process and produced a detailed analysis of the tribal dwellings:

> From a pole stuck in that spot of ground intended for the center of the fabric, a cord of upwards of 40 feet is extended, which carrying round the extremity is marked every ten feet by the insertion of a

small stick in the earth making an area of at least 100 feet in circumference. Forked poles eight feet high and four inches in diameter are next put firmly in the ground, taking the place of the pegs and marking the extreme of the circle. Across these are laid straight pieces of wood of the same size, and others considerably smaller, having one end in the earth are leaned against the last. Six string forks are then set up, halfway between the extremes and the center; twelve feet high on which powerful beams are placed as before, serving as a support to 120 poles running from the first elevation to the middle where a hole two feet wide is left to omit the smoke.

Willow are laid across the last poles everywhere with a good covering of straw firmly attached thereto and one foot of earth being tramped down hard over all completes the mansion, excepting the entrance, from whence runs out an erection of similar materials seven feet high, six feet wide and ten long. The door is generally an elk or buffalo hide. The floor is one and half feet lower than the earth outside, and for a fireplace the ground in the center of the building is scraped away so as to make it the lowest place in the lodge and from near it a pole surpassing in height any put in the roof is put out at the chimney where are suspended their medicine bags and war budgets carefully concealed in innumerable wrappers which effectively protect them from the influence of the weather.

BY THE EVENING of April 15, the craft was completed. Stuart again admired the Otos' craftsmanship. "Our canoe . . . [is] composed of poles and willows 20 feet long, 4 feet wide and 1½ feet deep making a vessel somewhat shaped like a boat, very steady and with the aid of a little mud of the seams, remarkably tight."

Despite a nasty, gusting wind that roiled the surface of the Platte, the traders departed early the following morning, leaving Rosinante with her new masters. On this, their third attempt to navigate the Platte, they were successful. On Sunday, April 18, 1813, Robert Stuart and his six companions emerged from the mouth of the Platte into the rapid, muddy currents of the Missouri, bound now for St. Louis six hundred miles downriver.

CHAPTER 34

ST. LOUIS AND NEW YORK

THEIR NEWLY CONSTRUCTED CANOE WASN'T STURDY enough to deal with the fast-moving, flood-swollen waters of the Missouri. With crude oars that Stuart and the others had fashioned themselves, they did their best to avoid trees and branches that extended into the elevated waters of the Missouri. Some were immobile—so-called planters. Others (sawyers) had been torn from their roots and floated on the river's surface or just beneath it. If struck, they could split and sink a frail skin canoe in an instant.

Stuart was well aware of the danger. "A rapid current . . . the water intolerably muddy, and every bend of it pretty well supplied with Sawyers and Planters occasioned by the falling in of the banks, which carrying the trees along with them, the roots become immovably fixed in the bed of the river and form an object of considerable risk to persons unaccustomed to such navigation."

Crooks and McClellan pointed out familiar landmarks as the current swept the traders downstream. On April 19 they traveled more than sixty miles, encamping across from the Bald-Pated Prairie, so named by Lewis and Clark because of its barren, treeless hills. Confronted with strong head winds and some nasty weather, their pace slowed the next few days as they floated by the Little Nemaha River, the Black Snake Hills, and the Nodaway River, the site of Hunt's winter camp.

On April 22, they pulled ashore in midmorning near today's St. Joseph, Missouri, to repair their leaky craft. "We passed the remainder of the day making a new frame for our canoe as [ours] . . . had become unfit for the purpose for which it was originally intended," wrote Stuart, who sent two hunters out that afternoon to bring back dinner. They soon returned with a deer and four wild turkeys.

The new frame wasn't much of an improvement. Fortunately, at a deserted traders' camp, where they stopped for the night on April 23, Stuart and his companions found two abandoned old canoes. Requisitioning the larger of the two, they reached Fort Osage the following afternoon.

Setting out up the Missouri in 1804, Lewis and Clark had selected this site as a likely spot for a fort. Six years later, Clark had Fort Osage built by a company of army dragoons under Captain Eli Clemson. Set on a spectacular bluff overlooking the Missouri, the triangular post was the only government garrison west of the Mississippi. It had been constructed to counteract British influence and, as Stuart noted, to reduce "the turbulent Kansa [nation] to a proper sense of their true relation in which Indians stand with their civilized neighbors."

These Indians, the Kansa or Kaw people, were then in possession of much of present-day northern and eastern Kansas, which they fiercely defended from intrusions by whites or neighboring tribes. They frequently robbed American traders who visited them, then brazenly sold their furs to their British rivals. According to David Lavender, after Meriwether Lewis had been appointed Governor of Louisiana Territory, he became so angered by the Kaw's conduct that he sanctioned a policy by which the government encouraged other tribes to make war on them.

At the garrison, the returning traders received a friendly reception. "We . . . were hospitably entertained by Lt. Brownson [First Lieutenant John Brownson] who commands in the absence of Major Clemson. He furnished us very generously with a sufficiency of pork and flour to carry us to St. Louis."

The lieutenant, a genial, young Vermonter, confirmed that war with the British had been underway for ten months. His account of the conflict amounted to a grim litany of defeat. The entire upper Great Lakes region, including Detroit and the great American fur-trading factory on Mackinac Island, was entirely in the hands of the enemy. The British and a number of Canadian fur traders led by the imposing, red-headed Scot, Robert Dickson, had enlisted the Indian

Elizabeth and Robert Stuart, circa 1848.
COLLECTION OF THE AUTHOR.

tribes of the upper Mississippi, including the Sioux, in their cause. Dickson, in fact, had helped to recruit fourteen hundred Indians to fight on the side of the British at Detroit and more recently led another eight hundred warriors by canoe across northern Wisconsin and Michigan. The citizens of St. Louis feared they might be Dickson's next target. Certainly, Lieutenant Brownson was on the alert for any enemy activity on the Missouri.

Ironically, Ramsay Crooks had worked for Dickson as a clerk at Mackinac when Crooks first started in the Indian trade, a coincidence he surely had the wisdom not to mention to the young American lieutenant at such a perilous time. As far as Brownson knew, the Scottish trader and his companions could have been British spies.

On April 26, Stuart's party set off again down the muddy Missouri, passing Fiery Prairie and Bonne Femme Fatale Creek, the Osage River, the Indian pictographs of Tavern Rock, and the old, long-deserted Osage village, which Lewis and Clark had reckoned was 256 miles above the Missouri's mouth. As they neared St. Louis, they could smell wood smoke from rough frontier settlements where unkempt children waved from the riverbank and gaunt, hard-eyed men and women looked up apprehensively at the passing strangers.

These "Christian settlements extend 198 miles up the Missouri," Stuart wrote. They'd been "made principally by emigrants from Kentucky who [if it had not been for the present war] would have advanced much farther, but at present content themselves within the fortifications they have constructed on account of the Indians and raise a bare sufficiency for the subsistence of their families."

IT WAS A LITTLE before sunset on April 30, 1813, when Stuart's party reached St. Louis, landing their canoe on the long sandbar at the river's edge where the barges, keelboats, and other canoes and pirogues tied up. In recording the moment, Stuart took note of the group's extraordinary good fortune. Not only had he and the other six members of the expedition survived many dangers, hardships, and fatigues—but "we were . . . all in the most perfect health after a voyage of 10 months from Astoria. We underwent . . . may I say, all the privations human nature is capable of."

The arrival of Stuart and his companions caused a sensation. Theirs was the first intelligence of Hunt's expedition in almost two years and the first news of Astor's establishment on the Columbia to reach this hub of the expanding American empire. In the taverns, members of the Missouri militia, Indian traders, and merchants in tall hats and frock coats—many of them Hunt's acquaintances or old friends of Crooks, Miller, and McClellan—stood them to drinks and pressed them for news about their journey and the fur trade of the far west.

What most captured the imaginations of many of those who pumped the returning traders for news was the electrifying information that there was a more southerly route to the Rockies and beyond that could be traveled entirely by wagon. For Indian traders accustomed to the painfully slow passage up the Missouri by keelboat—and frequent harassment by the Kaws, the Sioux, and other Indians along the way—this was priceless information, especially now that the upper Missouri was under the control of the British and their native allies.

The editor of the weekly Missouri *Gazette*, Joseph Charless, ran a brief item about Hunt's trip and Stuart's expedition in his May 8 issue but devoted the entire front page and half of the second to the story on May 15, drawing principally on interviews with Stuart and Crooks. "No other single item, war stories included, ever received comparable emphasis in the *Gazette*," David Lavender noted. "Today we can only guess at the excited talk which the account released like a heady elixir in St. Louis; the speculations about the Far West . . . Lewis and Clark all over again—renewed visions of an untouched continent waiting to be exploited."

Never much of a self-promoter, Stuart recounted some of the highlights of the return expedition in his low-key, reticent fashion, failing to mention how he had refused to leave Crooks behind to die despite the demands of the others in the party; how at gunpoint he had thwarted the cannibalistic inclinations of at least one of his starving comrades; how on more than one occasion he had rallied his companions, who had been willing simply to lie down and die; or how his restraint in not retaliating against the fleeing Crow horse thieves had likely kept the traders from being killed. Nor apparently did he mention—for reasons that probably had more to do with embarrassment than modesty—getting lost in pursuit of Miller's River.

In his self-edited account of the return journey, Stuart related the story of John Day going "perfectly insane"; the fortunate meeting with Miller, Hoback, and the others on the Snake; and the loss of the party's horses to the Crows with their "unbounded insolence." As a result, he explained, the expedition, having by Stuart's estimates already traveled 1,704 miles, had to continue on for an even greater distance by foot—much of the journey through entirely uncharted wilderness.

Wrote Charless:

Some idea of the situation of those men may be conceived, when we take into consideration that they were now on foot, and had a journey of 2,000 before them, 1500 of which was entirely unknown as they intended and prosecuted it considerably south of Messrs. Lewis and Clark's route. The impossibility of carrying any quantity of provisions on their backs, in addition to the ammunition and bedding, will occur at first view. The danger to be apprehended from starvation was imminent. They, however, put the best face on their prospects, and pursued their route towards the Rocky Mountains at the headwaters of . . . the Spanish River, and stood their course E.S.E. until they struck the headwaters of the great River Platte, which they undeviantly followed to its mouth.

Stuart, Crooks, and the others clearly understood the importance of their discovery of South Pass and the Platte River Road and what historian Merrill Mattes described as the "providential relationship" between the two. For the better part of three centuries, European, Canadian, and American explorers, most recently Lewis and Clark, had been seeking a Northwest Passage, an unimpeded watercourse to the Pacific. No such passage existed, but Stuart's party had found the next best thing: a continuous lane across the Great American Desert, through the Rocky Mountains, and on to the western sea. In his story, Charless told the world for the first time of this new road, in his enthusiasm exaggerating the ease by which it could be traveled:

By information received from these gentlemen, it appears that a journey across the continent of N. America might be performed with a wagon, there being no obstruction in the whole route that any person would dare call a mountain in addition to its being much the most direct and short one to go from this place to the mouth of the Columbia River. Any future party who may undertake this journey, and are tolerably acquainted with the different places, where it would be necessary to lay up a small stock of provisions, would not be impeded, as in all probability they would not meet with an Indian to interrupt their progress; although on the other route more north there are insurmountable barriers.

FOR CROOKS, MCCLELLAN, Miller, Jones, and the Canadians, St. Louis was the end of the line, but Stuart still had to get back to New

York with the dispatches for Astor. After drawing back pay and travel expenses for himself and his companions from the company account with W. P. Hunt's establishment and paying off Crooks and the others, Stuart purchased a horse and again started east, leaving on May 16.

Stuart traveled by horseback across present-day Missouri and Illinois, stopping for the night at Jordan's station (Frank Jordan Fort) at the site of today's Locust Grove, Illinois, a few days after one man was killed and another wounded by Indian allies of the British. The terrified settlers and soldiers had watched from behind the garrison walls, Stuart noted with disgust, while both men were scalped within one hundred yards of the blockhouse.

As Stuart crossed into Indiana, a white man riding a mile or so ahead of him was shot and killed by Indians. Hearing the gunfire, Stuart concealed himself and his horse and passed out of reach of the guns.

Travel weary and impatient to reach New York, Stuart was unimpressed with what he glimpsed of life east of the Mississippi. The sporadic entries in his journal reflect his irritability and exhaustion. Reaching Shaunian Town (Shawneetown), on the west bank of the Ohio River, on May 22, he found that the river had flooded. Here, he wrote, there was "a situation extremely disagreeable and unhealthy on account of the overflowing . . . river which swept off a considerable part of the houses, fences and a great proportion of the cattle in the spring. The inhabitants are a set of the most wretched and ragamuffin-looking animals I have yet met with—indeed, the accommodation all along between here and St. Louis is horrible."

Once he arrived at Green River, Kentucky, he sold his horse and switched to public convenience—the stage—traveling first to Baltimore, then Washington and Philadelphia. When he reached New York on June 23, Astor was expecting him. The *Gazette* stories had been reprinted earlier in several of the New York newspapers including the *Herald* and *Commercial Advertiser*. Astor had seen them and was wildly impatient to hear Stuart's news firsthand.

At the debriefing at Astor's offices at 69 Pine Street, Stuart gave his employer the dispatches, the year-old letter from Hunt, and his two journal books. In his unembellished, straightforward fashion, he told Astor of the sea voyage round Cape Horn, of clearing the forest and building the fort that bore Astor's name on the banks of the Columbia, of the posts his uncle and the other partners had established in the interior, and of colossal mountains and great rivers no white men had yet seen—"large and extensive rivers in that part of the country of which we had no knowledge," Astor later wrote in summarizing the meeting to Thomas Jefferson. "They found the Indians in the vicinity peaceable and friendly, and . . . in 1811 sent several parties into the interior and along the coast to explore the country which they found to abound with fish and game and the quantity of valuable furs far exceeding our most sanguine expectations."

Astor already knew about the *Tonquin*, of course, and the deaths of Thorn, McKay, and the crew, but the details that Stuart related were even more horrific than had been reported in the papers. Astor masked his shock and sorrow. As he said to a friend later that evening, "What would you have me do? Would you have me stay at home and weep for what I cannot help?"

He listened attentively to Stuart's account of his return journey, but it was the security of Astoria that really concerned him. More than anything, he feared the British were going to take possession of the Columbia and "destroy our establishment." For the first time, he learned that McDougall was in charge of the post—in fact, had been all along—and that his man Hunt had sailed off aboard the *Beaver* with Captain Sowle. The news, as Washington Irving later would make clear, alarmed and angered him.

At least Stuart was able to reassure his employer that that Columbia River post was "so well situated that a small force could defend it against 300 or 400 men." Stuart also believed that "having gained the confidence and good will of the natives," the Astorians could count on their support against the British.

That was the good news, but realistically, Astor's remaining traders couldn't hold out for long without help, particularly since, as Stuart had explained, at least half the men were in the interior trading with the Indians. For months now, Astor had, he told Stuart, been pressing Washington to send troops to the Columbia, but he'd had no response. Recently, in desperation, he had—at the recommendation of his friend Secretary of the Treasury Albert Gallatin—turned to Secretary of the Navy William Jones for help.

In April, Astor had written Jones suggesting that the navy send a warship—Gallatin had recommended the speedy USS *Hornet*—to intercept the Nor'Westers' *Isaac Todd* as it entered the Columbia. So far, Jones had failed to respond, but now, with the intelligence Stuart brought back with him, Astor would renew his campaign. Perhaps he and Stuart would even travel to Washington together in hopes of gaining Jones's backing.

When the interview was over, both men went out into the gathering early summer dusk. Astor, whose views of his Scottish partners had been colored by Captain Thorn's harsh words, was guarded with his praise. Stuart's report was "satisfactory," he later wrote his friend the merchant John Dorr. Unfortunately, Astor was slated to go to the theater; otherwise, he would have offered to buy his young partner the best dinner in New York.

Stuart had plans of his own. After he and Astor parted company, Stuart walked the few blocks to the waterfront where a lifetime ago he had embarked on the *Tonquin*, a ghost ship now, for the far Columbia. In the fading light, he looked for another vessel, this one to ferry him across the river to Brooklyn and the house on the corner of Fulton and Nassau. There, if his luck held, Betsy Sullivan would be awaiting his return.

AFTERWORD

ROBERT STUART AND BETSY SULLIVAN WERE MARRIED on July 21, 1813, at the First Presbyterian Church on Cedar Street in Manhattan. The Reverend Samuel Miller, a family friend, performed the ceremony. The newlyweds lived with Betsy's mother in Brooklyn while Stuart returned to the fur trade, traveling occasionally to Albany and upstate New York where he bought and sold pelts for himself as well as Astor.

Modest as they were, these endeavors came at a fortuitous time. Stuart's back pay, a little over three hundred dollars, had long since run out and Betsy—"Mammy," as he called her affectionately—was pregnant. On June 27, 1814, the Stuarts had their first child, Mary Elizabeth, from whom I am descended.

After the War of 1812 ended with the signing of the Treaty of Ghent on Christmas Eve 1814, Stuart and Ramsay Crooks started a trading venture of their own, backed by Astor. In 1816, Stuart joined the resuscitated AFC with Crooks, both as coagents. Three years later on May 14, 1819, he, Betsy, Mary, and a second child, David, moved from New York to the frontier settlement on remote Mackinac Island where the AFC had its northwestern headquarters. For the next fifteen years, Stuart remained at Mackinac supervising the AFC's dealings in the upper Great Lakes region and the upper Mississippi Valley and with Betsy rearing their eight children, three of whom died young.

In 1834, the Stuarts moved to Detroit, where they built the city's first brick house, a comfortable two-story residence on Jefferson Avenue. Three years later, Betsy had another child, a son, who died as an infant. While living in Detroit, Stuart served as the state treas-

urer of Michigan, then federal superintendent of Indian affairs in the
region of Michigan, and finally secretary of the Illinois & Michigan
Canal Company.

Robert Stuart died on October 18, 1848, at the Sherman House
Hotel in Chicago. Like his father, he had been sitting by the fire when
he suffered an apparent heart attack. Betsy, who discovered his body
the following morning, died on September 26, 1866.

AFTER STUART'S RETURN, John Jacob Astor renewed his
efforts to keep Astoria from the Nor'Westers. Based on the intelligence Stuart brought back with him, Astor made the case to Secretary of the Navy William Jones in a July 7 letter that Astoria, "is not
only the mean of a wide and extensive trade on the coast but also a
trade not only of great value in the interior, but one which in a very
few years will give us a complete control over all the Indians on this
side of the Mississippi and Missouri rivers. . . . Mr. Stuart is of the
opinion that the journey may be performed from the mouth of the
Columbia to St. Louis in 4 months, that is, after having some estab-
lishments on this side of the Rocky Mountains."

In late July, Astor sent Stuart to Washington to deliver his journal
and a letter to President Madison stressing the importance of securing Astoria. Stuart makes no mention in his own correspondence of
this trip or his meeting with the president, but in an October 18,
1813, letter to Thomas Jefferson, Astor noted that Stuart "kept a
journal . . . of his voyage across the country which he left with the
President. Should you feel a desire to read it, I am sure the President
will send it to you. You will see that there are large and extensive
rivers in that part of the country which we had no knowledge of."

Preoccupied with the British war and in poor health during the
summer of 1813, Madison failed to send troops or a ship to the
Columbia, but it was already too late to save the trading venture. In
October 1813, McDougall sold Astoria, the ancillary posts and all the
company furs to the Nor'Westers for forty-two thousand dollars,
plus another fourteen thousand dollars in back pay that was due the
Astorians. Several months later, McDougall signed on as a partner
with the NWC but not before marrying one of Comcomly's daugh-

ters. The liaison vastly enhanced his worth to his new employers, who were eager to win over the Chinooks and their still powerful chief, now McDougall's father-in-law.

The news could not have been entirely unexpected, but still Astor was shocked and angered when he learned that Astoria had been sold. On November 12, 1814, he placed a brief notice of its demise in the New York *Gazette* and *General Advertiser*. It read simply, "The firm of the Pacific Fur Company is dissolved." Astor blamed McDougall for the loss of the Columbia post and never forgave him for what he believed was the Canadian's treachery.

AFTER THEIR RETURN from the Columbia, Andre Valle, Francis LeClair, and Joseph Miller dropped out of sight. Benjamin Jones purchased a farm outside St. Louis but not long after went off to New Mexico for four years, presumably to trap and trade. On his return, Jones resided on a farm on Gravious Creek near St. Louis with his family. He died in June 1835 of cholera.

Robert McClellan was imprisoned for debt a month after his arrival in St. Louis. After his release, he opened a store in Cape Girardeau, Missouri, selling goods that had been supplied by a St. Louis businessman. In ill health, McClellan closed down the business after only six months, retiring to a farm owned by a friend, Abraham Gallatin. On May 24, 1815, McClellan fought against the Sac and Fox Indians at the Battle of the Sinkhole. He died five months later and was buried on the farm of his old friend General William Clark.

Borrowing $310 from a friend, Ramsay Crooks followed Stuart to New York, where he stayed with the Stuarts in Brooklyn and lobbied Astor for financing to start over in the fur trade. Encouraged by Commander Oliver Perry's decisive victory over the British on Lake Erie in September, Astor on October 8, 1813, loaned Crooks the funds to travel to the Ohio Valley with instructions to buy as many furs as he could on behalf of John Jacob Astor & Company. In 1814, again with Astor's backing, he and Stuart started their own trading company and two years later he became a coagent with the AFC. Crooks eventually became president of the company after buying out

Stuart and Astor's interests in 1834. He died on June 6, 1859, at his home on St. Marks Place in New York, the last surviving member of the Stuart expedition.

ON APRIL 4, 1814, ninety men including David Stuart left Astoria in seven canoes and barges. The elder Stuart, who had refused a position with the NWC, arrived in Montreal in early September, remaining there as an independent trader. In recognition of his achievements as a trader and explorer of the Okanogan River region, Stuart was elected to the Beaver Club in 1816. Several years later, "Old Uncle" retired to Mackinac, where he made his home with the Stuarts and continued to live with them when they moved to Detroit. He died on October 18, 1853.

STUART'S ACCOMPLISHMENTS were largely forgotten after his return. This was in part due to Astor's reluctance to make Stuart's narratives public. Astor viewed Stuart's journal as proprietary since it contained extensive intelligence of the fur trade, and he retained it as company property along with other documents and records pertaining to Astoria. Only after leaving the fur trade did Astor finally turn Stuart's narratives over to Washington Irving, in 1834 or 1835, as a perquisite to Irving writing *Astoria; or Anecdotes of an Enterprise beyond the Rocky Mountains*. The book, which drew heavily on both Stuart's and Hunt's journals without attribution, was published in 1836, while Stuart's narratives were first published in the United States in 1935, almost a century after his death.

SOUTH PASS AND the Oregon Trail were rediscovered in 1823 when fur trappers employed by William H. Ashley returned east using Stuart's route. Nine years later, Captain Benjamin Bonneville led an expedition of trappers up the Platte and came though South Pass, making the first crossing of the Continental Divide by wagon.

The first of the emigrant expeditions, the so-called Bidwell-Bartleson party, led by the mountain man Thomas Fitzpatrick, traveled Stuart's route on its way to Oregon in the summer of 1841. In the ensuing years, the Platte River Road and the mountain pass that linked the two halves of the United States were traversed by a seemingly endless succession of mountain men and trappers, caravans of pioneers in their great ox-drawn prairie schooners, Mormons pushing their handcarts all the way to the Great Salt Lake, and Forty-Niners rushing to the gold fields of California. Between 1841 and 1866, when the last of the great wagon trains left for the West, between 300,000 and 350,000 emigrants made their way through the Rockies by way of Stuart's route. Some eventually returned East, disappointed and disillusioned. Most established new homes, settling the vast territory Thomas Jefferson had acquired from France in 1803 and the land beyond.

NOTES

Foreword

5 "Compared with all the other overland diaries": Philip Ashton Rollins, ed., *The Discovery of the Oregon Trail: Robert Stuart's Narrative of His Overland Trip Eastward from Astoria in 1812–13. To which is added: An Account of the* Tonquin's *Voyage and of Events at Fort Astoria (1811–1812) and Wilson Price Hunt's Diary of His Overland Trip Westward to Astoria in 1811–1812* (New York: Edward Eberstadt, 1935), lxvi. Stuart's original journal and traveling memoranda are part of the William Robertson Coe Collection of Western Americana at the Yale University Library.

Chapter 1

7 Based on the ambitious proposal: John Jacob Astor to Thomas Jefferson, 17 Feb. 1808, (Library of Congress [LC]).

10 "Governor speaks well of Astor": Henry Dearborn to Thomas Jefferson, 13 April 1808 (LC).

10 "All beyond the Mississippi": Thomas Jefferson to John Jacob Astor, 13 April 1808 (LC).

11 "a most excellent man": Thomas Jefferson to Meriwether Lewis, 17 July 1808 (LC).

Chapter 2

13 "an affectionate": Helen Stuart Mackay-Smith Marlott, *The Letters of Robert and Elizabeth Sullivan Stuart*, vol. 1 (n.p., 1961), 108.

14 "to exchange a few blows": Sir Walter Scott, *Rob Roy*, Waverly Novels, The Centenary Edition, vol. 3, Edinburgh: Adams & Charles Black, 1870), 29.

16 "We were poor": Elizabeth Stuart to Kate Stuart, *Stuart Letters*, vol.1, 22 July 1850.

16 "educated according to the usages": Rollins, *Oregan Trail*, xxxvi.

18 "Lords of the Lakes": Washington Irving, *Astoria; or Anecdotes of an Enterprise beyond the Rocky Mountains*, 2 vol. (Philadelphia and New

York: J. B. Lippincott Company, 1836; reprint, Keystone Western Americana Series, Philadelphia: Lippincott, 1961), 11.

19 The intake was enormous: Peter C. Newman, *Caesars of the Wilderness: The Story of the Hudson's Bay Company,* vol. 2 (Toronto: Penguin Books Canada Ltd., 1987), 7.

20 "one of those intrepid souls": Charles C. Trowbridge to B. O. Williams, 23 March 1880, Michigan Pioneer Collections, 1879–1880 (10 vols. with index. Available at various Michigan libraries), III, 209.

Chapter 3

22 "Many times I have seen": Kenneth Wiggins Porter, *John Jacob Astor, Business Man,* vol. 1 (Cambridge, Mass.: Harvard University Press, 1931), 38.

23 "Mr. Astor is horrid": *James Gallatin, A Great Peacemaker: The Diary of James Gallatin, Secretary to Albert Gallatin, 1813–1827* (New York: Charles Scribner's Sons, 1914), 24.

23 "a set of men highly respectable": William Henry Atherton, *Montreal 1835–1914* (Montreal: S. J. Clarke Publishing Co., 1914), 65

25 "It was his purpose": Porter, *John Jacob Astor,* 169.

25 "just imported an elegant assortment": Ibid., 32.

Chapter 4

32 "The relation of the trader to the Indian": Hiram M. Chittenden, *History of the American Fur Trade of the Far West.* vol. 1 (New York: Harper, 1902; reprint, Lincoln: University of Nebraska Press, 1986), 11.

Chapter 5

35 "very respectful gentleman": John Jacob Astor to Thomas Jefferson, 14 March 1812 (LC).

36 Drawn up by hand: The agreement can be found in the Baker Library, Harvard University.

Chapter 6

39 "We sang, and the sight of a birch-bark": Gabriel Franchere, *Journal of a Voyage on the North Coast of North America during the Years 1811, 1812, 1813, and 1814* (Toronto: Champlain Society, 1969), 45.

39 "I found New York most agreeable": Ibid., 46

43 "He had the diffidence": Elizabeth Stuart to Kate Stuart, 1 August 1850, *Stuart Letters,* vol.1, 115.

43 "Being somewhat indisposed": Robert Stuart to Elizabeth Sullivan, September 1810, *Stuart Letters,* vol 1.

44 "they should be respected": Franchere, *Journal of a Voyage,* 130.

44 "To him I owe everything": Robert Stuart to Mary Stuart, 27 January 1834, *Stuart Letters,* vol.1, 17.

Chapter 7

45   "To prevent any misunderstanding": Irving, *Astoria Anecdotes*, 34.

46   "I must recommend you:" Ibid., 34.

47   "All was bustle": Alexander Ross, *Adventures of the First Settlers on the Oregon or Columbia River: Being a Narrative of the Expedition Fitted Out by John Jacob Astor, to Establish the Pacific Fur Company; with an Account of Some Indian Tribes of the Coast of the Pacific* (London: Smith, Eden and Co., 1849), 16.

48   "He was very self-conceited": Letter by Elisha Loomis to Chester Loomis, relating an account by Robert Stuart of his journey, Mackinac, 3 April 1831. For the letter in full see Kenneth A. Spaulding (ed.), *On the Oregon Trail: Robert Stuart's Journey of Discovery* (Norman, Okla.: 1953), 174–77.

51   "When thwarted of their cravings for delicacies": Irving, *Astoria Anecdotes*, 36.

51   "without having a Fly Market": Ibid., 38.

51   "as foolish a pedant as ever lived": Ibid., 37.

51   "the brutal way the ship's officers": Franchere, *Journal of a Voyage*, 50.

52   "They [the passengers] were determined": Irving, *Astoria Anecdotes*, 49.

52   "The customary ceremony": Robert F. Jones, ed., *Annals of Astoria: The Headquarters Log of the Pacific Fur Company on the Columbia River, 1811–1813* (New York: Fordham University Press, 1999), 2.

52   "rolling mountains": Ross, *Adventures*, 23.

53   "Wild fowl": Ibid., 25.

53   "Had excellent diversion": Jones, *Annals of Astoria*, 2.

54   "We knew too well": Ross, *Adventures*, 27.

56   "All the former feuds": Ibid., 29.

Chapter 8

57   "The women are handsome in person": Ross, *Adventures*, 59.

58   "They are very amorous": Franchere, *Journal of a Voyage*, 66.

61   "We soon came to terms": Ibid., 63.

62   "It would be difficult to imagine": Irving, *Astoria Anecdotes*, 55.

63   "The tools used": Ross, *Adventures*, 42.

Chapter 9

64   "The sight filled every heart with gladness": Ross, *Adventures*, 59.

65   "He was told it would be certain death": Elisha Loomis, 3 April 1831.

65   "Mr. Fox, if you are afraid": Ross, *Adventures*, 60.

65   "My uncle was drowned here": Ibid., 60.

66   "When the boat": Elisha Loomis, 3 April 1831.

66   "was without a rudder": Jones, *Annals of Astoria*, 4.
67   "A man caught hold": Elisha Loomis, 3 April 1831.
67   "the sight of which was appalling": Ross, *Adventures*, 66.

Chapter 10

70   "The armorer made his": Jones, *Annals of Astoria*, 5.
70   "They got him aboard": Ibid., 5.
72   "This morning Captain Thorn": Ibid., 8.
72   "The weather was magnificent": Franchere, *Journal of a Voyage*, 77.
74   "These four nations": Rollins, *Oregon Trail*, 4.
74   "An Indian from the Rapids:" Jones, *Annals of Astoria*, 14.
77   "If you ever see us safe back": Ross, *Adventures*, 89.

Chapter 11

79   "This gentleman is one of the first shots": Ibid., 181
80   "detested the volatile gaiety": Ibid., 175.
80   "No more Canadian voyageurs": Ibid., 175.
81   "Every nook and cranny": Ibid., 176.

Chapter 12

90   "The fur trading post of Mr. J. J. Astor": David Thompson, *Narrative of His Explorations in North America* (Toronto: Champlain Society, 1916), 501.
91   "Nothing was too good": Ross, *Adventures*, 93.
91   "a maneuver of the North West policy": Ibid., 93.
93   "Permit me to congratulate": David Thompson to Duncan McDougall, David Stuart and Robert Stuart, 15 July 1811, William Robertson Coe Collection of Western Americana, Yale University Library; reprinted in *The Yale University Library Gazette* XXIV, October 1949, 52–53.
94   "We have the pleasure to acknowledge": Ibid., 52–53.
94   "They had been unable:" Thompson, *Narrative*, 507.
95   "offering a prayer": Ibid., 511.

Chapter 13

97   "Their manner of singing": Rollins, *Oregon Trail*, 13.
97   "are rarely permitted": Ibid.
97   "The women are": Ibid., 10.
97   "Their lodges are": Ibid., 13.
99   "the aerial regions": Ibid., 8.
99   "all the literati": Ibid., 9.
99   "A day or two": Ibid., 9.
100   "Their manner of courtship": Ibid., 9.

101 "put their hands": Ross, *Adventures*, 87.
102 "It is his [Stuart's] opinion": Jones, *Annals of Astoria*, 27.
103 According to information": Fanchere, *Journal of a Voyage*, 88.
104 "All hands employed": Jones, *Annals of Astoria*, 37
105 "His sole purpose": Ibid., 42.
105 "Old Comcomly sent": Franchere, *Journal of a Voyage*, 90.

Chapter 14

106 "a very inferior species": Rollins, *Oregon Trail*, 8.
106 "The country is": Ibid., 5.
108 "Mr. Mumford returned": Franchere, *Journal of a Voyage*, 93.
109 "The incredible number": Rollins, *Oregon Trail*, 32.
109 "I navigated with six men": Ibid.
109 "Jan. 1st, Wednesday": Jones, *Annals of Astoria*, 65.
110 "The sudden change": Ibid., 67.

Chapter 15

111 "safe and sound": Franchere, *Journal of a Voyage*, 110.
111 "It had rained all night": Rollins, *Oregon Trail*, 308.
112 "Mr. Hunt . . . informed me": John Bradbury, *Travels in the Interior Parts of America in the Years 1809, 1810 and 1811* (Liverpool: Smith and Galway, 1819), journal entry for 17 March 1810.
113 "He seemed to have a great": Ibid.
113 "We had a view of the bluffs": Ibid., journal entry for 31 May 1810.
114 "The purport of the speech": Ibid.
115 "I found Mr. Lisa furious": Henry M. Brackenridge, *Views of Louisiana; Together with a Journal of Voyage up the Missouri River in 1811* (Pittsburgh: Cramer, Spear, and Eichbaum, 1814), journal entry for 5 June 1810.
115 "He told Lisa that the matter": Ibid.
116 "The gentlemen of the expedition": Missouri *Gazette*, 15 May 1813.
117 "The country was bare," Rollins, *Oregon Trail*, 281.
117 "I there bought thirty-six horses": Ibid.
117 "we now had horses enough": Ibid.
117 "The road was irksome": Ibid., 282.
118 "The great heat, the bad road": Ibid., 283.
118 "a very bad fellow": Ibid., 284.
118 "He accepted these terms": Ibid., 285.
119 "The mountains drew nearer": Ibid., 286.
119 "one of the hunters": Ibid.
120 "We should have continued": Ibid., 288.
120 "On the 17th, all being ready": Ibid., 290.
121 "The force of the current": Ibid.

121 "only by an extreme exertion": Missouri *Gazette*, 15 May 1813.

121 "Our situation had become critical": Rollins, *Oregon Trail*, 292.

122 "confined between precipices": Ibid., 80.

123 "a series of hardships and privations": Missouri *Gazette*, 15 May 1813.

124 "What was my astonishment": Rollins, *Oregon Trail*, 297.

124 "Poor man!": Ibid., 298.

124 "I counted on buying": Ibid.

124 "Whereupon, my men grumbled": Ibid.

125 "was shocked to find": Irving, *Astoria Anecdotes*, 264.

125 "Vague, almost superstitious terrors": Ibid.

125 "Starvation had bereft J. B. Provost": Missouri *Gazette*, 15 May 1813.

126 "one of Mr. Crooks's men": Rollins, *Oregon Trail*, 299.

126 "I had another horse killed": Ibid.

Chapter 16

128 "He had to distribute leaf tobacco": Thompson, *Narrative*, 514.

128 "To say there is not a worse path": Ross, *Adventures*, 122.

128 "Being dusk before": Rollins, *Oregon Trail*, 55.

129 "Two loads were only": Ibid., 56.

129 "No sooner did the canoes": Ibid.

129 "[He] had just enough time": Ibid., 57.

130 "Mr. Stuart, however, was unwilling": Franchere, *Journal of a Voyage*, 113.

130 "We found Mr. Reed": Rollins, *Oregon Trail*, 69.

130 "This was executed in a twinkling": Ibid.

131 "This ludicrous affair" Ibid.

131 "Our answer was *NO*": Ibid., 59.

132 "self-possessed and fearless man": Franchere, *Journal of a Voyage*, 157

132 "He saw everything": Ross, *Adventures*, 158.

132 "After leaving this place [Fort Okanogan]": Ibid.

Chapter 17

140 "I offered myself to go in his place": Elisha Loomis, 13 April 1831.

140 "Resolved, that it, being necessary": Rollins, *Oregon Trail*, lxxx.

140 "The mission was one of peril": Irving, *Astoria Anecdotes*, 313.

Chapter 18

143 "six feet two inches high": Ibid., 111.

144 "brave, honest and sincere": McClellan was buried on the farm of General William Clark. This is how he was described on the tombstone written by Clark. Rollins, *Oregon Trail*, xcv.

146 "I was much aided": Rollins, *Oregon Trail*, 59.

Chapter 19

147 "All hands were stirring": Jones, *Annals of Astoria*, 100.

149 "Every man was nearly drunk": Ross Cox, *The Columbia River*, ed. Edgar I. Stewart and Jane R. Stewart (1831; reprint, Norman, Okla.: University of Oklahoma Press, 1957), 121.

149 "In the afternoon of Monday": Rollins, *Oregon Trail*, 3.

149 "We had not been on shore": Cox, *Columbia River*, 121.

Chapter 20

152 "At its commencement was favored": John Jacob Astor to Thomas Jefferson, 14 March 1812 (Coe Collection, Yale University Library).

153 "I am sorry your enterprise for establishing": Thomas Jefferson to John Jacob Astor, 24 May 1812 (Coe Collection, Yale University Library).

Chapter 21

155 "A few minutes only": Rollins, *Oregon Trail*, 28.

156 "are very forward in their deportment": Meriwether Lewis, *Expedition of Captains Lewis and Clark 1804–5–6* (1814; reprint, Chicago: A. C. McClurg & Co.), 108.

156 "had been partially unsettled": Irving, *Astoria Anecdotes*, 314.

156 "an immense swamp": Rollins, *Oregon Trail*, 29.

157 "It is situated on a beautiful": Ibid.

158 "beautiful high prairies": Rollins, *Oregon Trail*, 30.

159 "become not only an": Ibid., 31.

159 "good health without": Jones, *Annals of Astoria*, 115.

160 "He might embroil": Rollins, *Oregon Trail*, 31.

160 "That large and beautiful": Ibid.

161 "The country nearly to the falls": Ibid., 32.

161 "the antique towers and fortifications": Ibid., 34.

161 "In low water": Ibid., 36.

162 "as if boiling": Ibid., 35.

162 "Had the canoe filled": Ibid.

163 "All mix promiscuously": Ibid., 54.

164 "The operator hardly ever": Ibid., 52.

164 "saucy, impudent rascals": Ibid.

164 "The fellow gave a dreadful": Cox, *Columbia River*, 132.

165 "They behaved very much": Rollins, *Oregon Trail*, 53.

166 "In language, dress and manners": Cox, *Columbia River*, 133.

166 "This mountain is entirely detached": Rollins, *Oregon Trail*, 59.

168 "the most hospitable, honest": Lewis, *Expedition*, 279.

168 "They are good Indians": Rollins, *Oregon Trail*, 62.

169 "The females . . . were distinguished": Cox, *Columbia River,* 145.

169 "I gave merchandise to the amount": Rollins, *Oregon Trail,* 62.

Chapter 22

170 "without the least appearance": Ibid., 75.

171 "a most enchanting tract": Ibid., 77.

172 "greatly agitated as if boiling": Ibid., 79.

172 "incredible multitudes of the": Ibid., 78.

172 "saw no less than 19 antelope": Ibid., 79.

172 "It is about 400 yards": Ibid., 80.

174 "on which they rode swift as a deer": John C. Ewers, *The Blackfeet, Raiders on the Northwestern Plains* (Norman, Okla.: University of Oklahoma Press, 1958), 21.

174 "They live in a wretched state of poverty": Lewis, *Expedition,* 446.

175 "Hearing that there is": Rollins, *Oregon Trail,* 84.

177 "From his former conduct": Ibid.

177 "with the best our small pittances": Ibid., 87.

178 "He was one of the first settlers": Bradbury, *Travels in the Interior,* journal entry, 26 May 1810.

179 "traveling about 950 miles": Rollins, *Oregon Trail,* 86.

179 "All the unknown Indians": Ibid.

180 "Was generally the rankest grass": Ibid., 108.

180 "of wretched Indians": Ibid.

181 "Their spears are a small straight": Ibid., 109.

181 "With the greatest facility": Ibid.

182 "By this day's march": Ibid., 111.

183 "Nothing that walks": Ibid., 112.

184 "an excellent species of trout": Ibid., 113.

184 "as far as lay": Ibid.

Chapter 23

186 "these abominable . . . shrubs": Rollins, *Oregon Trail,* 115.

187 "Ordinarily a lodge trace": Ibid., 123.

187 "Last night we made": Ibid., 115.

187 "This I would not have": Ibid., 127.

189 "This being the water course": Ibid., 128.

189 "hoping by this route": Ibid.

189 "After walking a considerable distance": Ibid.

190 "We thought it advisable to": Ibid., 129.

190 "Mr. Miller at once pronounced": Ibid.

Chapter 24

191 "Their chief came forward": Irving, *Astoria Anecdotes,* 333.

193 "Knowing the adroitness": Rollins, *Oregon Trail,* 131.

193 "Their behavior was insolent": Ibid.

193 "moved him backwards": Irving *Astoria Anecdotes,* 334.

194 "The chief now said": Elisha Loomis, 3 April 1831.

194 "to prevent an open": Rollins, *Oregon Trail,* 131.

194 "It is difficult to": Chittenden, *American Fur Trade,* Vol.1, 208.

195 "signals for the purpose": Rollins, *Oregon Trail,* 131.

195 "On striking this watercourse": Ibid., 132.

196 "Having thus lost the intended track": Ibid.

197 "the most horribly discordant howling": Ibid., 135.

197 "as if a legion of infernals": Ibid.

197 "[These] made us desist": Ibid., 134.

197 "the savages whose yells": Ibid.

198 "an insulting": Elisha Loomis, 3 April 1831.

Chapter 25

199 "Destitute of horses": Ibid.

199 "we have hopes of meeting": Rollins, *Oregon Trail,* 135.

199 "Should we fail in this": Ibid.

200 "We have just": Ibid.

200 "To prevent the villains": Ibid.

201 "Forty-five trout": Ibid., 148.

202 "This leads us to believe": Ibid., 137.

202 "Many older men among": Ewers, *The Blackfeet,* 40.

203 "that they might be informed": Lewis, *Expedition,* 378.

203 "had murdered and probably butchered": Ewers, *The Blackfeet,* 51.

204 "We remained in the same": Rollins, *Oregon Trail,* 138.

204 "The prime object": Ibid., 255.

205 "The body of the mountains": Ibid., 138.

206 "fearing the Blackfeet": Ibid., 139.

206 "A little to the side of our camp": Ibid., 150.

207 "a good deal indisposed": Ibid.

207 "We reached the other side": Ibid.

208 "by any delay": Ibid.

208 "Such a prospect": Ibid., 152.

208 "The phantoms": Ibid.

209 "We immediately moved": Ibid.

209 "[The sweat] had a good effect": Ibid., 153.

209 "On our way here": Ibid.

209 "Mr. C. mends slowly": Ibid.

Chapter 26

212 "The track is often so": Rollins, *Oregon Trail,* 154.

213 "sagebrush plains immense beyond seeing": David Lavender, *The Fist in the Wilderness* (Lincoln: University of Nebraska Press, 1964), 176.

213 "We were surrounded by mountains": Rollins, *Oregon Trail*, 287.
213 "a stream about 60 yards": Ibid., 155.
213 "We had great hopes": Ibid.
214 "When we arrived": Ibid., 156.
214 "He said it was just as well": Ibid.
214 "After dark [we] returned": Ibid.
215 "with the firm resolution to fire": Ibid., 157.
215 "My thoughts began to ruminate": Ibid.
216 "So ravenous were": Ibid., 158.
216 "I was very much alarmed": Ibid.

Chapter 27

217 "This was not a time": Rollins, *Oregon Trail*, 255.
219 "At their head were two": Ibid., 159.
219 "too bad to be eaten": Ibid., 160.
220 "Poor but hospitable in the extreme": Ibid., 161.
220 "the most rugged": Ibid., 255.
220 "There is a species of clay": Ibid., 161.
221 "It undoubtedly was those": Ibid.
221 "When we told them the day": Ibid.
222 "easy loads compared to what": Ibid., 162.
222 "We . . . made the best of our way": Ibid., 255.
222 "The ridge of the mountains": Ibid., 162.
222 "Being somewhat apprehensive": Ibid.
223 "were again obliged to take refuge": Ibid., 163.
224 "Let him [to whom] difficulties": Ibid., 155.

Chapter 28

227 "We at once concluded": Rollins, *Oregon Trail*, 165.
227 "a march truly disagreeable": Ibid., 166.
228 "scampered before we could": Ibid.
228 "We discovered to our great joy": Ibid., 167.
228 "feeling ourselves, as well as our": Ibid.
229 "by far the most delicious": Ibid., 187.
229 "To form somewhat of an adequate idea": Ibid., 188.
230 "The spray extends at least a quarter": Ibid.
231 "Seeing that the river still": Ibid., 189.
232 "their worthy relations": Ibid., 190.

Chapter 29

235 "I have just now a letter": John Jacob Astor to Secretary of State James
     Monroe, February 1813 (Coe Collection, Yale University Library).
236 "If such were there": Ibid.

Chapter 30

237 "even the prying investigation of Indian spies": Rollins, *Oregon Trail*, 191.

238 "The mountains to the southeast": Ibid.

238 "After the first surprise was over": Ibid., 192.

239 "They have a keen sense of humor": Virginia Cole Trenholm and Maurine Carley, *The Arapahoes, Our People* (Norman, Okla.: University of Oklahoma Press, 1970), 6.

239 "was far more regular and decent": Rollins, *Oregon Trail*, 192.

240 "We are poor now": Irving, *Astoria Anecdotes*, 366.

240 "Well, when you bring the horses": Ibid.

240 "the villains who robbed Mr. Miller": Rollins, *Oregon Trail*, 192.

240 "We determined to abandon": Ibid., 193.

Chapter 31

241 "As a result our feet": Ibid.

242 "These narrows are composed": Ibid., 195.

243 "Soon after leaving camp the country": Ibid.

243 "Up to this morning": Journal of Thomas N. Eastin, Merrill J. Mattes, *Platte River Road Narratives* (Urbana and Chicago: University of Illinois Press, 1988), 153.

244 "remarkably rugged and bluffy hills": Rollins, *Oregon Trail*, 196.

244 "How can I describe the scene": Mattes, *Platte River Road Narratives*, 153.

244 "Not a twig to be seen eastward": Rollins, *Oregon Trail*, 196.

244 "the wretchedness of our situation": Ibid., 197.

245 "This being so different": Ibid.

245 "Friday 1st, January 1813": Ibid., 207.

Chapter 32

246 "Labor of every kind": Jones, *Annals of Astoria* 143.

246 "that may be seen this season": Ibid., 144.

248 "Having maturely weighed": Franchere, *Journal of a Voyage*, 166.

248 "The only hope to be cherished": Jones, *Annals of Astoria*, 14.

Chapter 33

249 "We . . . found ourselves once more": Rollins, *Oregon Trail*, 256.

250 "Finding an Indian pen": Ibid., 209.

251 "seven miles past our last station": Ibid.

251 "the fur captains again": Mattes, *Platte River Road Narratives*, 17.

251 "blew with violence": Rollins, *Oregon Trail*, 210.

252 "Nothing but a boundless prairie": Ibid.

253 "They are but seldom larger": Ibid., 218.

253 "or as they are called": Ibid., 212.

253 "For the past 3 days march": Ibid., 211.

253 "It is thickly wooded": Ibid.

254 "Here at long last": Merrill J. Mattes, *The Great Platte River Road* (Lincoln: University of Nebraska Press, 1969), 282.

254 "We . . . are at a loss to say": Rollins, *Oregon Trail*, 213.

254 "From all appearance": Ibid.

256 "but our beloved friend": Rollins, *Oregon Trail*, 214.

256 "abandoned to their fate by their savage relatives": Ibid., 219.

256 "great bodies of timber": Ibid.

257 "lovers of sexual pleasure": Ibid., 350.

258 "These Indians come to their towns": Ibid., 221.

259 "As to the distance of the town": Ibid., 233.

259 "the disagreeable intelligence": Ibid., 235.

260 "They have resided together": Ibid.

260 "From a pole stuck in that spot": Ibid., 236.

260 "Our canoe . . . [is] composed of poles": Ibid.

Chapter 34

262 "A rapid current": Rollins, *Oregon Trail*, 240.

262 "We passed the remainder": Ibid., 237.

263 "the turbulent Kansa": Ibid., 238.

263 "We . . . were hospitably entertained": Ibid.

265 "Christian settlements extend": Ibid., 239.

265 "we were . . . all in the most perfect health": Ibid.

266 "No other single item": Lavender, *Fist in the Wilderness*, 193.

266 "Some idea of the situation": Missouri *Gazette*, 15 May 1813.

267 "By information received": Missouri *Gazette*, 8 May 1813.

268 "a situation extremely disagreeable": Rollins, *Oregon Trail*, 260.

269 "large and extensive rivers": John Jacob Astor to Thomas Jefferson, 18 October 1813 (LC).

269 "What would you have me do?": Arthur D. Howden Smith, *John Jacob Astor, Landlord to New York* (Philadelphia: J. B. Lippincott Co., 1929), 74.

269 "so well situated that a small force": John Jacob Astor to William Jones, 6 July 1813 (Coe Collection, Yale University Library).

270 "satisfactory": John Jacob Astor to John Dorr, 7 July 1813, James P. Ronda, *Astoria and Empire*, (Lincoln: University of Nebraska Press, 1990), 269.

BIBLIOGRAPHY

Books

Atherton, William Henry. *Montreal 1535–1914.* Montreal: J. Clarke Publishing Co., 1914.

Brackenridge, Henry M. *Views of Louisiana; Together with a Journal of Voyage up the Missouri River in 1811.* Pittsburgh: Cramer, Spear, and Eichbaum, 1814.

Bradbury, John. *Travels in the Interior Parts of America in the Years 1809, 1810 and 1811.* Liverpool: Smith and Galway, 1819.

Bryce, George. *The Remarkable History of the Hudson's Bay Company.* London: Sampson Low Marston & Company, 1900.

Chittenden, Hiram M. *History of the American Fur Trade of the Far West.* 3 vols. New York: Harper, 1902. Reprint, Lincoln: University of Nebraska Press, 1986.

Cox, Ross. *The Columbia River.* Edited by Edgar I. Stewart and Jane R. Stewart. 1831. Reprint, Norman Okla.: University of Oklahoma Press, 1957.

Ewers, John C. *The Blackfeet, Raiders on the Northwestern Plains.* Norman, Okla.: University of Oklahoma Press, 1958.

Franchere, Gabriel. *Journal of a Voyage on the North Coast of North America during the Years 1811, 1812, 1813, and 1814.* Toronto: Champlain Society, 1969.

Gallatin, James. *A Great Peacemaker: The Diary of James Gallatin, Secretary to Albert Gallatin, 1813–1827.* New York: Charles Scribner's Sons, 1914.

Gass, Patrick. *A Journal of the Voyages and Travels of a Corps of Discovery under the Command of Captain Lewis and Captain Clark.* Edited by David McKeehan, 1807. Reprint, Minneapolis: Ross and Haines, 1958.

Goetzmann, William H. *Army Exploration in the American West, 1803–1863.* Lincoln: University of Nebraska Press, 1979.

Irving, Washington. *Astoria; or, Anecdotes of an Enterprise beyond the Rocky Mountains.* Philadelphia and New York: J. B. Lippincott Company, 1836. Reprint, Philadelphia: Lippincott, 1961, Keystone Western Americana Series, introduction by William H. Goetzmann.

Jones, Robert F., ed. *Annals of Astoria: The Headquarters Log of the Pacific Fur Company on the Columbia River, 1811–1813.* New York: Fordham University Press, 1999.

———. *Astorian Adventure: The Journal of Alfred Seton, 1811–1815.* New York: Fordham University Press, 1993.

Josephy, Alvin M., Jr. *The Nez Perce Indians and the Opening of the Northwest.* New Haven: Yale University Press, 1965.

Lavender, David. *The Fist in the Wilderness.* Lincoln: University of Nebraska Press, 1964.

Lewis, Meriwether. *Expedition of Captains Lewis and Clark 1804–5–6,* 1814. Reprint, Chicago: A. C. McClurg & Co., 1905.

Lowie, Robert H. *The Crow Indians.* Lincoln: University of Nebraska Press, 1983.

Mackenzie, Alexander. *Alexander Mackenzie's Voyage to the Pacific Ocean in 1793.* Chicago: The Lakeside Press, 1931.

Mattes, Merrill J. *The Great Platte River Road.* Lincoln: University of Nebraska Press, 1969.

———. *Platte River Road Narratives.* Urbana and Chicago: University of Illinois Press. 1988.

Nadeau, Remi. *Fort Laramie and the Sioux.* Lincoln: University of Nebraska Press, 1982.

Newman, Peter C. *Caesars of the Wilderness: The Story of the Hudson's Bay Company.* Volume 2. Toronto: Penguin Books Canada Ltd., 1987.

———. *Company of Adventurers: The Story of the Hudson's Bay Company.* Volume 1. Toronto: Penguin Books Canada Ltd., 1987.

Phillips, Paul D. *The Fur Trade.* 2 vols. Norman, Okla.: University of Oklahoma Press, 1961.

Pinkerton, Robert. *Hudson's Bay Company.* New York: Henry Holt and Company, 1931.

Porter, Kenneth Wiggins. *John Jacob Astor, Business Man.* 2 vols. Cambridge, Mass.: Harvard University Press, 1931.

Rollins, Philip Ashton, ed. *The Discovery of the Oregon Trail: Robert Stuart's Narrative of His Overland Trip Eastward from Astoria in 1812–13. To Which is Added: An Account of the Tonquin's Voyage and of Events at Fort Astoria (1811–1812) and Wilson Price Hunt's Diary of His Overland Trip Westward to Astoria in 1811–1812.* New York: Edward Eberstadt, 1935.

Ronda, James P. *Astoria and Empire.* Lincoln: University of Nebraska Press, 1990.

———. *Lewis and Clark among the Indians.* Lincoln: University of Nebraska Press, 1984.

Ross, Alexander. *Adventures of the First Settlers on the Oregon or Columbia River: Being a Narrative of the Expedition Fitted Out by John Jacob Astor, to*

Establish the Pacific Fur Company; with an Account of Some Indian Tribes of the Coast of the Pacific. London: Smith, Eden and Co. 1849. Reprint, with an introduction by William G. Robbins, Corvallis: Oregon State University Press, 2000.

Sprague, Marshall. *The Great Gates: The Story of the Rocky Mountain Passes.* Lincoln: University of Nebraska Press, 1981.

Stuart, Robert. *Letters.* 2 vols. N.p., 1961.

Thompson, David. *Narrative of His Explorations in North America.* Toronto: Champlain Society, 1916.

Trenholm, Virginia Cole, and Maurine Carley. *The Araphoes, Our People.* Norman, Okla.: University of Oklahoma Press, 1970.

———. *The Shoshonis, Sentinels of the Rockies.* Norman, Okla.: University of Oklahoma Press, 1964.

Periodicals and Documents

Bridgewater, Dorothy Wildes. *The Yale University Library Gazette* 24 (October 1949), 47–68.

Howay, F. W. "The Loss of the *Tonquin.*" *The Washington Historical Quarterly* 13 (1932), 83–92.

Neilson Barry J. "Astorians Who Became Permanent Settlers." *Washington Historical Quarterly* 24 (1933), 221–31, 282–301.

Pacific Fur Company Partnership Agreement. Manuscripts Department, Baker Library, Harvard Business School.

ACKNOWLEDGMENTS

If this book has any merit, give credit to Charlotte Sheedy, my marvelous agent, and Liz Stein, an extraordinary editor. They both have my admiration and untold gratitude. Special thanks also to Carolyn Kim, Jenny Lawrence, Susan Banker, John Snyder, Colleen Daly, the late Nicholas Fischer, Mary Cullen, Katia Barrow, Stephanie Fairyington, and the wonderful staff at The New York Society Library.

INDEX

Page numbers in *italics* refer to illustrations.

ABOUT THE AUTHOR

LATON MCCARTNEY is an award-winning journalist and magazine editor. He is the author of the national bestseller *Friends in High Places*. He lives in New York and Wyoming.